# POETIVITI

## GUIDING CREATIVE POETIC EXPRESSION SUCCESSFULLY IN THE ELEMENTARY GRADES

## PRIMARY LEVEL

**by James Wainwright**

**illustrated by Paul Manktelow**

Cover by Jeff Van Kanegan



ISBN No. 0-86653-484-9

Printing No. 987654

**GOOD APPLE, INC.**
**BOX 299**
**CARTHAGE, IL 62321-0299**

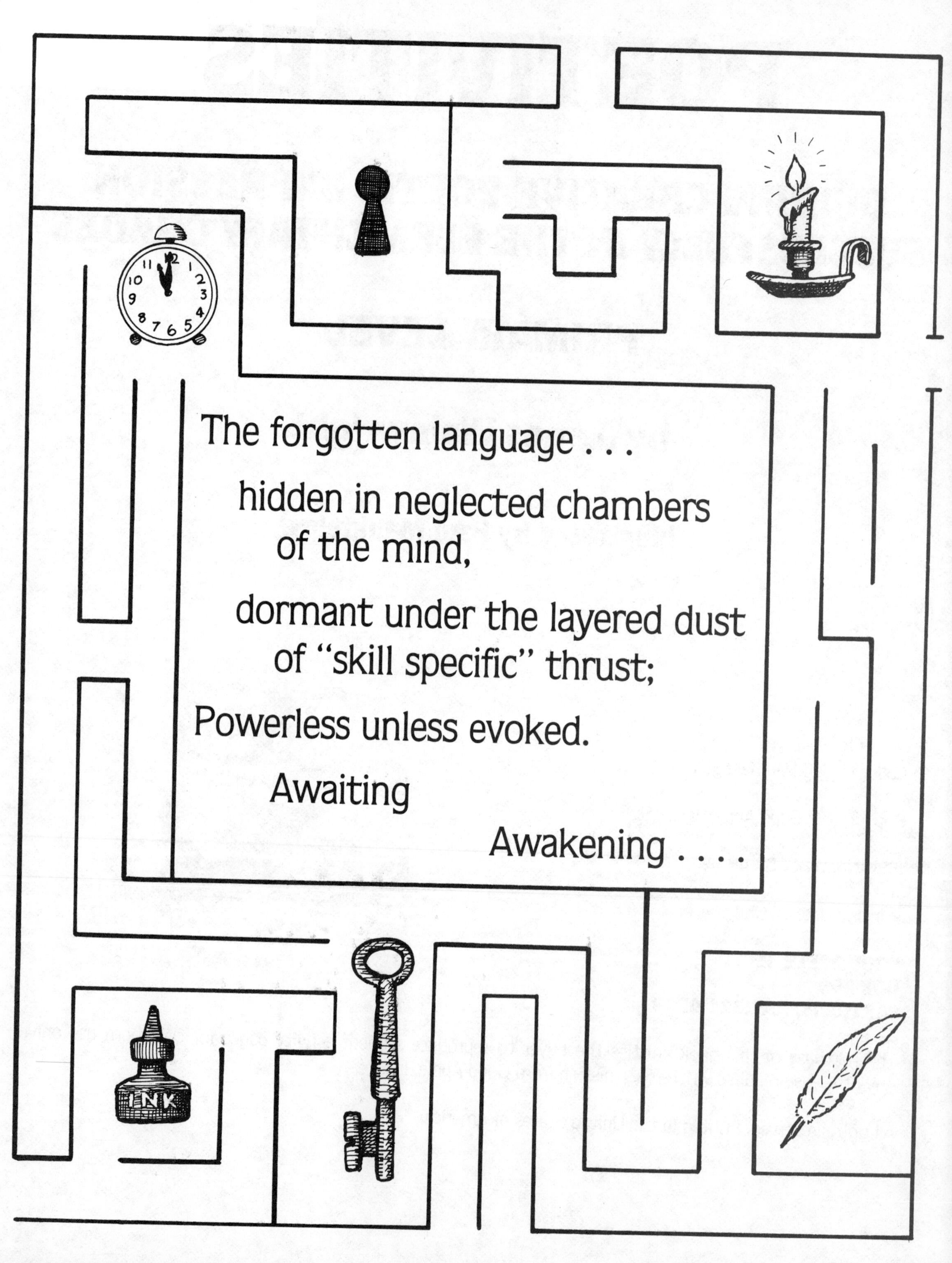


The forgotten language . . .

hidden in neglected chambers
of the mind,

dormant under the layered dust
of "skill specific" thrust;

Powerless unless evoked.

Awaiting

Awakening . . . .

# Table of Contents

# Introduction

*Poetivities,* a self-created word synthesized from poetry and activities, is an effort to stress the concept that poetry is a skill and, therefore, can be taught.

Each of us is born with much more than an innate desire to communicate our environmental situational experiences. We also seek an avenue for creative expression by which we can communally share the creative expression of our innermost thoughts, dreams, beliefs, feelings, and enigmas. We seek to move another's soul as well as register another's cognitive recognition. Poetry is one of the vehicles that allows us to fulfill this desire.

It is therefore an educational imperative that creative expression in young children be nurtured and developed. A true education must not only serve the logical practicalities of man's functioning within the framework of nature. and society, but must also provide an awakening and involvement in the philosophical and metaphysical questions that have underlined mankind's existence from the very start. Poetry is the metaphorical language that bridges man's perceptions of reality with a greater reality beyond mere sensory data.

The plethora of self-help books and talk show topics often can be distilled into a single problematic realization—that mankind has lost the ability to creatively communicate its inner spirit, getting mired down in the restraints of coexisting in a cognition-based technological society.

This book is a guide to unlock the forgotten language of poetic free verse. It is comprised of multi-step lessons designed for the free thinking, free wheeling teacher who seeks to guide very young children into creative expression. It is a developed "idea book" and, like any good manual, should soon be filled with your own personal notes, as teaching, like learning, is not a single-path, static journey but rather an ever changing revisionary as well as visionary process.

I have merely provided a series of field-tested ideas. To utilize this handbook efficiently, you will want to instill your own individual essence into each developed exercise—noting what worked well, what could be expanded, what could be refined for you as an individual. As teachers, if we're not constantly involved in the struggle to reinvent the wheel, then we're destined to roll only so fast, only so smooth, and only on roads on which we feel safe.

The Poetivity lessons are also carefully designed to provide integration primarily in language arts, but also in cross-curriculum disciplines as well. The lessons, particularly the Prewrite Activities, will strengthen grammatical components skills far better than handfuls of English book pages and dittos in that they evoke application from within rather than mere recognition from without.

The lessons and the high degree of involvement that they generate will certainly stimulate vocabulary enrichment and will serve to strengthen reading skills, particularly in inferential comprehension. They will also coincide with many of the standard curriculum objectives covered in most science and social studies units typically taught at the elementary level.

Finally, and probably most importantly, *Poetivities* will help break down the invisible barriers of poetry confusion and poetry resistance so common in children. It will subtlely lead your students into both an awareness of poetry's flexible intents and an appreciation of poetry's art.

# Poetry: Misunderstood Child of Communication

Preconceptions and misinformation have prevented the successful teaching of poetry writing for years. Poetry has mistakenly been looked upon as some kind of quasi-spiritual expression of elitist souls conceived by tormented minds and understood solely by literary intellectuals.

This is both tragic and completely wrong.

Poetry is actually our first venture into shared language expression. Toddlers speak in clipped syntax that is often symbolic of greater meaning than the mere word coupling. *Juice*, for example, actually stands for the unstated meaning of, "I'm thirsty and would like to drink some juice to rid myself of this thirst." This is the very heart of poetry—condensed linguistic lexicons that represent both hidden and multi-level semantical meaning.

The toddler is successful at it and never loses this ability with the infusion of sentence structure. Simply put, the elementary teacher needs only to strip this imposed structure and return to the language foundation in order to insure excellent poetic expression.

This manual will expand upon the simplistic premise stated above and offer devices, methods, and ideas to generate an exciting poetry writing experience for children of all ages.

# The Trash Compactor

Analogies often clarify foggy new information. In fact, we process all incoming knowledge dependent on our preexisting knowledge base.

Unfortunately, for most children, the preexisting knowledge base in poetry consists solely of Mother Goose and similar silly sing-songy rhymes. This, in turn, makes it somewhat difficult to redirect the thinking of poetic expression in a child who is well-conditioned in these established rhyme and meter patterns. This is not to say that these forms don't play a valid role in child development, but just as a child's dinner menu should reflect some nutritional variety, so too should his literary menu.

The analogy of the trash compactor works well in giving new poetic direction. It is also quite an accurate simplified analogy.

A trash compactor merely alters the form of the collected rubbish. It condenses the volume but in no way alters or eliminates the contents.

Poetry has the same action on prose. It greatly condenses the volume, but it in no way alters or eliminates the intended meaning. Thought and mood that might take five pages to develop and illuminate might effectively be communicated in a poem of five lines.

And, just as the weight of compacted trash is intensified into a smaller area, so too is the power and impact of poetry intensified into a significantly smaller area. This is one of the prime factors that gives poetry the intellectual and emotional "knockout punch" effect.

The "trash compactor" concept can be initiated and grasped at an early age. The younger grades will obviously require a physical demonstration of the concept, but by third grade mere verbalization should suffice. By establishing this understanding, you have created a foundation that poetic masterpieces can be erected upon, and I guarantee you won't believe the powerful poetry that your students will generate.

We teachers are but guides along the pathway to creativity, but it pays to have a flashlight along the way.

# Prewriting

All of the poetry writing activities or "Poetivities" as I refer to them, begin with prewriting activities. Simply stated, prewriting provides the direction, focus, and springboard for the successful completion of any writing task. It is not only a prudent approach, but it is actually essential if writing energy and productivity is to be achieved.

Prewriting is analogous to a baseball pitcher warming up before the actual game, to an engine idling before being run on a cold winter day, to an actor rehearsing a scene before it's shot.

A blank piece of paper and a vague general writing task is quite an obstacle, even for a fluid, experienced writer. A writer must know where he's going, how to get there, and how to get the ballpoint rolling so to speak. Parameters need to be established, and strategies need to be devised. Writing is at best a difficult task; it embraces any assistance it can receive.

This is the area where teaching skills are best utilized. The teacher in prewriting sets the purpose, guides the process, and motivates the outcome. Successful prewriting practically guarantees successful final writing.

The prewriting steps within the "Poetivities" are really nothing more than calculated compasses, generators, and catalysts. They create a positive atmosphere of unity while simultaneously insuring the grasping of the intended concept or task and its subsequent completion. No one hits a bull's-eye without first taking aim.

# Writing Poetry in the Primary Grades

The need to communicate is never stronger than it is in the first seven years of a child's life. It is compounded by the enigma of having a racing thought-filled mind that is often stymied by language constraints. The words are just not always there.

By realizing the struggle between communicative enthusiasm and frustration, the teacher can begin to bridge the gap and minimize internal negativism. Most teachers of primary grade children are masters at this bridging technique. They provide frequent oral opportunities and often utilize parents or upper grade children in story transcription.

The following "Poetivities" often revolve around a group participatory piece. This provides a thought-word interactive process in which all the children can feel connected, and, in fact, they each share in the success of the final product making them equal authors and imprinting future language manipulation.

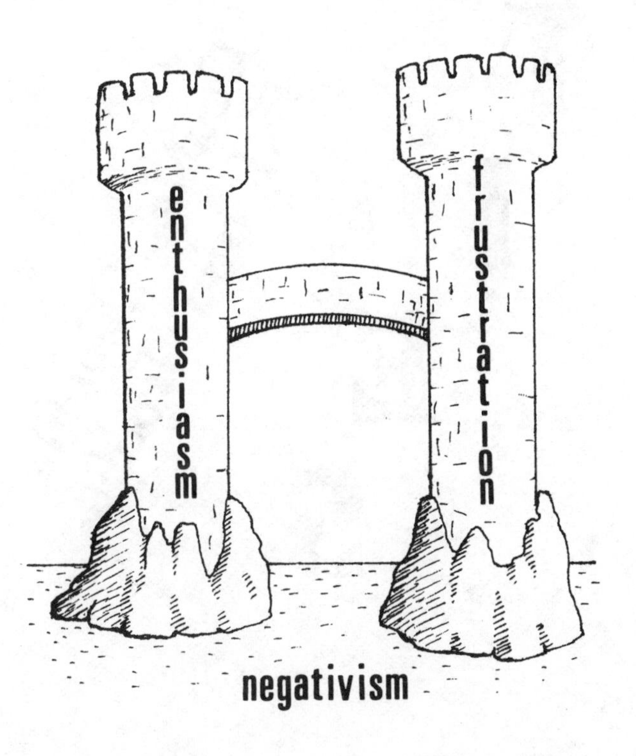


Also, since poem construction is not harnessed by "right or wrong" responses, the freedom and ease for sharing is very high, and embarrassment becomes virtually nonexistent.

Primary grade teachers are the hardest working, most gifted, and most important teachers within the educational system. You'll have a classroom full of poets in no time.

# POETIVITIES

"Yea, though I walk through the valley of the shadow of death...."

"In Xanadu did Kubla Khan
A stately pleasure-dome decree...."

"I think that I shall never see...."

"Double, Double
Toil and Trouble...."

"I took the one
less traveled by,
And that has
made all the
difference."

# Toy Parade

Poetry Objective: Free expression/Formatting

Language Objective: Noun-verb relationships/Word endings

Reading Objective: Classifying objects

## Prewrite Activities

1. Bring a Teddy bear to class.
2. Discuss the part that toys play in our lives.
3. Share all the things that you can do with your bear.
   Example: hold, cuddle, wave, kiss, dance, etc.

# Toy Parade

1. Have each child bring his favorite toy to class.
2. Create a "group poem" on the board.
   Setup: Tell children you're going to pretend that the toys they brought in are going to be part of a big toy parade.

   The contents of the poem merely will be the toy mentioned, followed by an action that the toy would do.

   Be sure to print it on the board in stacked lines.

Example:
The doll smiled,
The truck honked,
The baseball bounced,
The monkey jumped,
The soldier saluted,
The baby cried,
The gun fired,
The doggie barked,
All in the toy parade.

Be sure to include every child's toy and to use their ideas. Chime in only when the class is stuck. Guide them in word choice if duplication and repetition arise. They know many synonyms without realizing it.

## Expansion Ideas

1. Introduce the concept of descriptive writing (adjectives) by going back and inserting a word that describes the toy.
2. Place all the toys on a large table and group them by similar features.
3. Generate numerous creative writing opportunities with the table full of toys. (Tell about a toy party . . . pretend all the toys were as big as children and came to life . . . if toys had feelings, what would a typical "toy day" be like?)

# Sounds Abound

Poetry Objective: Sensory awareness

Language Objective: Word creation (introduction to onomatopoeia)

Reading Objective: To show how action is sometimes expressed so as to make the intended experience more vivid and real. Vowel sounds/consonant blends.

## Prewrite Activities

1. Find and play an album of sound effects. (If not in your library/learning center, most public libraries will have one.)
2. Pick selected album sounds and attempt to write them on the board.

   Example: The sound of a race car motor,
   Vvvvrrrroooommmm . . . errrrrooom

   Have *fun* with it. You're dealing with sounds, not words.
3. Lead into the generation of an onomatopoeia word list (crack, boom, bang, drip, etc.).

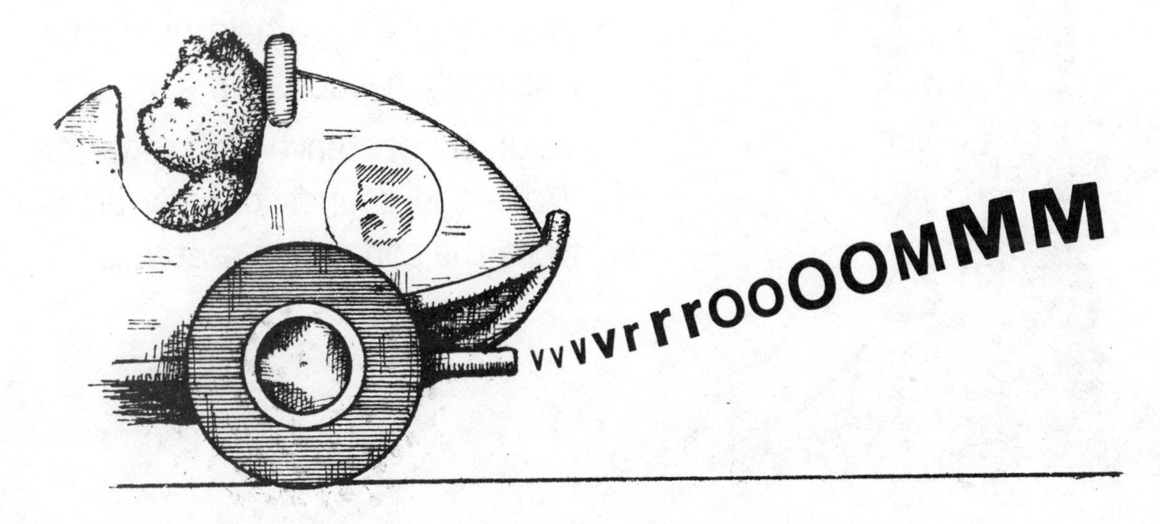

# Sounds Abound

1. Have the following sentence story on the board:
   a. Andy and Randy were crying because they were lost in the woods.
   b. It was getting dark and the wind began to blow.
   c. Off in the distance, they heard a coyote.
   d. An owl called from a tree.
   e. It started to storm.
   f. They ran through the leaves and sticks as fast as they could.
   g. They were tired and breathing heavily.
   h. Andy fell into a big puddle.
   i. Randy cut his arm on a branch and yelled in pain.
   j. Their friend Sandy fired three shots into the air to help them find their way back.
   k. They ran towards the sounds and when they spotted the cabin they cheered.
   l. They ran inside and shut the door very hard.
   m. Andy and Randy went straight to bed and fell asleep.

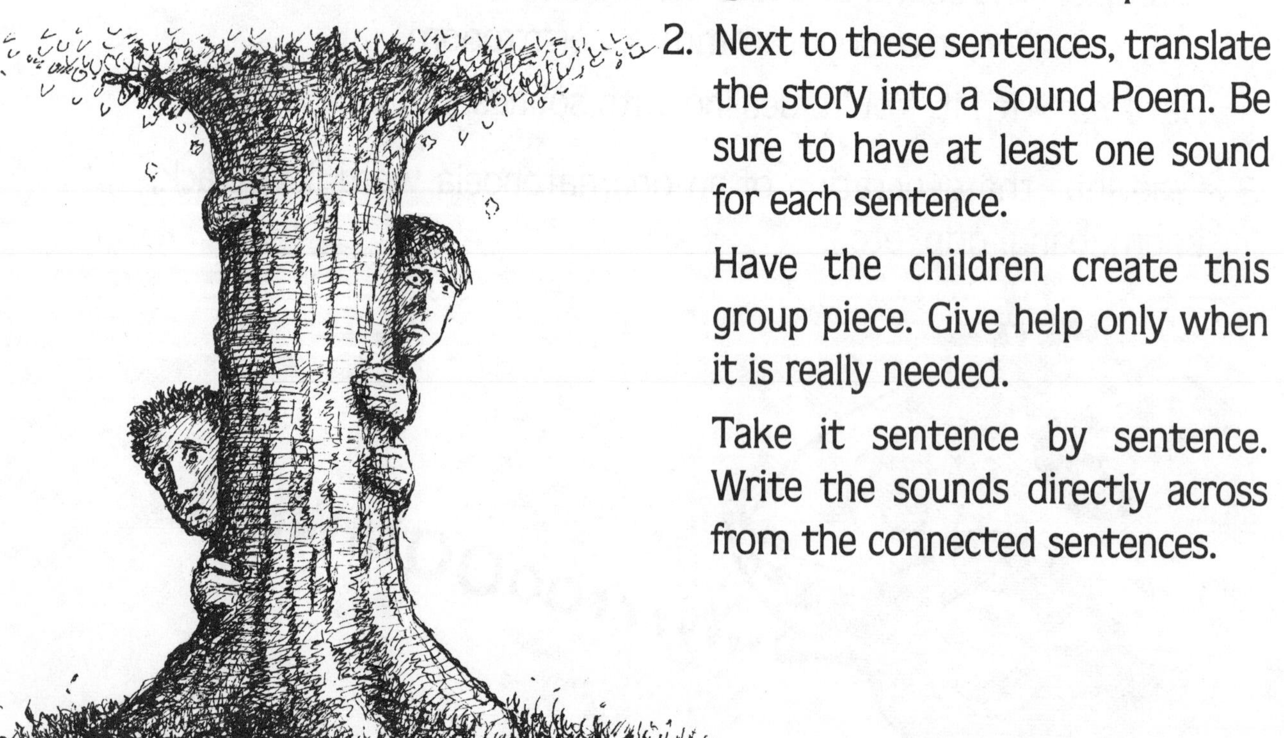

2. Next to these sentences, translate the story into a Sound Poem. Be sure to have at least one sound for each sentence.

   Have the children create this group piece. Give help only when it is really needed.

   Take it sentence by sentence. Write the sounds directly across from the connected sentences.

The completed poem should look something like this:

Lost and Found

Waaaaa . . .
Wewwww . . . Swishhhhhhhhhhh . . .
Arr . . . arr . . . arr . . . arooooooooo . . .
Whoooo . . . whoooo . . .
Crack . . . Ba . . . Boom!
Crunch . . . crunch . . . crackle . . . Snap . . .
Huhh . . . huhh . . . whewww . . .
SPLASH!
Owwwwwww!!!!
Bang! Bang! Bang!
Yea . . .
Slam!
Zzzzzzzzzzzzzz . . . .

## Expansion Ideas

1. After sharing the story poem, discuss why the poem version is more exciting.
2. Have the children put it on tape. They'll have a ball doing it and listening to it.
3. Older primary classes can break into small groups and create their own Sound Poems.

# Something's Fishy

Poetry Objective: Relating and expressing the external

Language Objective: Word associations

Reading Objective: Personification/Point of view

## Prewrite Activities

1. Do a group pantomime where students act out a variety of animals (dog, lion, rabbit, snake). After each pantomime, discuss what kind of things *might* be going through the animal's mind.
2. Read "Goldilocks and the Three Bears." List the ways the bears act like people (a lesson in personification). . . . family unit . . . live in a house with furniture . . . speak . . . cook . . . think . . . .
3. Discuss the story from the bears' point of view, emphasizing that they were merely minding their own business, going about their normal lives, when Goldilocks actually broke into their house, (crime), stole their food, (crime), and broke their personal belongings, (crime). Generate a brainstorming discussion on what the bears might have thought and what the bears might have felt.
4. Arrange to have a goldfish in a fishbowl for the students to observe and either distribute the following sheet or do together on the board.

# Goldie

# Something's Fishy

1. Take the "fish notes" and compose a group goldfish thought poem.

   Example:

   Inside Goldie's Mind

   What are these people staring at?
   I'm bored . . . .
   I'm lonely.
   This food tastes like paper!
   Hope my gold is gleaming.
   Least there's no fisherman to bother me.

2. Brainstorm a list of all the fish the students know.
3. Their task is to write a poem from their chosen fish's point of view, speculating on what its thoughts may be. (Odds are that the vast majority of boys in particular will choose the shark, so try to make other fish sound interesting in the setup.)

## Expansion Ideas

1. Coordinate poetivity with a science unit on fish.
2. Make papier-mâché fish to go with their poems.
3. Arrange a field trip to a local aquarium if possible.
4. Put an aquarium in the room and create an interest center to go with it.

# The BL Monster

Poetry Objective: Working with sounds

Language Objective: Alliteration

Reading Objective: Consonant blends

## Prewrite Activities

1. Concentrate current reading skills on consonant blends.
2. Have children draw and color large made-up monsters.
3. Do some fun tongue twisters with the class to reinforce beginning sound repetition (alliteration).

   Example:
   Loud lazy Larry loves licking luscious licorice lollipops.

4. Give each child his own consonant blend.
5. This is a great opportunity for a dictionary experience as you have the students use the dictionary to create word lists for their blends.
6. Students are then to use their word lists and create blend poems for their monsters.

## Expansion Ideas

1. Team children with a partner and have them combine their monsters to create a story or play.
2. Have the children create their own tongue twisters.
3. Put the pictures and poems together into a class book.
4. Create make-believe background information for the monsters.
5. Have the students give names to their monsters and for one entire day use the monster names to call on the children.

# The BL Monster

1. Take the monster that *you* drew and tape it on the front chalkboard.
2. Call it the BL Monster.
3. Create a group poem that uses as many BL blends as possible.
4. It will probably be necessary in the earlier grades to begin with BL word lists.

Example: black, blast, blaze, bleed, blind, blink, blob, block, blood, blow, blue, blur

BL Monster

Black and blue blockhead,
A big blue blob,
Blinking blind eyes that blur,
A mouth that blows blazing fire
And blasts away blue blood enemies.

# Where Am I?

Poetry Objective: Word choosing/Condensing

Language Objective: Nouns

Reading Objective: Establishing clues to setting

## Prewrite Activities

1. Have each child share his favorite place during share time or show and tell.
2. Have a variety of pictures of places available.
3. Classify the places into similar features (places that are quiet, places that are busy, places that are fun, etc.).
4. Distribute the following Flower Outline/Place Page. Students are to determine the petal pictures and write the word on the petal line. They are then to write the place they think all these things can be found.

   Acceptable Answers: Forest, woods, outdoors, park, mountains, wilderness.

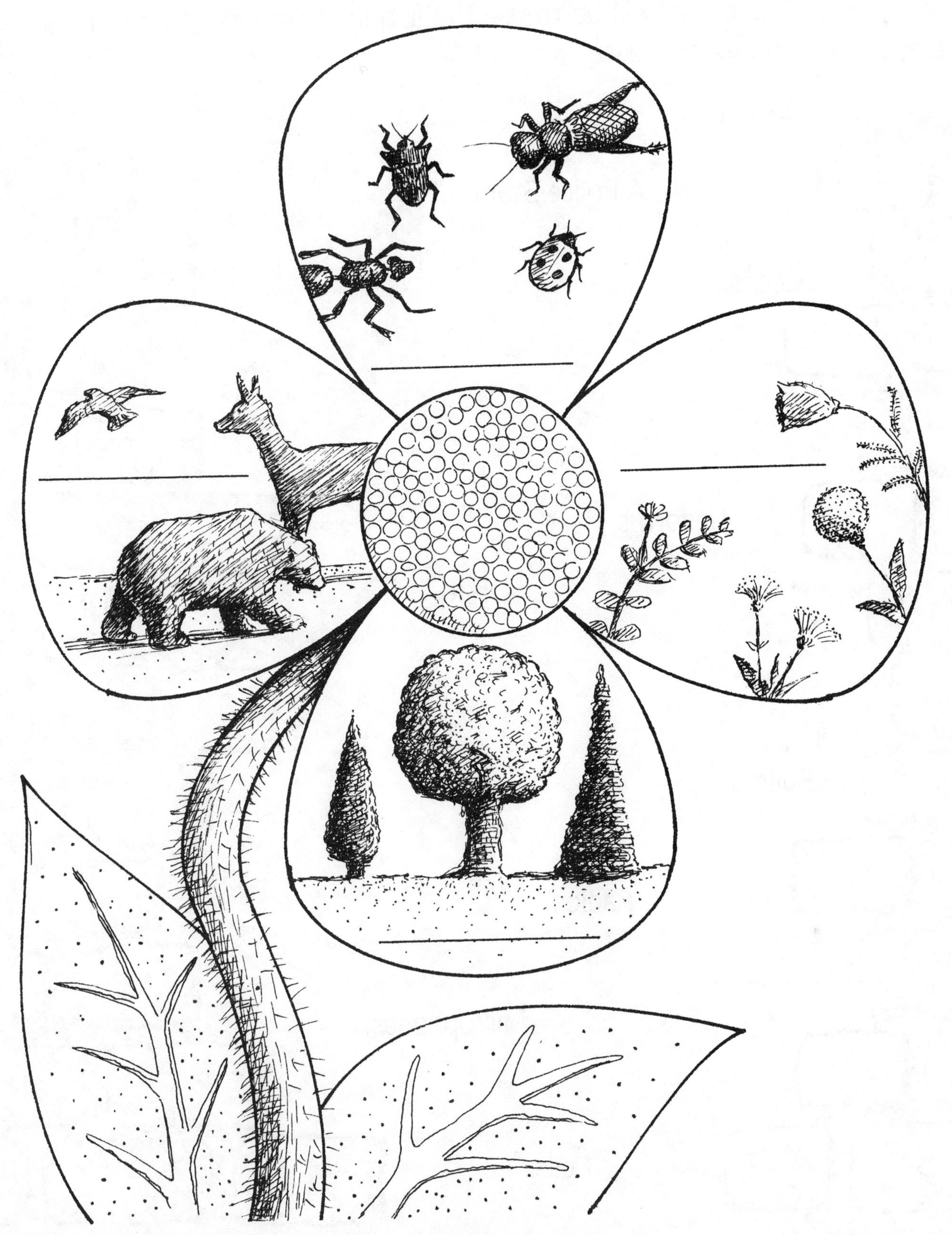

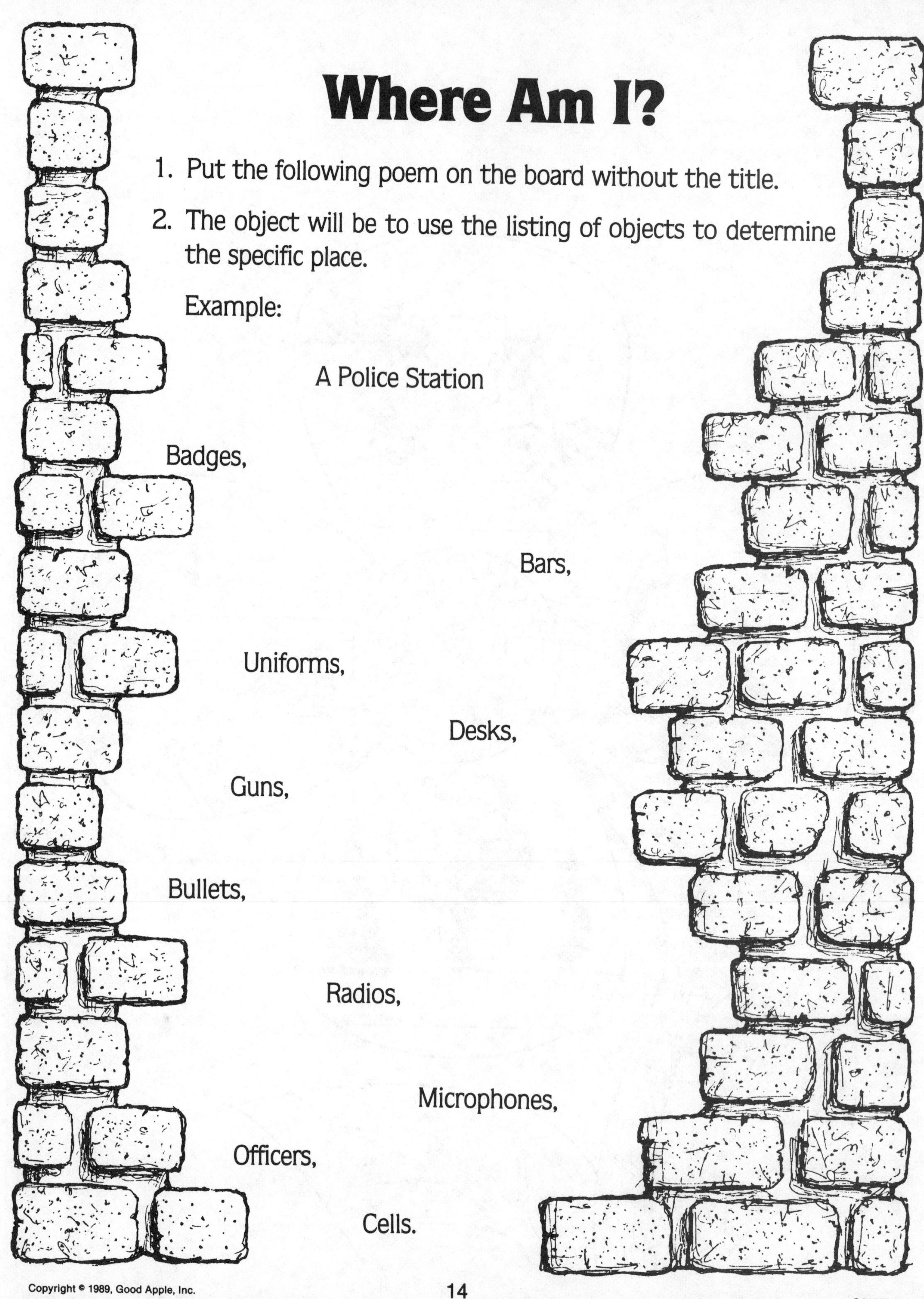

# Where Am I?

1. Put the following poem on the board without the title.
2. The object will be to use the listing of objects to determine the specific place.

Example:

A Police Station

Badges,

Bars,

Uniforms,

Desks,

Guns,

Bullets,

Radios,

Microphones,

Officers,

Cells.

3. Upon sharing the group poem, give children their own individual places to work with (amusement parks, playgrounds, zoos, supermarkets, schools, museums, airports, etc.).
4. They are to write in a free-form fashion objects that are found in their particular places.
5. Children take turns sharing their poems as classmates guess the places.

## Expanion Ideas

1. Have the children go back and put describing words in front of the nouns in their poems (adjectives).
2. Convert the noun poems into picture poems.
3. Create a favorite place bulletin board, complete with pictures and poems.
4. Have children do similar exercises using the various rooms in their houses.

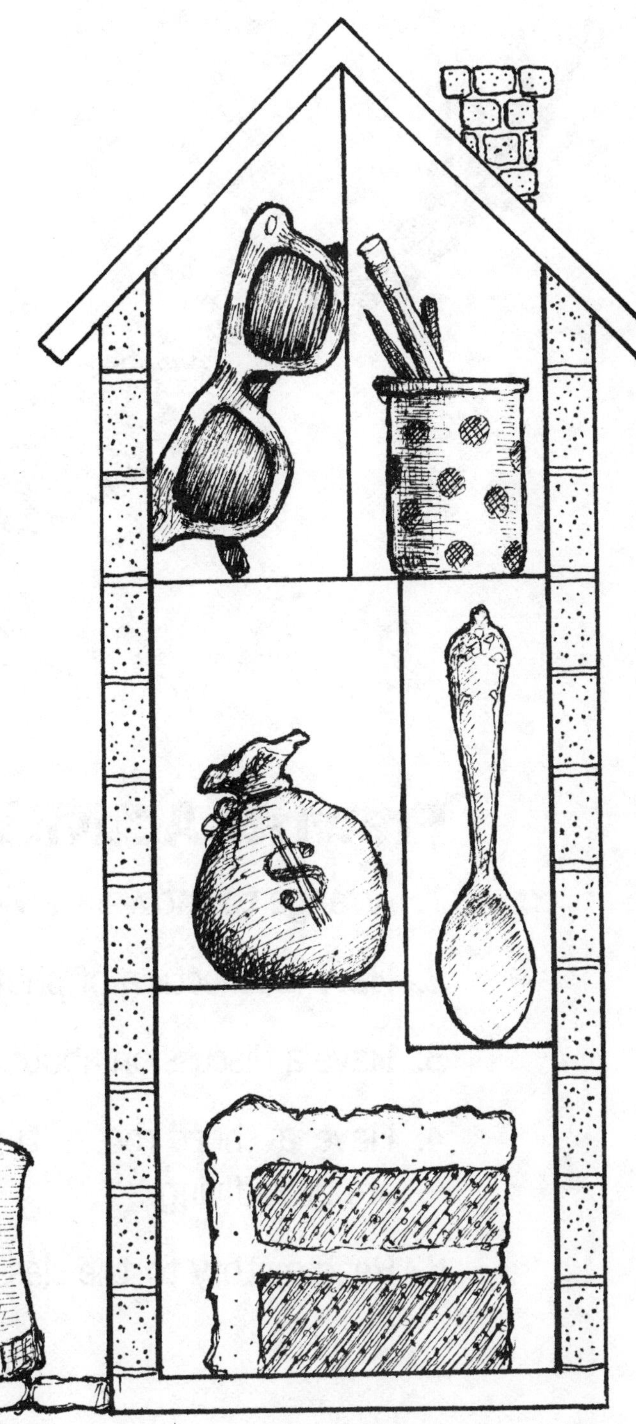

# Flying Free

| | |
|---|---|
| Poetry Objectiv:: | Developing out-of-experience expression/ Creating mood |
| Language Objective: | Word building (suffixes)/Adjectives, verbs |
| Reading Objective: | Comprehending character actions |

## Prewrite Activities

1. Arrange to show a movie/filmstrip of birds in flight.
2. Have a collection of photographs of birds available.
3. Have a discussion about what it would be like to fly.
4. Have a short recess time in which the children pretend they are birds flying.
5. Read a story to the class about birds.

# Flying Free

1. Turn the lights out and have the children either sit on top of their desks or lie on their backs on the floor, if you have carpeting.
2. Tell the children they are birds.
3. They are to describe how and what they are feeling as they fly through the skies.
4. Transcribe what they share. Try to guide them into the use of all of their senses.

Possible Outcome:

Up into the beautiful skies.
Wind blowing around my wings,
As I float and glide above the trees.
The noisy town far below doesn't even notice me.
The air is cool and crisp and smells wonderful.
It is so fresh.
I roll and twist in the breeze,
Such fun!
I love it.
I want to fly forever and ever,
The sky is my friend.

## Expansion Ideas

1. Tie the flying poems in with some bird artwork.
2. Have the class make paper wings and beaks and have a Bird Day in school.
3. Read them one of the numerous children's books that has a bird as a central character.
4. Tie in with a short science introduction to the many different kinds of birds and the way they live.
5. Pick a selection of some of the most popular birds in the class and make a bridge to geography by either pinning or taping little bird cutouts onto a map, reinforcing where a particular type of bird can be found.
6. Create a bird interest center.
7. Make a bulletin board depicting all the various birds that are on the endangered species list.

# It's a Secret

Poetry Objective:
To build to a greater unstated meaning

Language Objective:
Word choice

Reading Objective:
Associations/Sequence/Subtle introduction to inference

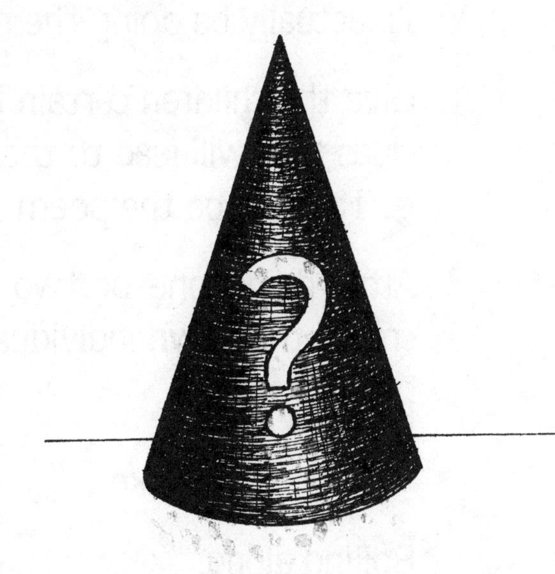


## Prewrite Activities

1. Do some standard riddles with the children.
   Example: What's black and white and "red" all over?
   A newspaper!

2. Have some large jigsaw style cutouts of various items. Present one piece at a time, and have children guess at what it is.

3. Tell small selected bits of well-known children's stories, and have children guess what story it is.
   Example: This sure is a long walk .... Where are you going? ... The woods are dangerous .... The dentist should get a look at those big teeth .... Get your axe, Woodcutter .... I want my Grandma!

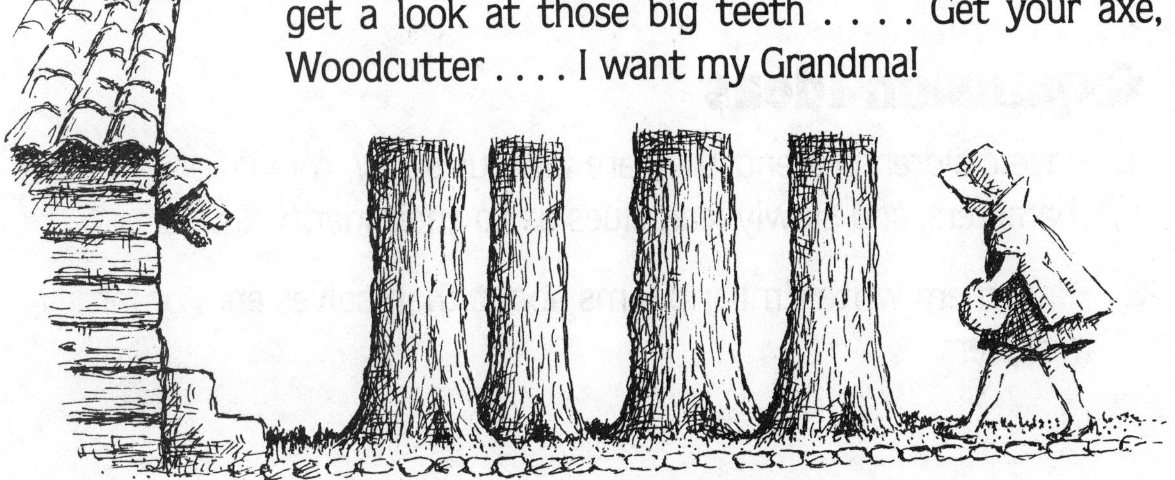

# It's a Secret

You'll actually be doing the reverse of the prewrite activities.

1. Give the children certain items and have them construct phrase clues that will lead to the final understanding of what the object is. This will be the poem.

2. After doing one or two group clue poems, have the children create their own individual poems.

   Example:

   A Bike

   Rolling along,
   Chain whipping around,
   Rubber skidding on clean pave-
   ment,
   Feet pushing hard on the pedals,
   Racing fast.

## Expansion Ideas

1. Have children pretend they are famous story, movie, or cartoon characters, and slowly leak clues as to their identities.

2. Have them write similar poems about themselves and/or family members.

# Synonym Cookies

| | |
|---|---|
| Poetry Objective: | Word choice (for intended meanings, and sound qualities) |
| Language/Reading Objective: | Introduction to synonyms |

## Prewrite Activities

1. Share similar branching words. Arrange to have an ice cube for each child to hold. Starting with the basic word *cold,* get the students to generate a list of words that mean "cold."

2. Discuss with the class what synonyms are and share the subtle differences in the words of their lists. Be sure to talk about the differences in the word sounds and the differences in the strength of word meanings.
   (Example: Which word is stronger, *cold* or *freezing*?)

3. Distribute the following outline picture of an elephant. Brainstorm and list all the words the class can come up with that mean "big." (*enormous, large, huge, magnificent, stupendous, humongous, gigantic,* etc.)

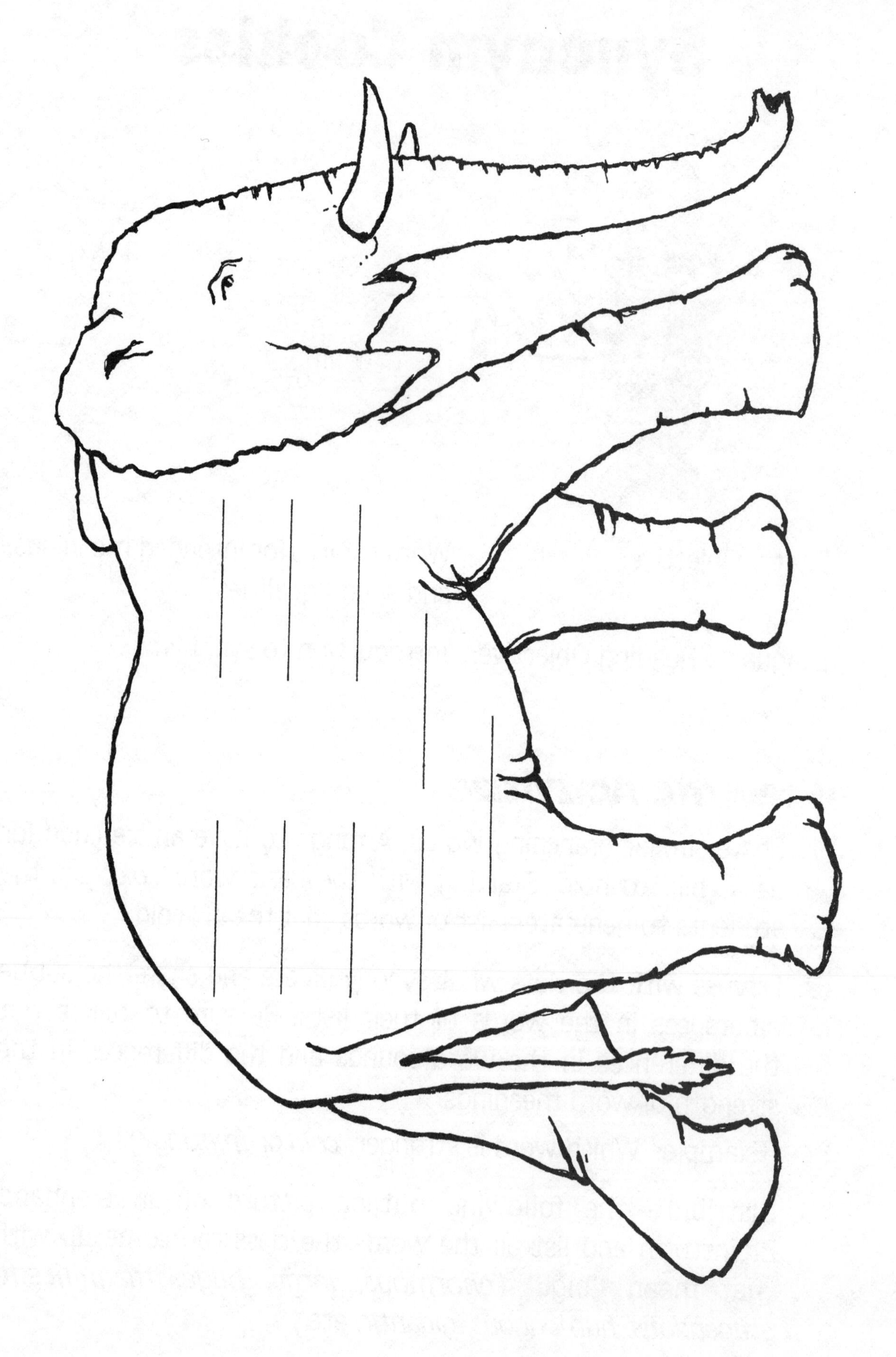

# Synonym Cookies

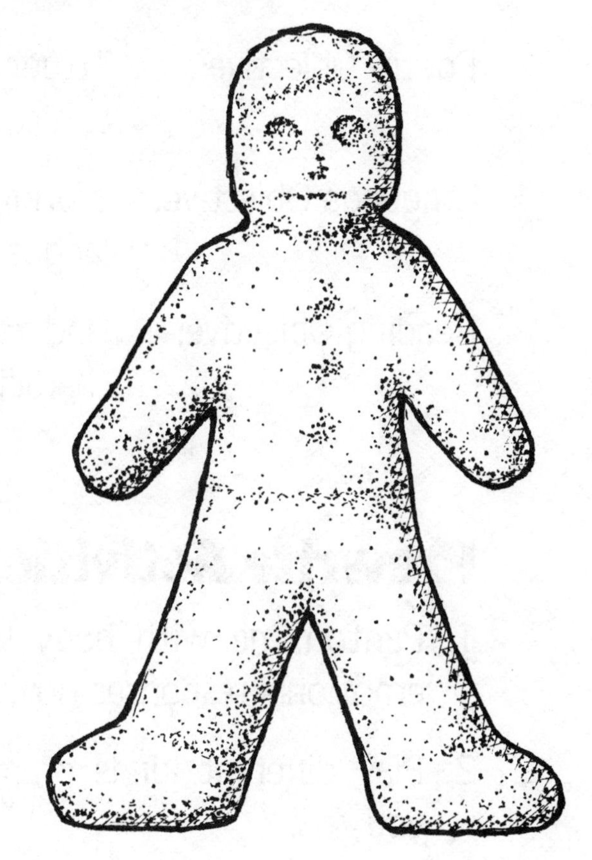

1. Make cookies with the class. Give each student some wax paper and cookie dough and have him shape the dough in whatever form he chooses. Then bake the cookies.
2. Give each student his baked cookie and have him draw a picture of it. The picture should be twice the size. Tell him that he should try to make the cookie picture look exactly like his cookie, complete with bumps, wrinkles, browned edges, etc.
3. Have the students eat the cookies.
4. Have the students write synonyms for the cookie's taste around the edges of their drawn cookies. Begin them with the word *good.*

## Expansion Ideas

1. Have them cut pictures out of magazines and do a similar write-around-the-edges activity.
2. Create Synonym Notebooks as a class.
3. Extend the cookie activity by having them write similes for the cookie through all five senses.

   Example: My cookie looks like . . . a tiny mountain.

# How Do You Feel?

| | |
|---|---|
| Poetry Objective: | To get in touch with emotional understanding and communicate the mood and feeling |
| Language Objective: | Working with expressive and descriptive language |
| Reading Objective: | Understanding character traits/Explaining character actions based on character feeling |

## Prewrite Activities

1. Pantomime with body language and facial expressions basic emotional responses (joy, sadness, anger, etc.).
2. Play different kinds of music and relate it to how it makes you *feel.*
3. Read the following situations and talk about how they would make you feel. Have the students put on the appropriate facial expressions as well.

a. A bully just broke your favorite toy.

b. You just got a new bike for your birthday.

c. Your dog Bosco just died.

d. You are next in line for Space Mountain at Disney World.

e. You just dropped a big chocolate milk shake in your lap.

f. Your best friend in the whole world just moved far away.

# How Do You Feel?

1. Turn the lights off and have children put their heads down.
2. Tell them we're going to drift back in time using our memories.
3. Give them an emotional response and force them to concentrate on a personal experience that is connected to that feeling (fear, anger, joy).

4. After about a minute of quiet concentration, turn the lights back on and have children write poems about their memories.

   Rule One: No rhymes
   Rule Two: No more than three words on a line

   Put the following example on the board as a guide:

   Worried
   Big dentist office
   White and scary
   Loud drills
   Will I gag
   Will it hurt
   I'm scared
   Please, God,
   A good checkup
   today
   OK.

## Expansion Ideas

1. To get the children comfortable with the loose structure of poems, have them write their scattered words around shape pictures. (A big heart for a love poem, a big smile for a happy poem, big bulging eyes for a scared poem, etc.)
2. Keep "feelings" diaries in the room.
3. Utilize the groundwork for positive student interaction with regard to one another's feelings.

# Cloud Dancing

| | |
|---|---|
| Poetry Objective: | Imagery |
| Language Objective: | Descriptive writing |
| Reading Objective: | Associations |

## Prewrite Activities

1. Using large construction paper, create a bunch of ink blots by dropping a "glob" of paint/ink in the center and folding and pressing.
2. Hold up the *large* ink blots one at a time and elicit responses from the class as to what images they see. (Be sure to turn the blot pictures in different directions as you do this.)
3. Have children take out plain pieces of white paper and black crayons. They are to close their eyes and wildly scribble as you count off, "One thousand one, one thousand two, one thousand three, STOP!"
4. Students are then to write their names on the backs of their scribble sheets.
5. Have the students then, on separate pieces of paper, write down descriptions of what they see in the scribbles.

6. Collect the "scribbles" and redistribute them in the class so that each child gets someone else's scribble.
7. On another sheet of paper they are to write what they see in this new scribble.
8. When they are finished, they are to return what they wrote and the scribble to the original artist, who will then compare what he wrote with what his classmate wrote.
9. Follow up with a discussion on why they think people see different images in nonspecific art.

# Cloud Dancing

1. Pick a day when the sky is full of thick, fluffy, white clouds.
2. Have the students get pencils and notebooks, and take them outside to cloud stare.
3. Every time they see a particular image in a cloud or cloud formation, they are to write down what they see, adding as much specific descriptive detail as possible.

It will be absolutely imperative for you to get them started with some "high-rev" modeling.

Example:

I see a fat, toothless, one-eared hippopotamus with a dragon's tail sitting on a beach ball . . . .

4. Back in the classroom, each student takes his notes and writes them on a large sheet of construction paper in any order or form he chooses, under the title of "Cloud Dancing."
5. Have the students decorate their "Cloud Dancing" by gluing cotton balls as three-dimensional clouds.

## Expansion Ideas

1. Tie in to an art lesson in modern art/surrealistic art.
2. A similar technique can be used to combine finger painting with creative writing.
3. Write a class story about some mythological cloud kingdom.
4. Do a science mini-lesson on clouds and their types and formations.

# Your Nature Is My Nature

Poetry Objective: Imagery/Mood

Language Objective: Descriptive writing/Adjectives

Reading Objective: Similes/Sensory comprehension

## Prewrite Activities

This Poetivity dovetails with the standard nature awareness aspect inherent in most primary curriculums.

1. Have a discussion on what it means to be observant.
2. Arrange to have a fellow teacher/administrator stop in the room for a moment.
3. After the adult leaves the room, have the children write down everything they can about the person's looks and clothes.
4. Share and reinforce the concept of observation.
5. Give each child a Ziploc bag and take the entire class on a nature hike around the building. Children are to find and place the following items in their bags: grass, leaves, bark, stones, weeds, flower petals.
6. Students use their nature "stuff" to fill in the following sheets (Observations Revisited).

# Observations Revisited

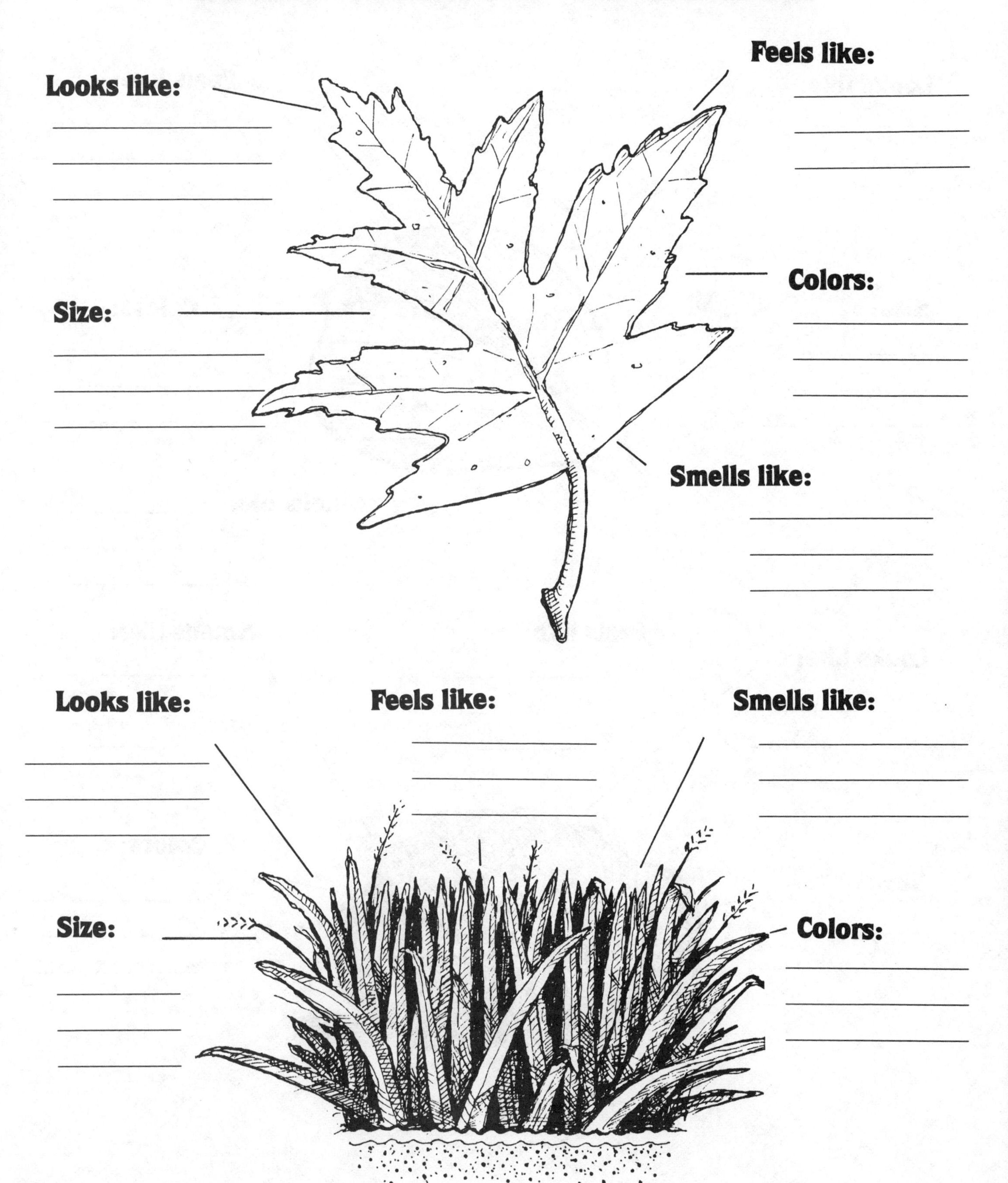

# Observations Revisited

**Looks like:**

**Feels like:**

**Size:**

**Colors:**

**Smells like:**

**Feels like:**

**Looks like:**

**Smells like:**

**Colors:**

**Size:**

# Your Nature Is My Nature

1. Give each student a large sheet of manila drawing paper and have him draw an outdoor nature scene. (It should include all the elements of his Ziploc bag collection.)

   Students' pictures should *not* have man or anything man-made in them and should have *plenty* of blank uncolored sections in them.

2. Students are then to select the simile parts of their nature sheets and write them in the blank spaces of their pictures.
3. Display the pictures and immediately break into a lesson on similes.

## Expansion Ideas

1. Integrate a science unit on plants or rocks.
2. Create a Simile Notebook with similes and corresponding pictures.

   Examples:

   My baby brother/sister is like a ______________________.

   My bedroom is like a ______________________.

   Recess is like a ______________________.

# What's Your Game?

Poetry Objective: Inferential clues

Language Objective: Specific nouns/Verbs

Reading Objective: Word associations/Sequence

## Prewrite Activities

1. Have a shared discussion on favorite nonsport games. Follow up with a brainstorming discussion on the value and importance of games. (Why are they fun? What do they teach us? Etc.)
2. Distribute Bingo cards and beans and play a few games of Bingo.
3. Write *Bingo* on the board and discuss how, although really a game of luck, there are "brain benefits." Write *Number/Letter Recognition* and *Listening Skills* on the board.
4. Make two columns on the board: *Nouns* *Verbs*
5. Under the Nouns column, brainstorm and list the "things" necessary to play Bingo: cards, beans, spinner/tumbler, tiles, caller.
6. Under the Verbs column, brainstorm and list the "actions" that take place during a Bingo game: spin, call, listen, look, pick, place, fill, win, shout.

7. Combine the words into a noun/verb poem being sure to string together the appropriate combinations.

   Example:

   Bingo

   Caller spins,
   Caller calls,
   Players listen and look,
   Beans picked,
   Beans placed,
   Column filled,
   Player shouts,
   Player wins.

   Emphasize how the understanding of the game is conveyed in a mere handful of words.

# What's Your Game?

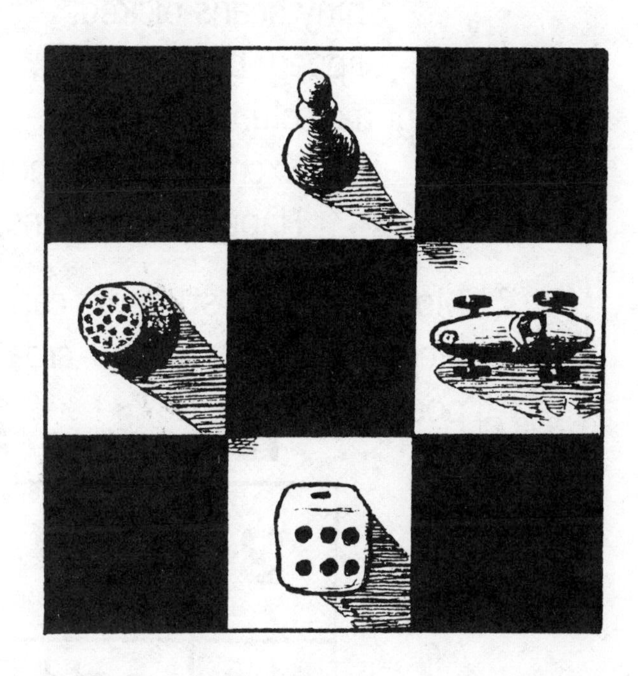

1. Have a variety of fairly simple board/card games available for class playing.
2. Divide the class into groups of three or four and distribute the games, avoiding duplication if possible.
3. Groups play their game and as a group repeat the prewriting activity of listing the nouns (things) and verbs (actions) in labeled columns.

4. Each group is then responsible to turn their selected words into a poem format similar to Bingo. Try to emphasize the order of the actions (sequencing).

5. After the games are collected and the poems are composed, each group shares their poem without mention of the game as other groups guess.

## Expansion Ideas

1. Further develop the clipped game poems by the addition of information words (adjectives/adverbs). Use "Bingo" as your example.

Bingo

Caller spins rapidly,
Caller calls clearly,
Anxious players listen carefully,
And look quickly,
Shiny beans picked,
Slippery beans placed,
Diagonal column filled,
Excited player shouts wildly,
Happy player wins.

2. More advanced students can be given cardboard, dice, and playing pieces and as a group create their own game and their own poem.

| B | I | N | G | O |
|---|---|---|---|---|
| 3 | 65 | 7 | 12 | 34 |
| 50 | 49 | 23 | 4 | 67 |

# A Day in the Life

Poetry Objective: Personification/Point of view

Language Objective: Writing to a defined purpose

Reading Objective: Character traits/Character motivation

## Prewrite Activities

1. This poetry exercise dovetails beautifully with a unit study on animals and especially a trip to the local zoo.
2. Have an activity/interest center where the children get the opportunity to receive as much information on various wild animals as possible.
3. Lead a discussion on the children's favorite animals, being sure to draw specific reasons for their choices.
4. Do a short class charades game with children acting out various wild animals.
5. Have the children make lists of ten wild animals that they think they know a lot about (a good time to introduce the concept of prioritized listing).

# A Day in the Life

1. Take the children's lists of animals and circle one, making sure to get a wide range of variety in the room.

2. After all the children have received their animals, have them close their eyes and turn the lights off. Guide the class into forgetting themselves, and, using the full power of their imaginations, they are to lock in to what it would be like if they were indeed their chosen animals. Give them frequent auditory clues so they really "lock in" on the particular setting where their animals would be found so that they fully visualize their surroundings.

3. Turn the lights back on while reinforcing that they are to stay in character.

4. Pass out the following animal information sheet. The students are to fill in the information as accurately as possible. Offer assistance when needed, and it would be a good idea to have the library's complete set of zoo books if possible (introduction to research).

# Animal Information

Type of animal: ____________________

Animal's first name: ____________________

Animal's last name: ____________________

Animal's home: ____________________

Animal's favorite food: ____________________

Animal's enemies: ____________________

____________________

Picture of Animal

____________________

Now, as your animal, write about your most interesting or exciting day. ____________________

____________________

____________________

____________________

____________________

____________________

____________________

____________________

5. Distribute a sheet of paper broken into fragmented present progressive verbs:

   Running through . . . .

   Hiding in . . . .

   Eating . . . .

   Playing . . . .

   Watching out for . . . .

   Thinking about . . . .

   Dreaming about . . . .

6. Children are to finish the fragmented phrases as they think their animals would answer.

   Example:

   Running through the jungle

   Hiding in thick tall grass

   Eating antelope

   Playing paw tag

   Watching out for hunters

   Thinking about my cubs

   Dreaming about being king

7. Upon finishing their clipped phrases, the children are to add two to four more "compacted" phrases from their interesting/ exciting experiences activity.

8. Have each child read his finished poem without mentioning the animal, and then have the rest of the class guess the animal.

## Expansion Ideas

1. Follow up the poetry experience by having the children write mini-reports about their animals, complete with art projects such as clay or papier-mâché models.

2. Have children make little paper cutouts of their animals and pin them to a large map reinforcing their geographical homelands.

3. Generate vocabulary lists on animal groups (herds, prides, flocks, etc.) and animal sounds (growls, roars, whistles, etc.).

4. Have a short late afternoon Animal Party where the children wear paper masks of their animals and eat Animal Crackers.

# Who Are You?

Poetry Objective: Self-understanding/Self-expression

Language Objective: Nouns/Adjectives

Reading Objective: Semantic word mapping

## Prewrite Activities

1. Demonstrate the old tried-and-true snowflake cutout to the class.
2. Give each child a piece of plain white paper and have him cut out one giant snowflake.
3. Display the snowflakes and lead a thorough discussion about the individual differences in each snowflake, springboarding into a discussion of the unique and special differences of each individual person.

4. Select two children to bring up to the front of the class. Have the students brainstorm the various differences between the two, beginning with the obvious physical differences and leading them into recognizing some of the basic differences in their personalities and their individualized likes and dislikes.
5. Give each student the following word mapping sheet. Students fill in their personal information.

# I Am . . .

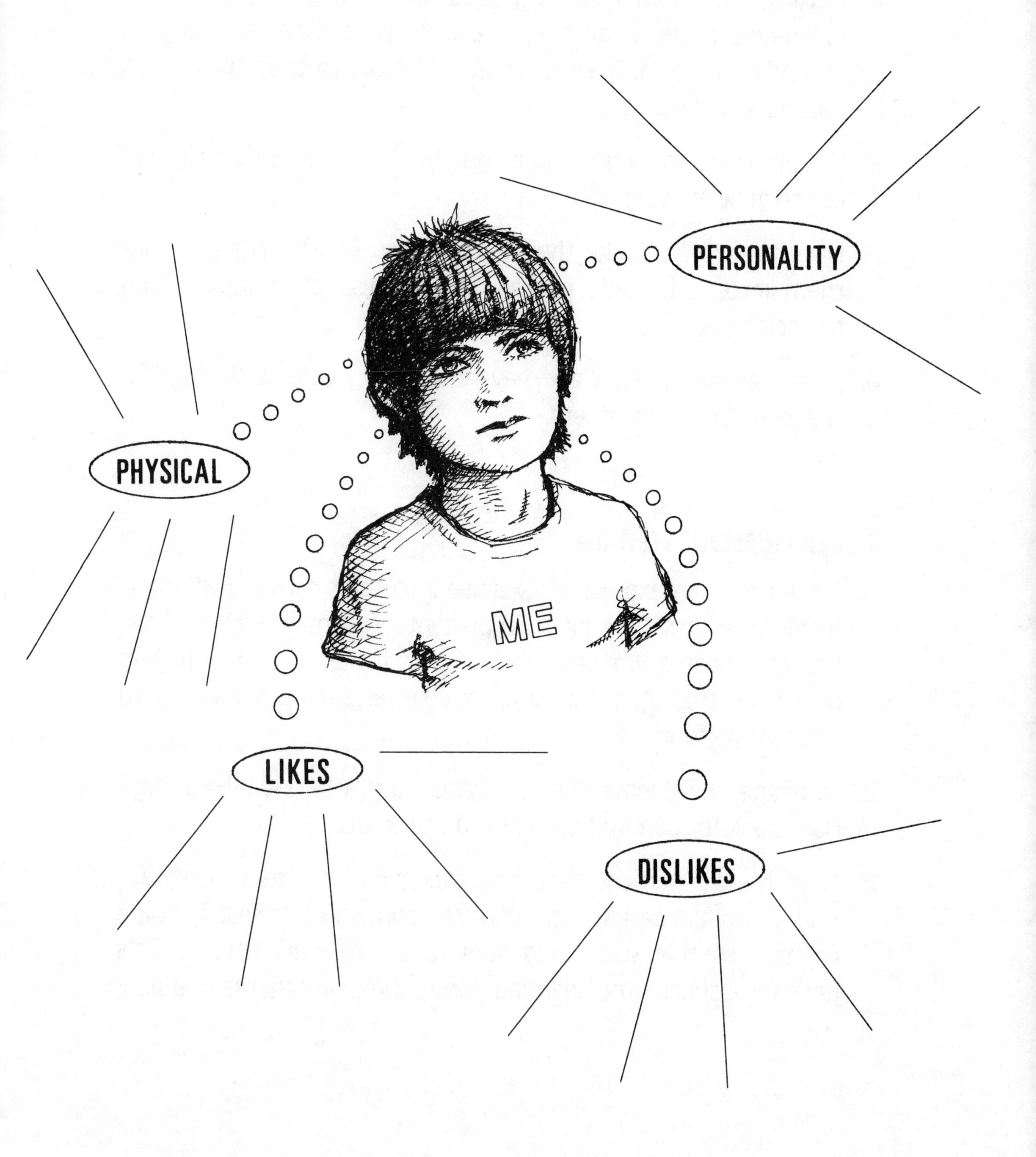

# Who Are You?

1. Return the snowflakes to the children, reviewing the basic differences again. Explain to the class that they are going to expand on those differences by adding color to their snowflakes (decorate and design).

2. Explain that words are what add the "color" in writing (mini-lesson in adjectives).

3. Have the children take their personalized word maps and turn them into "colorized" poems, adding descriptive information to their categories.

4. Share selected poems and have the class make guesses as to the identities of the poets.

## Expansion Ideas

1. Since this is an expression exercise into their own individuality, freedom in form is equally important. You may wish to have the final poems written on new snowflakes, over the fingers of a hand tracing, or on simplistic paper skeleton mobiles to hang in the room.

2. Laminate the poems with accompanying artwork into a large class book for parental display and checkout.

3. Have the children use their snowflakes and poems to decorate their individual desks; then work out some sort of seat hopping rotation so that each child gets to sit at every other child's desk for a short time, learning about their classmates in a new way.

# The Reasons of the Seasons

Poetry Objective: Figurative language

Language Objective: Symbols and connotations

Reading Objective: Categorize specific vocabulary

## Prewrite Activities

This Poetivity blends well with lessons involving learning the months and/or science units on weather.

1. Create a four-panel bulletin board with each section labeled one of the four seasons.

   Spring Summer Fall Winter

2. Distribute old magazines used for cutting purposes.
3. Students are to find, cut out, and paste pictures that pertain to a specific season, trying to find at least one picture for each season.
4. When the bulletin board is completed, point to particular cutouts and have that student explain why that picture goes under the selected season.
5. Distribute the following "seasonal pies" and guide the students through their chart fill-ins. Emphasize that what they write down has to be particular to the season.

# Seasonal Pie

List the different things you do in each season.

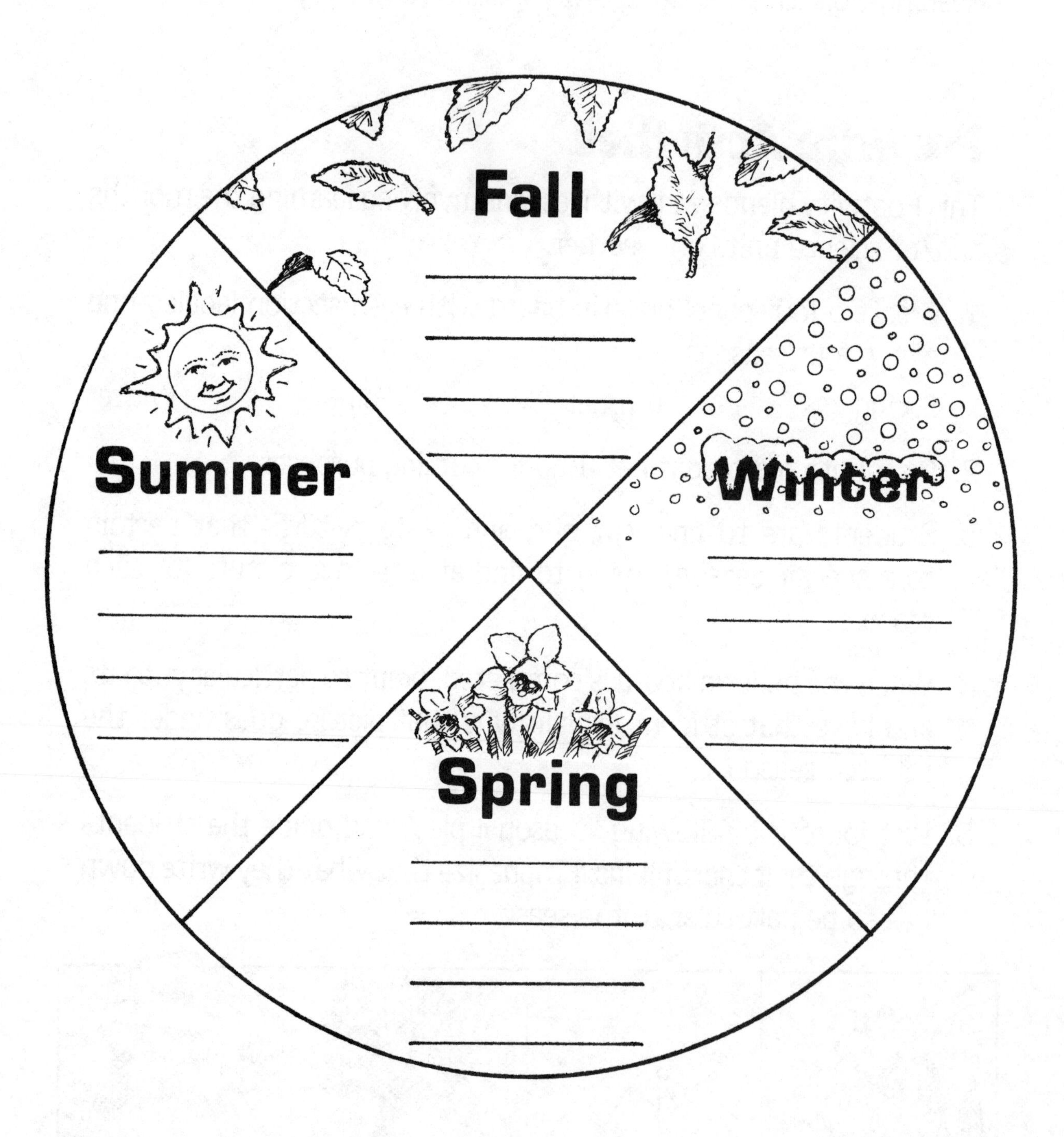

# Seasonal Pie

List the different things you see in each season.

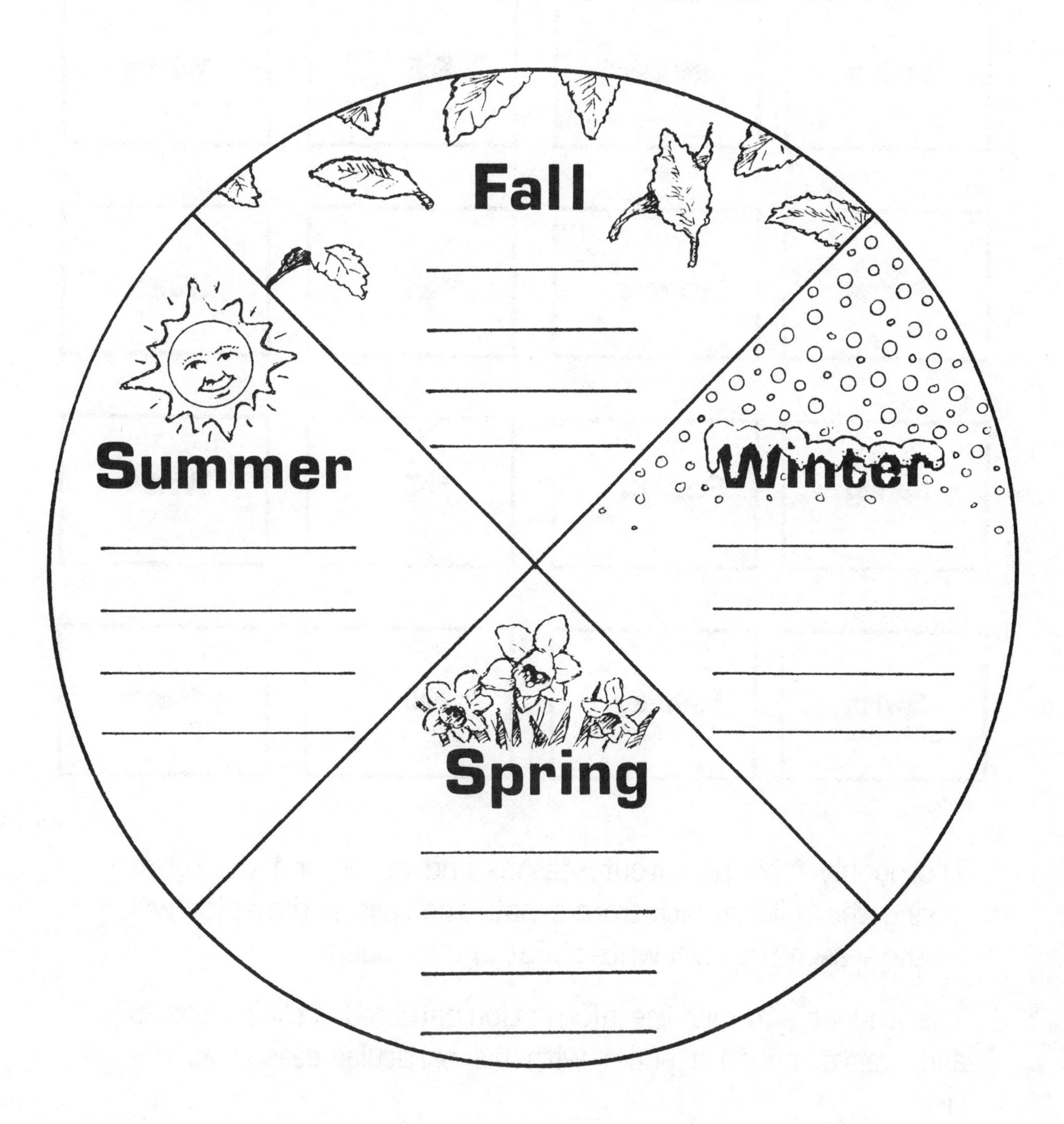

# The Reasons of the Seasons

1. Duplicate, cut and fold the following secret seasons:

| Spring | Summer | Fall | Winter |
| --- | --- | --- | --- |
| Spring | Summer | Fall | Winter |
| Spring | Summer | Fall | Winter |
| Spring | Summer | Fall | Winter |

2. Thoroughly mix the cutout seasons and go around the room having the children pick from a hat. The season they pick will be the season they will write about in their poems.

3. The student is to take the information gathered in the pie charts and weave it into a poem with his particular season as the title.

4. Upon completion, students take turns reading their poems while the class guesses the mystery seasons. (Make a game out of it.)

5. Have a post-poem discussion, reemphasizing how chosen select symbols automatically make a person associate with a particular season.

   Examples:

   sled . . . . winter
   swimming pool . . . . summer
   football . . . . fall
   Easter . . . . spring

# Expansion Ideas

1. Use the following ballot to have the students vote for their favorite season (a good experience in backing up an opinion with specific detail).

   I cast my vote for the season of ____________________

   This is the best season because ____________________

   ________________________________________

   ________________________________________

   ________________________________________

   ________________________________________

2. Do a creative writing/art project on make-believe seasons describing what they would be like.
   Sumall (a combination of summer and fall)
   Sprinter (a combinaton of spring and winter)

# For Consideration

Literary style is absorbed through exposure much in the same way that music and art appreciation are developed. One cannot minimize the strength of the oral tradition in seed-planting style variations as well as initiating a motivating interest and appreciation of any form of literature.

This is especially true in regard to poetry, as it is the one literary expression capable of generating such a vast variety of styles and formats. By reading poems to your class, you not only can fill short time gaps, but can open an awareness to thought and feeling that will reflect itself in each child's personal communications.

Again, the key is variety. Many teachers seem to restrict their poetry reading to Shel Silverstein. He is fantastic and entertaining, to be sure, but should definitely be augmented with other forms and intents. Children *do* have a strong capacity for dealing with serious and mood-provoking material; let's not underestimate their hearts, as we certainly can't afford to underestimate their minds.

Sprinkle your poetry reading wisely. In addition to Mr. Silverstein, share some Dickinson, some Poe, some Frost, some Whitman, even some Shakespeare. Even if the meaning is beyond their comprehension, and remember that poetry can be understood at many diverse levels, the richness and musicality of the language itself will seep in more than you could possibly realize.

History

# Teacher: Magician

Illusions . . . .
Vaporizing the confusions
with a wave of the wand
and a puff of smoke

Pulling rabbits out of a hat
is a snap
compared to pulling literacy out of a head

The great disappearing act—
dispelling the substance—less demons
who go by names as old as time:
"I don't know how," "I don't get it,"
"I don't want to," "I don't care"

The great appearing act—
Replacing the demons with substantial angels
who go by names as gold as time:
"Confidence," "Determination,"
"Enthusiasm," "Understanding"

Let the skeptical hecklers spout
For we don't doubt
that we possess the true magic

# FREE Test Taking Tips DVD Offer

To help us better serve you, we have developed a Test Taking Tips DVD that we would like to give you for FREE. **This DVD covers world-class test taking tips that you can use to be even more successful when you are taking your test.**

All that we ask is that you email us your feedback about your study guide. Please let us know what you thought about it – whether that is good, bad or indifferent.

To get your **FREE Test Taking Tips DVD**, email freedvd@studyguideteam.com with "FREE DVD" in the subject line and the following information in the body of the email:

a. The title of your study guide.

b. Your product rating on a scale of 1-5, with 5 being the highest rating.

c. Your feedback about the study guide. What did you think of it?

d. Your full name and shipping address to send your free DVD.

If you have any questions or concerns, please don't hesitate to contact us at freedvd@studyguideteam.com.

Thanks again!

# CDL Study Guide 2020 and 2021

## CDL Training Book 2020 and 2021 with Practice Test Questions for the Commercial Drivers License Exam [3rd Edition]

TPB Publishing

Written and edited by TPB Publishing.



ISBN 13: 9781628456677
ISBN 10: 1628456671

# Table of Contents

# Quick Overview

As you draw closer to taking your exam, effective preparation becomes more and more important. Thankfully, you have this study guide to help you get ready. Use this guide to help keep your studying on track and refer to it often.

This study guide contains several key sections that will help you be successful on your exam. The guide contains tips for what you should do the night before and the day of the test. Also included are test-taking tips. Knowing the right information is not always enough. Many well-prepared test takers struggle with exams. These tips will help equip you to accurately read, assess, and answer test questions.

A large part of the guide is devoted to showing you what content to expect on the exam and to helping you better understand that content. In this guide are practice test questions so that you can see how well you have grasped the content. Then, answer explanations are provided so that you can understand why you missed certain questions.

Don't try to cram the night before you take your exam. This is not a wise strategy for a few reasons. First, your retention of the information will be low. Your time would be better used by reviewing information you already know rather than trying to learn a lot of new information. Second, you will likely become stressed as you try to gain a large amount of knowledge in a short amount of time. Third, you will be depriving yourself of sleep. So be sure to go to bed at a reasonable time the night before. Being well-rested helps you focus and remain calm.

Be sure to eat a substantial breakfast the morning of the exam. If you are taking the exam in the afternoon, be sure to have a good lunch as well. Being hungry is distracting and can make it difficult to focus. You have hopefully spent lots of time preparing for the exam. Don't let an empty stomach get in the way of success!

When travelling to the testing center, leave earlier than needed. That way, you have a buffer in case you experience any delays. This will help you remain calm and will keep you from missing your appointment time at the testing center.

Be sure to pace yourself during the exam. Don't try to rush through the exam. There is no need to risk performing poorly on the exam just so you can leave the testing center early. Allow yourself to use all of the allotted time if needed.

Remain positive while taking the exam even if you feel like you are performing poorly. Thinking about the content you should have mastered will not help you perform better on the exam.

Once the exam is complete, take some time to relax. Even if you feel that you need to take the exam again, you will be well served by some down time before you begin studying again. It's often easier to convince yourself to study if you know that it will come with a reward!

# Test-Taking Strategies

## 1. Predicting the Answer

When you feel confident in your preparation for a multiple-choice test, try predicting the answer before reading the answer choices. This is especially useful on questions that test objective factual knowledge. By predicting the answer before reading the available choices, you eliminate the possibility that you will be distracted or led astray by an incorrect answer choice. You will feel more confident in your selection if you read the question, predict the answer, and then find your prediction among the answer choices. After using this strategy, be sure to still read all of the answer choices carefully and completely. If you feel unprepared, you should not attempt to predict the answers. This would be a waste of time and an opportunity for your mind to wander in the wrong direction.

## 2. Reading the Whole Question

Too often, test takers scan a multiple-choice question, recognize a few familiar words, and immediately jump to the answer choices. Test authors are aware of this common impatience, and they will sometimes prey upon it. For instance, a test author might subtly turn the question into a negative, or he or she might redirect the focus of the question right at the end. The only way to avoid falling into these traps is to read the entirety of the question carefully before reading the answer choices.

## 3. Looking for Wrong Answers

Long and complicated multiple-choice questions can be intimidating. One way to simplify a difficult multiple-choice question is to eliminate all of the answer choices that are clearly wrong. In most sets of answers, there will be at least one selection that can be dismissed right away. If the test is administered on paper, the test taker could draw a line through it to indicate that it may be ignored; otherwise, the test taker will have to perform this operation mentally or on scratch paper. In either case, once the obviously incorrect answers have been eliminated, the remaining choices may be considered. Sometimes identifying the clearly wrong answers will give the test taker some information about the correct answer. For instance, if one of the remaining answer choices is a direct opposite of one of the eliminated answer choices, it may well be the correct answer. The opposite of obviously wrong is obviously right! Of course, this is not always the case. Some answers are obviously incorrect simply because they are irrelevant to the question being asked. Still, identifying and eliminating some incorrect answer choices is a good way to simplify a multiple-choice question.

## 4. Don't Overanalyze

Anxious test takers often overanalyze questions. When you are nervous, your brain will often run wild, causing you to make associations and discover clues that don't actually exist. If you feel that this may be a problem for you, do whatever you can to slow down during the test. Try taking a deep breath or counting to ten. As you read and consider the question, restrict yourself to the particular words used by the author. Avoid thought tangents about what the author *really* meant, or what he or she was *trying* to say. The only things that matter on a multiple-choice test are the words that are actually in the question. You must avoid reading too much into a multiple-choice question, or supposing that the writer meant something other than what he or she wrote.

## 5. No Need for Panic

It is wise to learn as many strategies as possible before taking a multiple-choice test, but it is likely that you will come across a few questions for which you simply don't know the answer. In this situation, avoid panicking. Because most multiple-choice tests include dozens of questions, the relative value of a single wrong answer is small. As much as possible, you should compartmentalize each question on a multiple-choice test. In other words, you should not allow your feelings about one question to affect your success on the others. When you find a question that you either don't understand or don't know how to answer, just take a deep breath and do your best. Read the entire question slowly and carefully. Try rephrasing the question a couple of different ways. Then, read all of the answer choices carefully. After eliminating obviously wrong answers, make a selection and move on to the next question.

## 6. Confusing Answer Choices

When working on a difficult multiple-choice question, there may be a tendency to focus on the answer choices that are the easiest to understand. Many people, whether consciously or not, gravitate to the answer choices that require the least concentration, knowledge, and memory. This is a mistake. When you come across an answer choice that is confusing, you should give it extra attention. A question might be confusing because you do not know the subject matter to which it refers. If this is the case, don't eliminate the answer before you have affirmatively settled on another. When you come across an answer choice of this type, set it aside as you look at the remaining choices. If you can confidently assert that one of the other choices is correct, you can leave the confusing answer aside. Otherwise, you will need to take a moment to try to better understand the confusing answer choice. Rephrasing is one way to tease out the sense of a confusing answer choice.

## 7. Your First Instinct

Many people struggle with multiple-choice tests because they overthink the questions. If you have studied sufficiently for the test, you should be prepared to trust your first instinct once you have carefully and completely read the question and all of the answer choices. There is a great deal of research suggesting that the mind can come to the correct conclusion very quickly once it has obtained all of the relevant information. At times, it may seem to you as if your intuition is working faster even than your reasoning mind. This may in fact be true. The knowledge you obtain while studying may be retrieved from your subconscious before you have a chance to work out the associations that support it. Verify your instinct by working out the reasons that it should be trusted.

## 8. Key Words

Many test takers struggle with multiple-choice questions because they have poor reading comprehension skills. Quickly reading and understanding a multiple-choice question requires a mixture of skill and experience. To help with this, try jotting down a few key words and phrases on a piece of scrap paper. Doing this concentrates the process of reading and forces the mind to weigh the relative importance of the question's parts. In selecting words and phrases to write down, the test taker thinks about the question more deeply and carefully. This is especially true for multiple-choice questions that are preceded by a long prompt.

## 9. Subtle Negatives

One of the oldest tricks in the multiple-choice test writer's book is to subtly reverse the meaning of a question with a word like *not* or *except*. If you are not paying attention to each word in the question, you can easily be led astray by this trick. For instance, a common question format is, "Which of the following is...?" Obviously, if the question instead is, "Which of the following is not...?," then the answer will be quite different. Even worse, the test makers are aware of the potential for this mistake and will include one answer choice that would be correct if the question were not negated or reversed. A test taker who misses the reversal will find what he or she believes to be a correct answer and will be so confident that he or she will fail to reread the question and discover the original error. The only way to avoid this is to practice a wide variety of multiple-choice questions and to pay close attention to each and every word.

## 10. Reading Every Answer Choice

It may seem obvious, but you should always read every one of the answer choices! Too many test takers fall into the habit of scanning the question and assuming that they understand the question because they recognize a few key words. From there, they pick the first answer choice that answers the question they believe they have read. Test takers who read all of the answer choices might discover that one of the latter answer choices is actually *more* correct. Moreover, reading all of the answer choices can remind you of facts related to the question that can help you arrive at the correct answer. Sometimes, a misstatement or incorrect detail in one of the latter answer choices will trigger your memory of the subject and will enable you to find the right answer. Failing to read all of the answer choices is like not reading all of the items on a restaurant menu: you might miss out on the perfect choice.

## 11. Spot the Hedges

One of the keys to success on multiple-choice tests is paying close attention to every word. This is never truer than with words like almost, most, some, and sometimes. These words are called "hedges" because they indicate that a statement is not totally true or not true in every place and time. An absolute statement will contain no hedges, but in many subjects, the answers are not always straightforward or absolute. There are always exceptions to the rules in these subjects. For this reason, you should favor those multiple-choice questions that contain hedging language. The presence of qualifying words indicates that the author is taking special care with his or her words, which is certainly important when composing the right answer. After all, there are many ways to be wrong, but there is only one way to be right! For this reason, it is wise to avoid answers that are absolute when taking a multiple-choice test. An absolute answer is one that says things are either all one way or all another. They often include words like *every*, *always*, *best*, and *never*. If you are taking a multiple-choice test in a subject that doesn't lend itself to absolute answers, be on your guard if you see any of these words.

## 12. Long Answers

In many subject areas, the answers are not simple. As already mentioned, the right answer often requires hedges. Another common feature of the answers to a complex or subjective question are qualifying clauses, which are groups of words that subtly modify the meaning of the sentence. If the question or answer choice describes a rule to which there are exceptions or the subject matter is complicated, ambiguous, or confusing, the correct answer will require many words in order to be expressed clearly and accurately. In essence, you should not be deterred by answer choices that seem excessively long. Oftentimes, the author of the text will not be able to write the correct answer without offering some qualifications and modifications. Your job is to read the answer choices thoroughly and completely and to select the one that most accurately and precisely answers the question.

### 13. Restating to Understand

Sometimes, a question on a multiple-choice test is difficult not because of what it asks but because of how it is written. If this is the case, restate the question or answer choice in different words. This process serves a couple of important purposes. First, it forces you to concentrate on the core of the question. In order to rephrase the question accurately, you have to understand it well. Rephrasing the question will concentrate your mind on the key words and ideas. Second, it will present the information to your mind in a fresh way. This process may trigger your memory and render some useful scrap of information picked up while studying.

### 14. True Statements

Sometimes an answer choice will be true in itself, but it does not answer the question. This is one of the main reasons why it is essential to read the question carefully and completely before proceeding to the answer choices. Too often, test takers skip ahead to the answer choices and look for true statements. Having found one of these, they are content to select it without reference to the question above. Obviously, this provides an easy way for test makers to play tricks. The savvy test taker will always read the entire question before turning to the answer choices. Then, having settled on a correct answer choice, he or she will refer to the original question and ensure that the selected answer is relevant. The mistake of choosing a correct-but-irrelevant answer choice is especially common on questions related to specific pieces of objective knowledge. A prepared test taker will have a wealth of factual knowledge at his or her disposal, and should not be careless in its application.

### 15. No Patterns

One of the more dangerous ideas that circulates about multiple-choice tests is that the correct answers tend to fall into patterns. These erroneous ideas range from a belief that B and C are the most common right answers, to the idea that an unprepared test-taker should answer "A-B-A-C-A-D-A-B-A." It cannot be emphasized enough that pattern-seeking of this type is exactly the WRONG way to approach a multiple-choice test. To begin with, it is highly unlikely that the test maker will plot the correct answers according to some predetermined pattern. The questions are scrambled and delivered in a random order. Furthermore, even if the test maker was following a pattern in the assignation of correct answers, there is no reason why the test taker would know which pattern he or she was using. Any attempt to discern a pattern in the answer choices is a waste of time and a distraction from the real work of taking the test. A test taker would be much better served by extra preparation before the test than by reliance on a pattern in the answers.

# FREE DVD OFFER

Don't forget that doing well on your exam includes both understanding the test content and understanding how to use what you know to do well on the test. We offer a completely FREE Test Taking Tips DVD that covers world class test taking tips that you can use to be even more successful when you are taking your test.

All that we ask is that you email us your feedback about your study guide. To get your **FREE Test Taking Tips DVD**, email freedvd@studyguideteam.com with "FREE DVD" in the subject line and the following information in the body of the email:

- The title of your study guide.
- Your product rating on a scale of 1-5, with 5 being the highest rating.
- Your feedback about the study guide. What did you think of it?
- Your full name and shipping address to send your free DVD.

# Introduction

Each state is federally mandated to have certain minimum requirements for issuing commercial drivers licenses (CDLs).

This document is designed to serve as an informational guide to the various sections of the CDL test. It does not outline all the federal and state requirements that are necessary to operate a commercial motor vehicle (CMV). Information on specific CMV operation requirements may be obtained from your state Division of Motor Vehicles (DMV), or the Federal Motor Carrier Safety Administration (FMCSA).

There are three different types of CDLs:

- Class A: A combination vehicle with a gross combination weight rating of 26,001 pounds or more if the vehicle(s) being towed has a gross vehicle weight rating (GVWR) of more than 10,000 pounds

- Class B: A single vehicle with a GVWR of 26,001 pounds or more, or any such vehicle towing a vehicle with a gross vehicle weight that does not exceed 10,000 pounds.

- Class C: A vehicle intended to carry multiple passengers, including the driver (since the number varies from state to state, you will need to check with your local state DMV to find out the exact number of passengers requiring a CDL), OR any size vehicle that transports hazardous materials and requires federal placarding or is carrying material listed as a select agent or toxin. Rules for hazardous materials may also vary by state so check with your state DMV for specifics.

## *Commercial Driver License Tests*

Obtaining a commercial driver license (CDL) is a two-part process involving a knowledge (written) portion and a skills (driving) portion.

### Knowledge Tests

The knowledge portion consists of one or more knowledge tests. The one(s) you will need to take will depend on the license class and endorsements you are seeking to acquire. The CDL knowledge tests include:

- The general knowledge test, required for everyone taking the CDL exam.

- The passenger transport test, required for all bus drivers.

- The air brakes test, required for those who operate vehicles with air brakes, including air over hydraulic brakes.

- The combination vehicles test, necessary for those who wish to operate combination vehicles.

- The hazardous materials test, required for drivers hauling hazardous materials. A Transportation Security Administration (TSA) background check is also required for this endorsement.

- The tank vehicle test, necessary for drivers hauling liquid or gaseous substances in one or more tanks. Check with your state DMV for the specific individual rated capacity for your vehicle.
- The doubles/triples test, necessary for those operating double or triple trailers.
- The school bus test, necessary for school bus drivers.

### Skills Tests

Once you obtain a passing score on the required knowledge test(s), you will need to take the CDL skills tests, using the type of vehicle for which you seek to be licensed. You will be tested on three types of skills: pre-trip inspection, basic vehicle control, and on-road driving. When taking the Pre-Trip Inspection Test, you cannot use a vehicle with mechanisms that are marked or labeled in any way.

#### Pre-Trip Vehicle Inspection

This test will determine your knowledge of all the checks necessary prior to safe operation of your vehicle. You will need to perform a pre-trip inspection, specifying the vehicle components you would check and the reasoning behind each.

#### Basic Vehicle Control

This test determines how well you operate the vehicle. You will need to drive your vehicle forward and backward, and turn it within a designated space indicated by traffic lanes, cones, barriers, etc. The examiner will explain the specifics of each test segment.

#### On-Road Test

This test determines how well you safely operate your vehicle in various traffic conditions. After the examiner explains the route to you, you may be required to perform left and right turns, navigate intersections, railroad crossings, curves, hills, single or multi-lane roads, streets, or highways.

## *Medical Documentation Requirements*

As of January 30, 2014, if you apply for a CDL Permit (or renew, upgrade, add endorsements to or transfer a CDL from another state), you are required to provide information to your State or Tax Collector Driver's License Agency (STDLA) regarding the type of commercial motor vehicle you drive or plan to drive. Your STDLA may require a "certified" medical status as part of your driving record. If so, you will need to send in your current medical examiner's certificate and/or any pertinent medical adjustments (such as vision, diabetic or skills performance waivers, or other exemptions). Your STDLA will be able to tell you the procedure for submitting this documentation.

If you are given a "certified" medical status classification but you do not send in and/or keep your certification current, you will be deemed "noncertified" and may have your CDL taken away. The following explanations help clarify this updated self-certification process:

## Interstate vs. Intrastate Commerce

There are two types of commerce classifications for drivers who operate a CMV requiring a CDL. You will need to determine which pertains to you.

Interstate commerce involves operating a CMV:

- Across state lines or to a foreign country;
- From one location to another within the same state, but the vehicle crosses into another state or foreign country sometime during the trip; OR
- Between two places within the same state, but the vehicle's cargo or passengers are scheduled to terminate in another state or foreign country

Intrastate commerce involves operating a CMV within state boundaries only.

If your routes include both types of commerce classifications, you must choose interstate commerce.

## Inter/Intrastate Commerce: Status Non-excepted or Excepted?

There are four types of commerce that require self-certification:

- Interstate non-excepted
- Interstate excepted
- Intrastate non-excepted
- Intrastate excepted

After identifying your inter/intrastate commerce classification, you must determine if your driving status will be non-excepted or excepted.

### Interstate Commerce

Excepted interstate commerce involves driving a vehicle in interstate commerce *only* for any of these activities:

- To drive school children and/or school staff between home and school
- As federal, state or local government employees
- To carry human cadavers or people who are sick or injured
- Fire truck or rescue vehicle drivers responding to emergencies and other similar activities
- Primarily transporting propane winter heating fuel in response to emergencies needing urgent action such as damage to a propane gas system after a storm or flood situation
- When responding to a pipeline emergency that needs urgent attention such as a leak or rupture
- For custom farm harvesting or to drive farm machinery and materials for a custom harvesting operation to and from a farm or to drive custom harvested crops to storage or market locations
- The seasonal transportation of bees by a beekeeper

- A vehicle controlled and operated by a farmer that is not a combination vehicle (power unit and towed unit), and is used to drive agricultural products, farm machinery or farm materials (except those considered placardable hazardous) to and from a farm and within a radius of 150 air-miles
- As a private motor carrier of passengers for non-business purposes
- To transport migrant workers.

If your answer is yes to one or more of the above situations as your sole driving activity, your operating status is excepted interstate commerce—you DO NOT need a Federal medical examiner's certificate.

If your answer is no to all of the above situations, you operating status is non-excepted interstate commerce—you need to submit a current medical examiner's certificate (also known as a medical certificate or DOT card), to your State Driver Licensing Agency (SDLA).

In most cases, people with CDLs who drive CMVs in interstate commerce have non-excepted interstate commerce status. Drivers who operate in both excepted and non-excepted interstate commerce are required to choose non-excepted interstate commerce status in order to drive in both types of interstate commerce.

### Intrastate Commerce

Excepted intrastate commerce involves driving a CMV in intrastate commerce situations that are not deemed necessary to require medical certification by the state that issued your CDL. Since these vary by state, contact your SDLA for specifics.

Non-excepted intrastate commerce involves operating a CMV in intrastate commerce situations that do require medical certification by the state that issued your CDL. Since these vary by state, contact your SDLA for specifics.

Drivers who operate in both excepted and non-excepted intrastate commerce are required to have non-excepted intrastate commerce.

## Self-Certification Statements

You will need to indicate your self-certification status on your CDL application. The exact wording may vary from state to state, but the following examples will give you an idea of the type of statements to expect:

- Interstate non-excepted: I certify that I operate or expect to operate in interstate commerce. I am subject to and meet Federal DOT medical card requirements and must carry a medical examiner's certificate.
- Interstate excepted: I certify that I operate or expect to operate in interstate commerce. I am not required to obtain a medical examiner's certificate since my transport activities have been given excepted status.

- Intrastate non-excepted: I certify that I operate or expect to operate solely in intrastate commerce. I am subject to and meet the medical requirements for my state; and must carry a medical examiner's certificate.

- Intrastate excepted: I certify that I operate or expect to operate entirely in intrastate commerce. I am not subject to the medical requirements for my state; and not required to obtain a medical examiner's certificate.

# *Disqualifications*

## General

If you are disqualified for any reason, you will not be permitted to operate a CMV. This includes any violations you commit driving either a CMV or your own vehicle that result in the withdrawal of your driver's license.

The following are examples of the types of violations that may disqualify you from being able to legally drive a CMV. Again, since there are variations from state to state, it is best to check with your DMV to find out the specific laws for the state issuing your CDL.

## Alcohol, Leaving the Scene of an Accident, and Commission of a Felony

The following offenses will result in a one-year disqualification:

- If your BAC is .04% or higher
- Driving while under the influence of alcohol
- Refusing blood and/or breath testing
- Driving while under the influence of a controlled substance
- Leaving the scene of an accident
- Committing a felony that involves the use of CMV
- Driving with a suspended CDL
- Causing a fatality through negligent operation of a CMV

If a violation happens when operating a CMV placarded for hazardous materials, you will lose your CDL for at least three years.

A second offense will result in loss of your CDL for life.

If you use a CMV to commit a felony involving controlled substances, you will lose your CDL for life.

If you are found to have any detectable amount of alcohol under .04%, you will be put out-of-service for 24 hours.

## Traffic Violations

Serious traffic violations while driving a CMV include:

- Unnecessary speeding (going 15 mph or higher above the limit)
- Reckless driving
- Improper or inconsistent lane changes

- Tailgating (travelling too closely behind a vehicle)
- Traffic violations resulting in accident fatalities
- Not having a CDL or failure to have one in the vehicle
- Failure to have the proper CDL classification and/or endorsements
- Texting while driving
- Using a handheld mobile device

You will lose your CDL:

- For at least sixty days after two serious traffic violations within three years.
- For at least 120 days after three or more serious traffic violations within three years.

## Violation of Out-of-Service Orders

If you violate an out-of-service order, you will lose your CDL:

- For at least ninety days for a first violation
- For at least one year after two violations within ten years
- For at least three years after three or more violations within ten years

## Railroad-Highway Grade Crossing Violations

You will lose your CDL:

- For at least sixty days for a first-time violation
- For at least 120 days after a second violation within three years
- For at least one year after a third violation within three years

These violations involve breaking federal, state or local laws related to the following offenses:

- For drivers not required to always yield:
- Not stopping if the tracks are not clear
- Not slowing down to make sure there isn't a train approaching
- Not stopping before driving through the crossing
- Not having enough space to drive through the crossing without stopping
- Not following traffic control directions (of a device or enforcement official) at a crossing
- Not driving through a crossing because of low undercarriage clearance

## Hazardous Materials Endorsement Background Check and Disqualifications

If you plan to operate a vehicle with a hazardous materials endorsement, you will need to be fingerprinted and undergo a background check.

Your hazardous materials endorsement will be refused or confiscated if you:

- Are not a legal permanent U.S. resident
- Renounce your U.S. citizenship
- Are wanted or under indictment for certain felonies
- Have been convicted in military or civilian court for certain felonies.

- Have been judged mentally defective or spent time in a mental institution.
- Are considered a security threat by the Transportation Security Administration

Hazardous materials endorsement regulations differ from state to state, so check with your DMV for specifics.

## Traffic Violations in Your Personal Vehicle

CDL holders who violate particular traffic laws while driving a personal vehicle may be subject to CMV operation disqualifications, as per the Motor Carrier Safety Improvement Act (MCSIA) of 1999. These include:

- Loss of your CDL: If your personal driver's license is revoked, cancelled, or suspended due to traffic violations (parking violations do not apply).

- Loss of your CDL for one year: If your personal driver's license is revoked, cancelled, or suspended as the result of alcohol, controlled substances, or felony violations.

- Loss of your CDL for life: If you receive a second violation while driving either your personal vehicle or a CMV

## Other CDL Rules

The following federal and state rules pertain to all CMV drivers:

- CDL holders are not permitted to obtain licenses from more than one state. Violators may be subject up to $5,000 fine or time in prison. The court may also take the CDL issued by your resident state and send any others back.

- Traffic violation convictions (except parking) committed while driving your personal vehicle or a CMV must be reported to your employer within thirty days.

- Traffic violation convictions (except parking) committed while driving your personal vehicle or a CMV in another jurisdiction must be reported to your Department of Highway Safety and Motor Vehicles within thirty days.

- If your driving privileges are suspended, withdrawn, canceled or disqualified, you need to inform your employer within two business days.

- When seeking commercial driving employment, you are required to give your prospective employer a list of driving positions going back ten years.

- It is illegal to operate a CMV without a valid CDL. Violation of this regulation is subject to a $5,000 fine or time in jail.

- Drivers with hazardous materials endorsements must alert the state that issued his or her CDL and relinquish the endorsement within 24 hours in any of the following situations:

- If convicted or indicted in any civilian or military jurisdiction or found not guilty by reason of insanity of a disqualifying violation listed in 49 CFR 1572.103

- If adjudicated as a mental defective or committed to a mental institution as specified in 49 CFR 1572.109
- Renouncement of U.S. citizenship
- If you have more than one CDL, or it is suspended or rescinded, your employer may be subject to a $5,000 fine or time in prison.
- States can track CDL driver data through a singular computer system. Investigations on accident records can pinpoint holders of multiple CDLs.
- Talking on a handheld mobile device or pressing more than one button on a mobile phone while driving is forbidden.
- Sending or reading text messages while driving is forbidden.
- You are required to always wear a seat belt, for both your own safety and that of others. In the event of an accident, it will help keep you restrained and in control of the vehicle, decreasing the possibility of serious injury or death. Drivers failing to wear a seat belt are four times more likely to suffer fatal injuries if thrown from the vehicle.
- You will not be permitted to receive a "hardship" license to operate a CMV if your personal driver's license is revoked, cancelled, or suspended.

Other CDL rules and/or regulations may pertain specifically to the state issuing your CDL. Contact your DMV for specifics.

## *International Registration Plan International Fuel Tax Agreement*

Most CMVs used for interstate commerce need to be registered as part of the International Registration Plan (IRP) and the International Fuel Tax Agreement (IFTA). This is to ensure that vehicles operating within the forty-eight adjoining U.S. states and ten Canadian provinces are equally taxed.

It is the responsibility of each jurisdiction to register applicable vehicles. The process entails the following:

- Issuing license plates and cab cards or proper credentials
- Calculating, collecting and distributing fees
- Performing audits to guarantee distance and fees are properly reported
- Enforcing IRP requirements

Each licensee (motor carrier) is given an assigned base jurisdiction for IRP tax reporting and payment and identification that permits operation throughout all IFTA member areas.

Requirements for registration include:

- Applying for registration
- Providing proper documentation
- Paying fees

- Showing credentials
- Keeping correct distance records
- Having records available for review

IRP registrants and IFTA licensees may be either vehicle owners or operators.

IFTA fuel tax is determined by the distance traveled and the number of gallons (liters) used within member jurisdictions. Licensees report activities through IFTA member jurisdictions via filing a quarterly tax return with the base jurisdiction. The base jurisdiction is then responsible for submitting the taxes and representing the other jurisdictions throughout the tax collection process, including performing audits. Licensees are required to keep any documentation backing the tax return data.

Requirements for IRP vehicle plates and IFTA motor carrier licenses are defined by the IRP Plan and the IFTA for Qualified Vehicle and Qualified Motor Vehicle:

As per the IRP:

A Qualified Vehicle (except as outlined below) is operated or intended to be operated within two or more Member Jurisdictions and is utilized to transport people for hire or designed, used, or maintained mainly to transport goods, and:

- Has two axles and a GVWR or registered GVWR greater than 26,000 pounds (11,793.401 kilograms), or

- Has three or more axles, regardless of weight, or

- Is used in combination, when the combined GVWR is more than 26,000 pounds (11,793.401 kilograms).

As per the IFTA:

A Qualified Motor Vehicle is a vehicle (except recreational vehicles) that is utilized, intended, or maintained to transport people or goods and:

- Has two axles and a GVWR or registered GVWR greater than 26,000 pounds or 11,797 kilograms; or

- Is used in combination, when the combined GVWR is more than 26,000 pounds or 11,797 kilograms.

IFTA-licensed carriers operating IRP-registered vehicles must record the amount of fuel used and distance traveled for each trip. Many drivers use an Individual Vehicle Distance Record (IVDR), (also known as a Driver Trip Report) to fulfill this requirement. IVDR forms may differ, but the necessary data is the same across the board and must include:

## Distance

(According to Article IV of the IRP Plan)

- Beginning and end dates for the trip
- City and State or Province for the trip's source and endpoint
- Travel route(s)

- Odometer or hubodometer reading for start and conclusion of trip
- Total distance traveled
- Distance traveled within the jurisdiction
- Power unit or vehicle identification number

## Fuel

(According to Section P560 of the IFTA Procedures Manual)

Receipts/invoices must show (but are not limited to):

- Purchase date
- Name and address of seller
- Gallons/liters purchased
- Type of fuel
- Cost per gallon/liter or total sale price
- Vehicle unit number or other unique identifier
- Name of buyer

Include data for just one vehicle on each IVDR. To keep on track, record odometer readings as per the following schedule:

- When the day begins
- When leaving the state or province
- At the end of the trip/day

Log all trip data in descending order. This includes dates, routes, odometer readings and fuel purchases. Every state/province included on your route must be recorded on the IVDR. Make sure you retain all fuel receipts and submit them with your completed IVDR.

All logs and documentation must be properly recorded in order to ensure drivers and their carriers meet IRP and IFTA regulations. Keep IVDRs for four years for tax audit purposes. Failure to do so may result in fines or penalties or IRP/IFTA registration or license suspension or withdrawal.

Further questions about the IRP and its requirements can be directed toward your base jurisdiction DMV or IRP, Inc. (www.irponline.org). The IRP website has English, Spanish and French training videos on its home page. Further questions about IFTA and its requirements can be directed to your base jurisdiction agency or IFTA (http://www.iftach.org/index.php).

# Driving Safely

Information specific to CMV operation and safe driving practices are included in this section and will be featured on the CDL exam.

## *Inspection of Vehicle*

Federal and state laws require commercial drivers to inspect their vehicles to ensure their safety and the safety of other drivers on the road. Inspections can detect problems that could end up causing a vehicle to dysfunction or even crash. Your vehicle may also undergo inspection spot checks by federal and state inspectors. If your vehicle is deemed unsafe, it will be placed "out of service" until it is repaired.

### Three Types of Vehicle Inspections

- Pre-Trip Inspection: This helps discover problems that could cause a service malfunction or accident.

- During a Trip: For safety reasons you should check gauges frequently for signs of trouble and use your senses (sight, hearing, smell, and touch) to check for possible issues. Critical items to examine when you stop:

  - Tires, wheels and rims
  - Brakes
  - Lights and reflectors
  - Brake and electrical connections to trailer
  - Trailer coupling devices
  - Cargo securement devices

- After-Trip Inspection and Report: An after-trip inspection should be performed at the end of your trip, day, or driving time period. You may need to fill out a vehicle condition report listing any detectable defects—this alerts the motor carrier that the vehicle needs repairs.

### What to Look For

<u>Tire Problems</u>

- Tread separation
- Cuts or other damage
- Tires that are not the same size
- Too much or too little air pressure
- Radial and bias-ply tires used together
- Valve stems that are cut or cracked
- Dually situated tires coming in contact with each other or parts of the vehicle.
- Uneven wear. Front tires need at least 4/32-inch tread depth in every major groove; other tires need 2/32 inch. You should not see any fabric showing through the tread or sidewall.
- Regrooved, recapped, or retreaded tires on the front wheels of a bus. Wheel and Rim Problems
- Damaged rims
- Mismatched, bent, or cracked lock rings are hazardous

- Wheels or rims with prior welding repairs are not safe
- Missing clamps, spacers, studs, or lugs indicates a danger warning
- Rust around the wheel nuts. You should check the tightness as this could indicate the nuts are loose. After a tire has been changed, you should stop later and re-check tightness of the nuts.

### Bad Brake Drums or Shoes

- Cracked drums
- Shoes or pads stained with oil, grease, or brake fluid
- Shoes that are worn, thin, missing, or broken

### Steering System

- Missing nuts, bolts, cotter keys, or other parts
- Bent, loose, or broken parts (e.g. the steering column, steering gear box, or tie rods)
- If the vehicle has power steering, check the hoses, pumps, and fluid level; look for leaks
- Steering wheel movement greater than 10 degrees (approximately 2 inches at the rim of a 20-inch steering wheel) can make steering difficult

### Suspension System

The suspension system holds the axles in place while supporting the vehicle and its cargo, making any broken parts within the system very hazardous. Refer to diagrams below for specifics.

Look for the following:

- Spring hangers that allow the axle to move from its proper position
- Cracked or broken spring hangers
- Missing or broken leaves in any leaf spring. The vehicle will be deemed "out of service" if one quarter or more are missing, but any defect is dangerous.
- Broken leaves in a multi-leaf spring or leaves that have shifted, potentially causing them to come in contact with a tire or other part
- Leaking shock absorbers
- Any axle positioning parts that are cracked, damaged, or missing (e.g. torque rod or arm, u-bolts, or spring hangers)
- Damaged and/or leaking air suspension systems
- Loose, cracked, broken, or missing frame members

Here are the key suspension parts to be aware of:

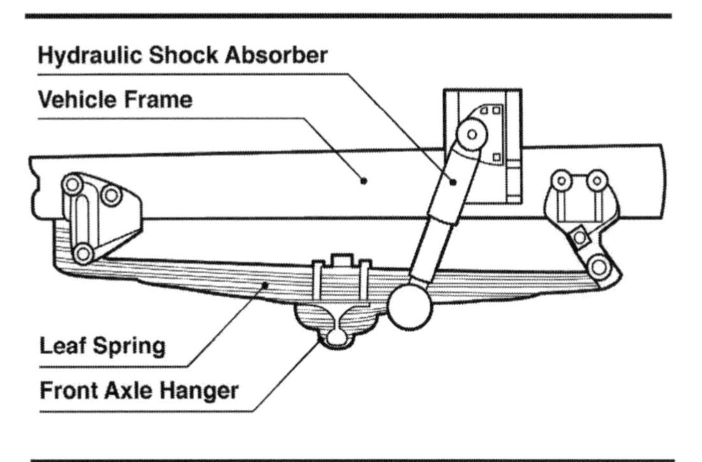


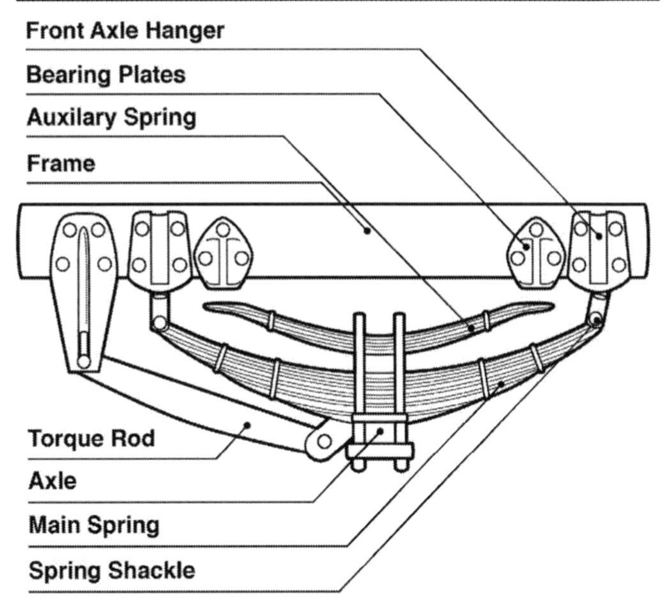


## Exhaust System

If the exhaust system breaks, toxic fumes can leak into the cab or sleeper berth.

Look for the following:

- Loose, broken, or missing exhaust pipes, mufflers, tailpipes, or vertical stacks
- Loose, broken, or missing mounting brackets, clamps, bolts, or nuts
- Exhaust system parts that are rubbing against fuel system parts, tires, or other moving parts of vehicle
- Leaking exhaust system components

### Emergency Equipment

Emergency equipment must be present on your vehicle.

Look for the following:

- Properly charged and mounted fire extinguisher(s) in working order
- Spare electrical fuses (unless the vehicle has circuit breakers)
- Emergency warning devices (e.g. three reflective warning triangles, six fuses or three liquid burning flares)

### Cargo (Trucks)

Prior to each trip, make sure your vehicle is not overloaded and the cargo is stable and secure. If you are hauling hazardous materials, make sure you have the necessary documentation and placarding.

## CDL Pre-Trip Vehicle Inspection Test

You will be asked to inspect your vehicle as you would prior to a trip to determine whether it is safe to drive. During this pre-trip inspection, you will need to describe the components you would check and why.

In order to understand and remember all the steps in the pre-trip inspection process, it should be performed the exact same way every time. Take note of the vehicle's overall condition. Check for damaged areas and whether the vehicle appears to be leaning to one side. Look underneath for evidence of fresh oil, coolant, grease, or fuel leaks. Check the area around the vehicle for possible obstructions to the proper operation of the vehicle (people, other vehicles or objects, low hanging wires or branches, etc.).

This seven-step inspection method is a good guide to follow:

### Step 1: Vehicle Overview

Review Last Vehicle Inspection Report. Drivers may need to generate a daily vehicle inspection report. Any items flagged as safety hazards must be directed to the motor carrier to make repairs and confirm these issues were fixed or not needed. Sign the report only after receiving validation from the carrier.

### Step 2: Check Engine Compartment

Make sure the parking brakes are on and/or wheel chocks are in place.

You may need to open the hood, tilt the cab (after securing loose items), or open the engine compartment door.

Check the following:

- Engine oil level
- Radiator coolant level and condition of hoses
- Power steering fluid level and hose condition (if so equipped)
- Windshield washer fluid level
- Battery fluid level, connections and tie downs (battery may be situated somewhere else in the vehicle)
- Automatic transmission fluid level (the engine may need to be running)

- Check belts (alternator, water pump, air compressor) for tightness and excessive wear—learn and be aware of how much "give" the belts should have when correctly adjusted, and check each one
- Engine compartment leaks (fuel, coolant, oil, power steering fluid, hydraulic fluid, battery fluid)
- Cracked or worn electrical wiring insulation
- Lower and secure the hood, cab, or engine compartment door

## Step 3: Start Engine and Inspect Inside the Cab

Get in the vehicle and start the engine.

- Make sure the parking brake is on.
- Put the gearshift in neutral (or "park" if automatic).
- Start the engine; listen for unusual noises.
- Check the Anti-lock Braking System (ABS) indicator lights if the vehicle is equipped with this feature. The dashboard light should briefly go on and then turn off. If it does not, there is a problem with the ABS. There is also a problem with the ABS if the vehicle has a trailer and the yellow light on the left rear does not turn off.

Look at the gauges.

- Oil pressure. Once the engine is started, it should show a normal reading within seconds.
- Air pressure. Pressure should build from 50 to 90 psi within three minutes. Build air pressure to governor cut-out (usually around 120 – 140 psi). Make sure you know your vehicle's requirements.
- Ammeter and/or voltmeter—should be within normal range(s).
- Coolant temperature—should gradually rise to normal operating range.
- Engine oil temperature—should gradually rise to normal operating range.
- Warning lights and buzzers for oil, coolant, charging circuit warning, and antilock brake system lights should turn off right away.

Check condition of controls. Check the following to make sure they are not too loose, stuck, damaged, or inadequately positioned:

- Steering wheel
- Clutch
- Accelerator ("gas pedal")
- Brake controls
- Foot brake
- Trailer brake (if vehicle so equipped)
- Parking brake
- Retarder controls (if vehicle so equipped)
- Transmission controls

- Interaxle differential lock (if vehicle so equipped)
- Horn(s)
- Windshield wiper/washer
- Lights
- Headlights
- Dimmer switch
- Turn signal
- Four-way flashers
- Parking, clearance, identification, marker switch(es)

Check mirrors and windshield. Check the vehicle's mirrors and windshield for cracks, dirt, illegal stickers, or other impediments to your view. Clean and adjust as needed.

Check emergency equipment. Make sure safety supplies include:

- Spare electrical fuses (unless the vehicle is equipped with circuit breakers)
- Three red reflective triangles, six fuses or three liquid burning flares
- Properly charged and safety rated fire extinguisher

Check for optional items such as:

- Chains (when required due to winter conditions)
- Tire changing equipment
- Emergency phone number list
- Accident reporting kit (packet)

Check safety belt. Make sure the safety belt is not ripped or frayed and that it is adjustable, securely mounted, and fastens correctly properly.

### Step 4: Turn Off Engine and Check Lights

After making sure the parking brake is set, turn off the engine and remove the key. Turn on the headlights (low beams) and four-way emergency flashers, and step out of the vehicle.

### Step 5: Do Walking Inspection

- Walk to the front of the vehicle and make sure the low beams are illuminated and the four-way flashers are both functioning correctly.
- Flick the dimmer switch to make sure the high beams go on.
- Turn off the headlights and four-way emergency flashers.
- Check that the parking, clearance, side-marker, and identification lights work properly.
- Turn on the right side turn signal, and begin your walk-around inspection.

#### *General*

- Walk around and inspect the outside of the vehicle.
- Clean all exterior lights, reflectors, and glass components.

#### *Left Front Side*

- Make sure the window glass on the driver's side door is clean.
- Check to see door latches and/or locks are in working order.

- Left front wheel
- Condition of wheel and rim—make sure they are properly aligned and there are no missing, bent, or broken studs, clamps or lugs.
- Condition of tires—make sure they have enough air and the valve stem and cap are working properly and free of serious cuts, bulges, or tread wear.
- Use a wrench to test any lug nuts with rust streaks, which can signify loosening.
- Make sure the hub oil level shows a correct reading, with no visible leaking.
- Left front suspension
- Check the condition of the spring, spring hangers, shackles, and U-bolts.
- Check the condition of the shock absorbers.
- Left front brake
- Check the condition of the brake drum or disc.
- Check the condition of the hoses.

### *Front*

- Inspect the condition of the front axle.
- Inspect the condition of the steering system.
- There should be no loose, worn, bent, damaged or missing parts.
- Grab the steering mechanism to check for looseness.
- Inspect the condition of the windshield.
- Check for damage and clean if dirty.
- Check windshield wiper arms for proper spring tension.
- Check wiper blades for damage, "stiff" rubber, and proper securement.
- Lights and reflectors
- Parking, clearance, and identification lights should be clean, operational, and the proper color (amber in the front).
- Reflectors should be clean and the proper color (amber in the front).
- Right front turn signal light should be clean, operational, and the proper color (amber or white on the forward facing signals).

### *Right Side*

- Right front: Inspect all items as per the left front procedure.
- Ensure the primary and secondary safety cab locks are engaged (if vehicle has a cab-over-engine design).
- Right fuel tank(s)
- Make sure it is securely mounted and not damaged or leaking.
- Make sure the fuel crossover line is secure.
- Make sure the tank(s) contain enough fuel.
- Make sure the cap(s) are on and secure.
- Condition of visible parts
- Check the rear of engine rear and make sure it is free of leaks.
- Check the transmission and make sure it is free of leaks.
- Check that the exhaust system is secure, not leaking, and not touching any wires, fuel, or air lines.
- Check the frame and cross members to ensure there are no bends or cracks.

- Check that the air lines and electrical wiring are properly secured against any snagging, rubbing, or wearing.
- Make sure that the spare tire carrier or rack is not damaged (if so equipped).
- Make sure the spare tire and/or wheel is securely mounted in the rack.
- Make sure the spare tire and wheel are the correct size and properly inflated.
- Cargo securement (trucks)
- Make sure the cargo is properly secured (blocked, braced, tied, chained, etc.)
- Make sure the header board is adequate and secure (if required).
- Make sure the sideboards and stakes are strong, undamaged, and properly secured (if the vehicle has them).
- If the cargo needs a canvas or tarp, make sure it is correctly in place so it does not tear, flap, or block mirrors.
- If the vehicle is oversized, make sure all necessary signals (flags, lamps, and reflectors) are safely and properly mounted and all the required permits are present.
- Make sure the curbside compartment doors are in good shape, securely closed, latched/locked and the required security seals are correctly positioned.

*Right Rear*

- Condition of wheels and rims—make sure there are no missing, bent, or broken spacers, studs, clamps, or lugs.
- Condition of tires—make sure they have enough air, and the caps and valve stems are in good working condition, with no serious cuts, bulges, or tread wear. Check that they are not rubbing against each other, or have nothing stuck between them.
- Make sure the tires are the same type, e.g., not mixed radial and bias types.
- Make sure the tires are evenly matched sizes.
- Make sure the wheel bearing/seals are not leaking.
- Suspension
- Check the condition of spring(s), spring hangers, shackles, and U-bolts.
- Make sure the axle is secure.
- Make sure no lube (gear oil) is leaking from the powered axle(s).
- Check the condition of the torque rod arms and bushings.
- Check the condition of the shock absorber(s).
- If the vehicle is retractable axle equipped, check the condition of the lift mechanism.
- If the vehicle is air powered, check for leaks.
- Check the condition of the air ride components.
- Brakes
- Inspect the brake adjustment.
- Inspect the condition of the brake drum(s) or discs.
- Inspect the hoses for any wear due to rubbing.
- Lights and reflectors
- Check that the side-marker lights are clean, operational, and the proper color (red in the rear, amber in other areas).
- Check that the side-marker reflectors are clean and the proper color (red in the rear, amber in other areas).

*Rear*

- Lights and reflectors
- Check that the rear clearance and identification lights are clean, operational, and the proper color (red in the rear).
- Check that the reflectors are clean and the proper color (red in the rear).
- Make sure the taillights are clean, operational, and the proper color (red in the rear).
- Make sure the right rear turn signal is operational, and the proper color (red, yellow, or amber in the rear).
- Make sure the license plate(s) are present, clean, and secured.
- Make sure the vehicle has correctly fastened splashguards, and they are not dragging on ground or rubbing against the tires.
- Make sure the cargo is secure (trucks).
- Make sure the cargo is properly secured (blocked, braced, tied, chained, etc.)
- Make sure the tailboards are up and properly secured.
- Make sure the end gates are undamaged and properly secured in the stake sockets.
- If a canvas or tarp is required, ensure it is properly secured to prevent tearing, flapping, or blocking of the rearview mirrors or rear lights.
- If the vehicle is over-length or over-width, make sure all signs and/or additional lights/flags are safely and properly mounted and you have all required permits.
- Make sure the rear doors are securely closed, latched/locked.

*Left Side*

- Check all items as done on right side, plus:
- Battery(ies) (if not mounted in engine compartment)
- Battery box(es)—securely mounted to vehicle.
- Battery box cover is securely in place
- Battery(ies) secured against movement
- Battery(ies) not broken or leaking
- Fluid in battery(ies) at proper level (except those that are maintenance-free)
- Cell caps in place and securely tightened (except those that are maintenance-free)
- Vents in cell caps are free of foreign material (except those that are maintenance-free)

## Step 6: Check Signal Lights

Get In and Turn Off Lights

- Turn off all lights.
- Turn on brake lights (apply trailer hand brake or have someone depress the brake pedal).
- Turn on left turn-signal lights.

Get Out and Check Lights

- Check that left front turn-signal light is clean, operating and the correct color (amber or white on signals facing the front).
- Check that the left rear turn signal light and both brake lights are clean, operating, and the correct color (red, yellow, or amber).

Get In Vehicle

- Turn off lights not required for driving.
- Make sure all necessary papers, trip manifests, permits, etc. are present.
- Make sure there are no loose articles in the cab that could impede driving or even strike you in the event of an accident.
- Start the engine.

### Step 7: Start the Engine and Check Test for Hydraulic Leaks.

If the vehicle is equipped with hydraulic brakes, pump the brake pedal three times, then firmly press and hold for five seconds. The pedal should stay firm. Any movement could indicate a leak or other problem that you will need to repair before driving the vehicle. If the vehicle has air brakes, perform the checks described in the Air Brake section.

#### *Brake System*

- Test Parking Brake(s)
- Fasten safety belt.
- Set the parking brake (power unit only).
- Release the trailer parking brake (if applicable).
- Place vehicle in low gear.
- Gradually pull forward against the parking brake to make sure it holds.
- If the vehicle has a trailer, perform the same steps with the trailer parking brake set and vehicle parking brakes off.
- If the parking brake does not hold the vehicle, it is faulty and needs to be fixed.
- Test Service Brake Stopping Action
- Drive slowly forward (about five miles per hour).
- Firmly depress the brake pedal.
- If the vehicle “pulls” to one side or the other, it could indicate brake trouble.
- Any unusual brake pedal "feel" or delayed stopping action might indicate faulty brakes

Federal and state regulations prohibit the operation of any CMV deemed a safety hazard. If you detect any safety issues during the pre-trip inspection, you must get them repaired.

## Inspection During a Trip

Check the vehicle operation often. The following is a list of items you should check:

- Instruments
- Air pressure gauge (if the vehicle is equipped with air brakes)
- Temperature gauges
- Pressure gauges
- Ammeter/voltmeter
- Mirrors
- Tires
- Cargo, cargo covers
- Lights

Use your senses. Inspect anything that looks, sounds, smells, or feels unsafe.

### Safety Inspection

Drivers of trucks and truck tractors transporting cargo must check that the cargo is securely in place within the first fifty miles of a trip and every 150 miles or every three hours during the trip (whichever comes first).

## After-Trip Inspection and Report

You may need to log a daily report regarding the condition of the vehicle(s) you operated. Report anything that could affect vehicle safety or cause a possible mechanical failure.

# *Basic Control of Your Vehicle*

To safely operate a CMV, you must be able to control its speed and direction, which requires the following skills:

- Accelerating
- Steering
- Stopping
- Backing up safely
- Shifting gears

Your seatbelt needs to be secured at all times when driving. When leaving your vehicle, make sure the parking brake is on.

## Accelerating

When you start up your vehicle, make sure it doesn't roll back as you may hit someone. To prevent rollback, use the parking brake whenever needed. If the vehicle is a manual transmission, partly engage the clutch before you take your right foot off the brake. You can also prevent rollback by disengaging the parking brake only after you have given the engine enough power. If the vehicle features a trailer brake hand valve, it can also be used to prevent rollback.

Accelerate slowly and smoothly to prevent jerking motions. If you accelerate roughly, it can damage the vehicle's mechanical system or the coupling (in vehicles hauling a trailer).

Accelerate slowly in rain or snow conditions, or anytime there is poor traction. Applying too much power can make the drive wheels spin and cause you to lose control of the vehicle. Lift your foot off of the gas pedal if the wheels begin to spin.

## Steering

Make sure you grip the steering wheel firmly with both hands placed on opposite sides of the wheel. If you do not have a firm grasp on the wheel, it could slip out of your hands if you hit a curb or a pothole.

## Stopping

When you need to stop, depress the brake pedal with a gradual motion so that the vehicle comes to a smooth, safe stop. The brake pressure required to come to a complete stop will depend on the vehicle's speed and how quickly you need to brake. If you have a manual transmission, depress the clutch when the engine is near the idling stage.

### Backing Safely

Backing up in a CMV is always dangerous and should be avoided whenever feasible, as it is impossible to see everything behind you. You can prevent this by parking the vehicle so that you can drive forward when leaving.

When you do need to back up, here are a few simple safety rules:

- Start in the proper position. Determine the type of backing you will need to do and position the vehicle in the best way to permit backing up safely.
- Look at your path. Check your line of travel before you begin. Get out and walk around the vehicle, observing the clearance to the vehicle sides and overhead, in and near the route your vehicle will take.
- Use mirrors on both sides. Frequently check the outside mirrors on both sides of the vehicle. If you are unsure, get out and check your path.
- Back up slowly. Always back up as slowly as possible, using the lowest gear. This makes it easier to fix any steering errors and stop quickly if needed.
- Back and turn toward the driver's side. It is more difficult to see clearly when you back to the right side. Instead, back to the driver's side so you can watch the rear of your vehicle by looking out the side window, even if it necessitates driving around the block to put your vehicle in this position. The added degree of safety is worth it.
- Use a helper. Use a helper whenever possible to help observe blind spots you cannot detect. The helper should stand near the back of your vehicle in clear sight. Prior to backing up, prepare a set of hand signals that you both understand, including a signal for "stop."

## *Shifting Gears*

It is very important to shift gears correctly. You will not be able to accurately control your vehicle if you cannot shift into the proper gear while driving.

### Manual Transmissions

Most CMVs equipped with manual transmissions require double clutching to change gears. Here is the method to follow:

- Release the accelerator, push in the clutch and shift into neutral simultaneously.
- Release the clutch.
- Let the engine and gears slow down to the rpm required for the next gear (this takes practice).
- Push in the clutch and shift to the higher gear at the same time.
- Release the clutch and press the accelerator at the same time.

It takes practice to shift gears using the double clutch method. If you remain in neutral too long, it may be hard to shift into the next gear. Rather than forcing this step, instead return to neutral position, release the clutch, increase engine speed to equal the posted speed, and try again.

### Knowing When to Shift Up

There are two ways of knowing when to shift:

#### *Use Engine Speed (rpm)*

Study the driver's manual for your vehicle so you are aware of the operating rpm range. Watch your tachometer, and shift up when your engine reaches the high end of the range. Some newer vehicles use "progressive" shifting: the shifting rpm becomes higher as you go up in the gears. Make sure you know the correct method for the vehicle you will operate.

#### *Use Road Speed (mph)*

Learn the optimum speeds for each gear so you will know when to shift up by checking the speedometer. With either method, engine sounds may also help you determine when to shift.

### Basic Procedures for Shifting Down

- Release the accelerator, push in the clutch, and shift into neutral simultaneously.
- Release the clutch.
- Press down on the accelerator; increase the engine and gear speed to the necessary rpm for the lower gear. Simultaneously depress the clutch and shift to the lower gear.
- Simultaneously release the clutch and press down on the accelerator.
- Downshifting, like upshifting, requires knowing when to shift. Use either the tachometer or the speedometer and downshift at the right rpm or road speed.

Situations where you should downshift:

### Before Starting Down a Hill

Slow the vehicle and shift down to a speed you can control without having to jam on the brakes, which may cause them to overheat and lose their braking power. Downshift before starting down the hill. Make sure you are in a low enough gear; this is typically a lower gear than you would need to climb the same hill.

### Before Entering a Curve

Slow to a safe speed and downshift to the correct gear. This allows you to maintain some power through the curve to help keep the vehicle stable and permits you to increase your speed as you exit the curve.

## Multi-Speed Rear Axles and Auxiliary Transmissions

Many vehicles feature extra gears through the use of multi-speed rear axles and auxiliary transmissions. They are typically controlled via a knob or switch on the gearshift lever of the main transmission. Since there are many different types of shift patterns, you will need to learn the correct way to shift gears in the vehicle you will operate.

## Automatic Transmissions

If your vehicle has an automatic transmission, it is important to select a low range when going down graded roads. This will allow you to better control engine braking and help prevent the transmission from upshifting beyond the selected gear (unless the governor rpm is exceeded).

### Retarders

Retarders on a vehicle help slow it down, reducing brake wear and providing another alternative to decreasing speed. There are four basic types: exhaust, engine, hydraulic, and electric. All can be switched on or off by the driver and some allow the power to be adjusted. When turned "on," retarders apply their braking power (to the drive wheels only) whenever you fully release the accelerator. Because these devices can be noisy, some areas restrict usage. Make sure you know if their use is permitted on your route.

Use caution. In poor traction conditions, the retarder may cause the drive wheels to skid. You should turn the retarder off whenever the road is wet, icy, or snow covered.

## *Seeing*

Many accidents are the result of distracted driving. It is essential that you are aware of your vehicle's surroundings at all times.

### Seeing Ahead

#### Looking Far Enough Ahead

Be aware of the traffic around the perimeter of your vehicle. It may require a great deal of space to stop or switch lanes—you'll need to foresee way ahead to make sure you can safely make these maneuvers.

#### How Far Ahead to Look

While on the road, you should anticipate approximately how far you would drive in twelve to fifteen seconds. That's driving about one block at a low speed (city driving) and a quarter of a mile at a higher speed (highway driving). Failing to anticipate ahead may require fast braking or hasty lane changes. However, items in closer range should not be ignored. You should strike a balance between near and far views.

#### Look for Traffic

Be aware of the vehicles around you. This includes those merging onto the highway, moving into your lane, turning, and braking. Looking far enough ahead gives you the ability to predict and compensate by altering your speed or switching lanes to prevent an issue. Begin to slow down if you are approaching a traffic light that has been green for a long time—it will likely turn red before you reach it.

### Seeing to the Sides and Rear

It is crucial to have an awareness of what's behind you and on both sides of your vehicle. This requires frequently inspecting your mirrors, particularly in special circumstances.

#### Mirror Adjustment

You should adjust your vehicle's mirrors before each trip when the trailer(s) is parked straight. Position each to see various views of the vehicle in order to have a point of reference.

#### Regular Checks

Frequently inspect your mirrors to ensure you can correctly see your vehicle and the vehicles around you.

## Traffic
Use your mirrors to check for passing vehicles and those beside and behind you in case you need to change lanes quickly. Be aware of "blind spots" your mirrors cannot reach. Vehicles traveling around you may move into these blind spots. Frequently check your mirrors to ascertain their location.

## Check Your Vehicle
Mirrors should also be used to watch for tire fires and help keep an eye on any open cargo you may be carrying. Be on the lookout for loose fastenings or a tarp that is fluttering or ballooning.

## Special Situations
Certain circumstances such as lane changes, turns, merges, and tight maneuvers necessitate heightened mirror checks.

## Lane Changes
When changing lanes, you will need to check your mirrors to confirm there are no vehicles beside or attempting to pass you. Check your mirrors:

- Prior to changing lanes to ensure there is enough room.
- After switching on your turn signal, to ensure a vehicle has not migrated into your blind spot.
- Right after you start changing lanes, to ensure the road is clear.
- Once the lane change is completed.

## Turns
When turning, use your mirrors to ensure the back of your vehicle will not strike anything.

## Merges
Check your mirrors when merging to ensure there is enough space between vehicles to safely enter traffic.

## Tight Maneuvers
Check your mirrors frequently whenever you are in a situation where you don't have much clearance around your vehicle.

## How to Use Mirrors
Accurate use of your mirrors requires inspecting them quickly while recognizing what you are viewing.

Switch your view between the mirrors and the road ahead but don't concentrate too long on the mirrors or you may drive quite a distance without an awareness of what's ahead.

The curved mirrors (also referred to as convex, "fisheye," "spot," or "bugeye") on large vehicles reflect a wider viewing area than flat mirrors, causing objects to appear smaller and farther away than they really are. It is important to keep this in mind when checking these mirrors.

# Communicating

## Signaling

Other drivers are unaware of what you are going to do until you tell them. It is essential to use your turn signals to alert them of your intentions. Here are some general rules for safe signaling.

### Turns

Follow these three rules for using turn signals:

- *Signal early*. Signal much before turning to prevent other vehicles from trying to pass.
- *Signal continuously*. In order to turn safely, keep both hands on the wheel. Complete the turn before cancelling the signal.
- *Cancel your signal.* Switch your turn signal off after you've turned (if not self-canceling).

### Lane Changes

Lane changes should be slow and smooth. Switch your turn signal on first to allow a driver in your blind spot to honk or stay clear of your vehicle.

### Slowing Down

If you need to slow down, warn drivers behind you by lightly hitting the brake pedal a few times (enough to flash the brake lights). If you need to drive very slowly or stop, use your vehicle's four-way emergency flashers. Send a warning to other drivers if experiencing any of these situations:

#### *Trouble Ahead*

If you see a problem that will require other vehicles to slow down, flash your brake lights to alert drivers behind you. Your vehicle's size may obstruct their view in seeing danger up ahead.

#### *Tight Turns*

Many car drivers are unaware how much you need to slow down to navigate a tight turn in a large vehicle. Brake early and slow down gradually to alert drivers behind you.

#### *Stopping on the Road*

If you need to stop on a busy road to unload cargo or passengers, or at a railroad crossing, alert drivers behind you by flashing your brake lights. Make sure you don't make any sudden stops.

#### *Driving Slowly*

If you need to drive at a slow speed for some reason, warn drivers behind you by using your emergency flashers if permitted. Flasher regulations vary from state to state. Check the laws of the states where you will drive.

### Don't Direct Traffic

Some drivers try to be helpful by alerting other vehicles when it is safe to pass. Do not attempt to do this, as it could cause an accident, putting you at fault.

## Communicating Your Presence

You should make other drivers aware of your presence in order to prevent accidents. Even when your vehicle is in clear view, others may not see it.

### When Passing

Other vehicles, pedestrians, or bicyclists can move into your path at any time. To make sure they are aware of your presence, gently honk your horn or flash your lights from low to high beam and back in areas where laws permit. Careful operation of your vehicle will help prevent an accident if they don't see or hear you.

### When It's Hard to See

You need to make your presence especially known at dawn or dusk, or in inclement weather such as rain, snow or fog. If you are having difficulties seeing other vehicles, presume they will be unable to see you clearly. Turn on your headlights to the low setting—the high beams can irritate other drivers.

### When Parked on the Side of the Road

Make sure you use your four-way emergency flashers if you need to pull over to the side of the road, particularly at night. Your taillights are not a warning signal—drivers have crashed into parked vehicles because they were unaware they were stopped.

You need to set up emergency warning devices within ten minutes anytime you are required to pull over and stop. Adhere to the following procedure:

- If you need to stop on or by a one-way or divided highway, place warning devices ten feet, 100 feet, and 200 feet ahead of approaching traffic.
- If you need to stop on a two-lane road that has traffic going in both directions or on an undivided highway, denote the location of your vehicle by putting warning devices within 10 feet of the front or rear corners and 100 feet behind and ahead of it on the shoulder or in the lane where you are parked.
- Park the vehicle beyond any hill, curve, or other obstacle that prevents other drivers from seeing it within a distance of 500 feet. If a hill or curve is blocking the line of sight, move the triangle closest to the rear to a point back down the road so drivers have enough warning.
- When placing the triangles around the vehicle, grasp them between yourself and the oncoming traffic so other drivers can see you.

### Use Your Horn When Needed

Use your horn only when necessary. While it can help prevent an accident by notifying others around you of your presence, the noise can surprise and frighten others when used needlessly.

## *Controlling Speed*

Many accidents are the result of speeding. It is imperative to modify your speed based on driving conditions such as traction, curves, visibility, traffic, and hills.

### Stopping Distance

$$Perception\ Distance + Reaction\ Distance + Braking\ Distance = Total\ Stopping\ Distance$$

### Perception Distance

The length traveled by your vehicle in ideal conditions—from the time you perceive a danger until it is acknowledged by your brain—is known as perception distance. It can be influenced by a variety of mental and physical factors, particularly the danger itself and visibility conditions. An observant driver has an average perception time of 1¾ seconds, which is about 142 feet when traveling 55 mph.

### Reaction Distance

This is the length of road you will continue to travel in optimum conditions prior to braking to avoid a danger ahead. The average driver's reaction time is ¾ second to one second, about 61 feet when traveling 55 mph.

### Braking Distance

This is the length of road your vehicle will travel in optimum conditions while you are braking, typically about 216 feet when traveling 55 mph on dry pavement with decent brakes.

### Total Stopping Distance

This is the entire length of road traveled by your vehicle in ideal conditions taking into account all factors (perception, reaction, and braking distance) prior to completely stopping your vehicle. It is typically a minimum of 419 feet when traveling 55 mph.

### The Effect of Speed on Stopping Distance

Speed is a major factor in the amount of time it takes you to stop and the impact of your vehicle in the event of a crash. At 40 mph, the impact and braking distance are four times greater than when driving 20 mph. At 60 mph, your impact and braking distance become nine times greater, with your stopping distance longer than the length of a football field. When your speed increases to 80 mph, the impact and braking distance are 16 times greater than when travelling 20 mph. High speeds significantly increase stopping distances and the severity of crashes. By reducing speed, you can greatly decrease the distance you need to stop.

### The Effect of Vehicle Weight on Stopping Distance

The brakes on heavier vehicles work harder and absorb more heat. However, the brakes, tires, springs, and shock absorbers on a CMV function best with a full payload; empty vehicles have less traction and require greater stopping distances.

## Matching Speed to the Road Surface

Traction—the friction between the tires and the road—is essential to steering and stopping a vehicle. Certain road conditions lessen the effects of traction, requiring lower speeds.

### Slippery Surfaces

When the road is slippery, it will be more difficult to turn without skidding and take longer to stop. Since wet roads can increase your stopping distance twice as much, you need to travel at a lower speed in order to brake in the same length of time as on a dry road. When driving on a wet road, reduce your speed by a third (from 55 to about 35 mph). When driving on a snow-packed road, slow your speed in half, or more. On an icy road, gradually reduce your speed and come to a complete stop as soon as you can.

### Identifying Slippery Surfaces

Sometimes it is difficult to determine whether the road is slippery. Warning signs include:

- Shaded Areas. Shady parts of the road stay icy and slippery much longer than other areas.
- Bridges. Bridge surfaces will freeze prior to the road. Extra caution is required when outside temps dip near 32 degrees Fahrenheit.
- Melting Ice. If ice melts even just a little bit, it becomes wet and much more slippery than ice that is not.
- Black Ice. When the temperature dips below freezing and the road looks wet, beware of black ice—a transparent layer of very thin ice. Although the road may appear wet, black ice will make it very slick.
- Vehicle Icing. To check for icy conditions, open the window and touch the front of the mirror, mirror support, or antenna. If you detect ice on them, the road surface is likely beginning to ice up as well.
- Just After Rain. Just after it starts to rain, rainwater swirls together with oil deposited on the road by vehicles. This makes the road very slick at first; if it keeps raining, the mixture will get washed away.
- Hydroplaning. Water or slush can collect on the road in certain types of weather, causing your vehicle to hydroplane. Similar to water skiing, the tires skim along the surface of the water and lose traction, making it impossible to steer or stop. Try to regain control by taking your foot off the accelerator and pushing on the clutch, which will slow your vehicle and allow the wheels to turn more easily. Do not use the brakes—depress the clutch if the drive wheels start to skid.
- Your vehicle can hydroplane while traveling at speeds as low as 30 mph if there is a lot of water. Tire grooves help repel water—if your vehicle's tire pressure is low, or the tread is worn, hydroplaning is more likely.
- Vehicles are more likely to hydroplane when traveling over surfaces where water collects. Be on the lookout for clear reflections, tire splashes, and rain on the road—all imply pooling water.

## Speed and Curves

Safely navigating curves requires modifying your speed. Driving too fast when approaching a curve can cause you to skid off the road or roll your vehicle, particularly if it has a high center of gravity. Prior to entering a curve you will need to slow down and then accelerate slightly as you follow through. This will help you control the vehicle and retain traction in the tires.

## Speed and Distance Ahead

As you are driving, you should always be able to stop within the length of road you see ahead of you. This parameter will vary depending on the situation—you will need to drive more slowly at night (particularly when using your vehicle's low beams), or in fog, rain, or other inclement weather.

## Speed and Traffic Flow

Follow the flow of traffic, matching the speed of the other vehicles on the road as best you can without speeding. Many states have lower speed limits for CMVs than cars. Vehicles traveling in the same direction at similar speeds are less likely to have accidents. Driving faster than other vehicles requires frequent passing, which increases the possibilities of a crash. Use extra care when passing.

## Speed on Downgrades

When traveling downhill, gravity will cause your vehicle's speed to build. It is essential to operate your vehicle at a speed that is not too fast for the:

- Weight of the vehicle and its cargo
- Length of the hill
- Steepness of the hill
- Road conditions
- Weather

Prior to driving down a hill, shift into a low gear and follow safe braking practices to control your speed. Heed to speed limit and grade postings specifying the hill's length and steepness. The brakes will have the most impact when your vehicle is in a lower gear and near the administered rpms. Use your brakes cautiously so you can safely slow or stop when conditions are hazardous. The section on "Mountain Driving" outlines how to carefully navigate down long, steep downgrades.

## Roadway Work Zones

Use extra caution when driving through roadway work zones. The main cause of injury and death in these zones is speeding. Always heed posted speed limits, paying careful attention not to increase your speed as you pass through extensive areas of road construction. Slow down when road and weather conditions are unfavorable, decreasing your speed even more if you spot any workers near the highway.

# *Managing Space*

Make sure there is enough space on all sides of your vehicle in order to give you enough time to safely react. Large, heavy vehicles take up a wider area and need more room to stop and turn.

## Space Ahead

It is essential to pay attention to and maintain the area in the front of your vehicle.

### The Need for Space Ahead

You must refrain from tailgating behind the vehicle in front of you in case you need to brake abruptly. Accident reports indicate these are vehicles CMVs crash into the most. It is important to remember that smaller vehicles can typically brake faster.

### How Much Space?

Here's a good rule of thumb regarding the distance between vehicles:

If traveling 40 mph, follow at least one second behind for each 10 feet of vehicle length. For example, allow four seconds for a 40-foot vehicle and six seconds for one that is 60-feet long. At higher speeds, tack on an additional second for safety. Thus, speeds over 40 mph require five seconds of space for a 40-foot vehicle and seven seconds for a 60-foot vehicle.

Use this method to determine the number of seconds: After the vehicle in front of you drives past a shadow or some other marking, slowly count "one thousand-and-one, one thousand-and-two" etc., until you get to the same place. Compare the number with the formula above. If you are driving too close, slow down a bit and don't forget you'll need quite a bit additional space if the road conditions are slick.

### Space Behind

It's impossible to prevent other drivers from tailgating, but there are some steps you can follow to increase safety.

#### Stay to the Right

Stick to the right lane if you are carrying a heavy load. CMVs often have difficulties maintaining speed, particularly when traveling uphill. Do not try to overtake another slow vehicle unless you can pass them quickly and safely.

#### Dealing with Tailgaters Safely

The size of a CMV often makes it difficult to determine if a vehicle is driving closely behind you. Situations where you may be tailgated:

- If you are driving slowly, essentially trapping the vehicle in back of you.
- During inclement weather, which can make it tough for the driver behind you to clearly see the road ahead.

In the event that you are tailgated, you can decrease the possibilities of an accident by doing the following:

- Avoiding abrupt movements. Give other drivers enough warning by switching on your turn signal and decelerating if you need to slow down or turn.
- Increasing the distance between you and the vehicle in front of you. This will help prevent the need to make any quick changes in your speed or direction and make it easier for the tailgater to pass you.
- Maintaining your speed. It's safer to be followed closely at a lower speed.
- Avoiding tricks. Don't switch on your taillights or flash your brake lights.

### Space to the Sides

Since CMVs are often wider and occupy a larger area than other vehicles on the road, you will need to wisely manage the space around you. The following two tips will help you keep on track:

#### Stay Centered in Your Lane

This allows for a safe amount of space on either side.

Strong winds can make it difficult to stay in your lane, and even more so for lighter vehicles, particularly when you are exiting a tunnel. If it is windy, try to avoid driving alongside other vehicles.

### Avoid Traveling Next to Others

This is hazardous for two reasons:

1. Another driver could make a sudden lane change and crash into you.
2. You may find yourself hemmed in if you need to switch lanes. It's best to locate an opening in the flow of traffic, which may be difficult when traffic is heavy. If you cannot avoid driving alongside another vehicle, do your best to allow as much room as you can between the two vehicles. Slow down or pull ahead to make sure the other driver notices you.

## Space Overhead

Driving a CMV requires an awareness of your vehicle's height. It is essential to keep the following in mind:

- Road maintenance or packed snow can decrease clearances on bridges and overpasses—don't presume that the posted figures are accurate.
- Hauling heavy cargo lowers the height of a CMV. You may not have the same clearance level when your vehicle is empty.
- Clearance signs are not always present on low structures such as bridges or tunnels. Proceed with caution if you are uncertain whether you can safely drive underneath. If it appears you cannot, then find an alternate route.
- Uneven surfaces can cause vehicles to sway, making it difficult to pass items located on the outside of the road such as signs, tree branches, or bridge supports. To prevent this issue, ease a little into the middle of the road.
- Prior to backing up your vehicle, get out and inspect for obstructions and other dangers that might not be easily spotted such as trees, branches, or electrical wires.

## Space Below

CMVs often have low clearances underneath, which can be even less when you are carrying a full load of cargo. Road drainage channels, railroad tracks, and uneven or poorly paved surfaces can aggravate the issue. Proceed through these areas with caution.

## Space for Turns

It is essential to consider the space required around a CMV when executing turns.

### Right Turns

Tips to help prevent right-turn crashes:

- Proceed very slowly to allow your vehicle and others more time in the event of an issue.

- If your vehicle cannot turn right without crossing into another lane, prevent other drivers from overtaking you on the right by turning widely, making sure the back end of your vehicle is hugging the curb.
- As you begin to turn, make sure you do not turn wide to the left, or vehicles behind you may assume you are making a left turn and attempt to pass on your right causing you to collide.
- If you need to cut into the oncoming lane to make a turn, look out for approaching vehicles and allow them clearance to pass by or stop. Do not back up or you could strike a vehicle in back of you.

#### Left Turns
Make sure you are in the middle of the intersection prior to making a left turn. If you turn too early, off tracking may cause the left side of your vehicle to collide with another vehicle. If the intersection has two left-turn lanes, always choose the one on the far right so you can easily see drivers to your left. Attempting the turn from the inside lane may require you to swerve to the right.

### Space Needed to Cross or Enter Traffic

Because of their larger size and weight, CMVs require more room than a car to enter into traffic. If you are carrying a full load of cargo it will take you longer to accelerate. Make sure you have enough space and time to make the turn and that you are able to drive all the way through before the approaching traffic.

## *Seeing Hazards*

### Importance of Recognizing Hazards

#### What is a Hazard?
Any road condition or other road user (driver, bicyclist, pedestrian) that poses a probable risk is considered a hazard. A good example of a hazardous situation: A car on the highway up ahead starts heading for an exit ramp but brakes hard all of the sudden. This could indicate that the driver is unsure about taking the exit and could re-enter the highway. If the vehicle then cuts you off, it becomes an emergency.

#### Spotting Hazards Allows You to be Prepared
Recognizing possible hazards in advance gives you more time to prevent them from turning into emergencies. Using the scenario above as an example, you may decide to slow down or switch lanes if the car suddenly cuts in front of you. Being aware and prepared decreases the need to brake abruptly or make sudden lane changes.

#### Learning to See Hazards
Clues to help spot hazards in advance become more obvious and routine with time and experience. Many are outlined in the following section.

## Hazardous Roads

### Move-Over Laws

Move-over laws have been instituted to help reduce the increasing number of accidents involving individuals working on or near the highway, such as police officers, emergency medical personnel, fire department employees, and road construction workers. Participating states have signs posted along the highway. As per these regulations, drivers approaching a roadside incident must slow down and switch lanes. If you see an authorized emergency vehicle stopped alongside the road or a work zone, approach the area slowly and move into a lane away from the emergency vehicle or work zone if possible. If you cannot safely switch lanes, slowly and carefully drive past the area as traffic conditions permit.

If you spot any of the following road hazards, slow down and proceed with caution:

#### *Work Zones*

Roadwork produces hazardous conditions such as narrower lanes, sharper curves, and uneven road surfaces. Construction workers and vehicles may obstruct your path and other drivers may become distracted. If necessary, use your four-way flashers or brake lights to alert drivers in back of you.

#### *Drop Off*

Sometimes the asphalt near the edge of the roadway has a sudden drop off. If your vehicle gets too close to the edge, it can sway to the side and clip objects such as signs and tree limbs. Crossing the drop off, pulling over to the side and re-entering the highway can also make it difficult to steer.

#### *Foreign Objects*

Be on the lookout for any objects scattered on the road, as they can be hazardous to your vehicle, particularly the tires, wheel rims, and electrical and brake lines. It is often difficult to tell what the objects are from a distance—boxes and bags may appear empty, but they could contain heavy items inside that could damage your vehicle. Spotting them in advance will help prevent you from having to swerve or brake to hitting them.

#### *Off Ramps/On Ramps*

Use extra caution when exiting and merging onto highways and other major roadways, particularly when navigating a downgrade and curve simultaneously as it may be difficult to slow your vehicle. The speeds posted for exits and on ramps often pertain to cars only. Make sure you are traveling at the proper speed prior to turning onto an on or off ramp.

## Hazards

Always be aware of other vehicles or people along your route that may pose a hazard. Some examples are listed below:

### Blocked Vision

Drivers with blocked or limited vision may not see you clearly. This includes:

- Vehicles with a blocked rear window.
- Rental trucks. Their drivers are often unaware that these vehicles have restricted side and rear views.

- Vehicles whose windows are covered with frost, ice, or snow.
- Vehicles partially concealed by blind intersections or alleys. If you cannot see the driver, he or she can't see you and could suddenly back out or swerve into your lane.

### Delivery Trucks
Delivery drivers are often in a rush and may make sudden or erratic movements. Parcels or the vehicle door also sometimes block their view.

### Parked Vehicles
When you see a parked vehicle, check to see if there are any passengers or a driver inside and if you see any exhaust or brake/backup lights. This could indicate that someone will soon exit the vehicle or drive away. Be especially aware of buses dropping off passengers—they could walk in front of or behind the bus, and may not see you.

### Pedestrians and Bicyclists
Walkers, joggers, and bicyclists traveling away from you will not be able to see or hear you approaching. Inclement weather days pose an additional danger since pedestrians may be wearing hats or carrying umbrellas that block their view and walking hastily with their head down to get to their destination.

### Distractions
Distracted drivers will not be completely alert, even if they appear to be looking in your direction. They might assume that they have the right of way.

### Children
Children playing in or near the road might not see you.

### Talkers
Drivers or pedestrians might be so engaged in conversation that they fail to see you.

### Workers
If you see people working alongside the work, beware of their movements, as they may not see you. Also be on the lookout for distracted drivers as the work itself interferes with traffic flow.

### Ice Cream Trucks
Children often congregate near ice cream trucks, so beware of sudden movements near the truck or stand.

### Disabled Vehicles
Look out for vehicles pulled over on the side of the road. If you see a raised hood or jacked up wheels, this could indicate that a driver is trying to check an engine or change a tire and may be unaware of the traffic around them.

### Accidents
Proceed with caution if approaching an accident scene—those at the scene may make sudden movements without regarding traffic. The accident itself also tends to cause rubbernecking, with other drivers abruptly slowing or braking.

### Shoppers

Pedestrians and drivers near shopping areas are often distracted, as they are focused on window shopping or driving around looking for stores or parking.

### Confused Drivers

Confused drivers often brake abruptly or make sudden movements, a common occurrence near highway and major junctions. Beware of drivers not local to the area, often signified by vehicles with car-top luggage carriers or out-of-state license plates, or drivers searching for house numbers or checking street signs or maps. They could be lost or unfamiliar with traffic patterns and drive hesitantly or erratically, therefore changing direction suddenly or stopping without warning.

### Slow Drivers

Spotting a slow vehicle in the distance can help avoid an accident. Some vehicles (mopeds, farm and construction machinery, etc.) are naturally slow, so be on the lookout for them—many are marked with a "slow moving vehicle" red/orange triangle symbol as a warning.

### Drivers Signaling to Turn

Drivers who are turning typically drive more slowly, particularly if the turn is tight. They may have to wait for traffic to make the turn or stop traffic themselves. Sometimes they fail to use their signal. All these situations are hazardous.

### Drivers in a Hurry

Impatient drivers can cut you off as they are trying to pass in front of you, and vehicles merging into traffic may speed up to get ahead of you so they are not stuck driving behind you, causing you to brake. Either scenario may cause you to brake suddenly.

### Impaired Drivers

Impaired drivers include those who are sleep-deprived, sick, or under the influence of drugs or alcohol. They may do any of the following:

- Weave or drift across the road.
- Drive off the road onto the shoulder or jump a curb while turning.
- Stop incorrectly (when a traffic light is green or linger too long at a stop sign, for example).
- Drive with the window open when it is cold outside.
- Abruptly increase or decrease speed.
- Be especially watchful for drunk and sleepy drivers late in the evening.

### Nonverbal Cues

The body language of other drivers can be a good indicator of their intentions, particularly if they fail to signal. Since drivers look in the direction they are turning, watch their head and body movements if they appear about to make a turn. Those looking back over their shoulder (especially those riding motorcycles and bicycles) may be getting ready to switch lanes.

### Conflicts

Be alert for conflict conditions where you have to alter your speed and/or direction to stop from colliding with another vehicle. High-risk situations include intersections, on and off ramps, necessary lane changes/merges, slow/stopped traffic, and accidents. Conflicted drivers may react in a way that places them in conflict with you.

### Always Have a Plan

Make sure you are always prepared for any type of hazardous situation. Stay alert at all times and think about how you will react based on your pre-planned strategy. A hazard can very quickly become an emergency. Using caution serves to protect both your own safety and the safety of other drivers.

## *Distracted Driving*

Driving while distracted is extremely dangerous for yourself and others around you. Not paying attention can cause you to crash, leading to vehicle or property damage, injury or even death. Distractions can come from either inside or outside your vehicle, including:

- Interacting with passengers
- Adjusting vehicle control knobs (e.g. radio, CD player, or temperature)
- Eating, drinking, or smoking
- Looking at maps or other reading material
- Reaching for an item that dropped
- Speaking on a cell phone or CB radio
- Reading or transmitting text messages
- Using an electronic device (such as a GPS, pager, tablet, computer, etc.)
- Being mentally preoccupied
- Traffic, other vehicles, or pedestrians
- Incidents such as police activity or an accident
- Sunlight/sunset
- Obstructions in the road
- Roadwork
- Billboards or other signs along the road

### Distracted Driving and Accidents

Some significant statistics to keep in mind regarding the correlation between distracted driving and accidents:

- Large-truck crashes:
- Eight percent were the result of CMV driver distractions outside the vehicle
- Two percent were the result of distractions inside the vehicle (LTCCS Large Truck Crash Causation Study)
- About 5,500 people die each year in road accidents
- Distracted driving plays a part in about 448,000 motor vehicle accidents a year (Source: NHTSA Traffic Safety Facts: Distracted Driving)
- Cell phone usage (even hands-free) – uses 39% of the energy the brain would typically devote to safe driving
- A driver who uses a hand-held device is more likely to get into a serious accident resulting in injury
- (Source: NHTSA distracted driving website, www.distraction.gov).

## Effects of Distracted Driving

Driving distracted can impair your awareness, causing you to see a potential danger too late or not at all. As a result, your reaction to the situation could be delayed or inadequate.

## Types of Distractions

There are three types of distractions, all hazardous.

- Physical distraction: something that makes you remove your hands from the steering wheel or take your eyes off the road—adjusting the heat control, for example.
- Mental distraction: behavior that deflects your concentration from the road, such as talking with a passenger or being preoccupied about a previous occurrence.
- Both physical and mental distraction: involves both your mental and physical state, such as using a cell phone to talk or to read/send text messages.

## Use of Cell/Mobile Phones

According to 49 CFR Part 383, 384, 390, 391 and 392 of the Federal Motor Carrier Safety Regulations (FMCSRs) and the Hazardous Materials Regulations (HMR), the use of hand-held mobile phones by CMV drivers is limited. Drivers who do not abide by this Federal constraint or who have been charged several times for violating state or local regulations regarding cell phone usage are subject to ineligibility sanctions. In addition, motor carriers cannot force or permit CMV drivers to use hand-held mobile telephones.

Hand-held mobile phone usage is defined by any of the following:

- Having a voice conversation while holding a mobile telephone with at least one hand
- Pressing more than just one button when dialing a mobile phone
- Reaching for a mobile phone while restrained by a seat belt

After two or more state violations of hand-held mobile phone regulations, your CDL will be deemed ineligible—60 days for the second offense within three years and 120 days for three or more offenses within three years. After just the first violation (and each one after that) of this license ban, drivers may be fined up $2,750 in civil penalties. Motor carriers may be fined up to $11,000 for sanctioning or ordering a driver to use a hand-held mobile telephone while driving. The only circumstance where CMV drivers are permitted to use a hand-held mobile phone is to communicate with police officers or other emergency personnel in a crisis situation.

According to research, CMV drivers who dial a mobile phone while driving are six times more likely to cause a safety-critical event (e.g., accident, near-accident, unintentional lane change) than those who do not. When dialing a phone, drivers take their eyes off the road for an average of 3.8 seconds, which is roughly 306 feet of roadway if traveling 55 mph (or 80.7 feet per second). A good deal could happen in that length of time—it is your responsibility as a CMV driver to pay attention to the road at all times.

It is important to keep in mind that hands-free devices are just as distracting as hand-held ones as they both reduce focus on driving. CMV drivers are permitted to use hands-free mobile phones only if located within a close proximity to the driver's seat and in compliance of voice communication rules.

## Texting

According to 49 CFR Part 383, 384, 390, 391, 392, the Federal Motor Carrier Safety Regulations (FMCSR), CMV drivers are forbidden to text while driving a vehicle for interstate commerce reasons. Drivers who do not abide by this Federal constraint or who have been charged several times for violating state or local regulations regarding texting while driving are subject to ineligibility sanctions. In addition, motor carriers cannot force or permit CMV drivers to text while driving.

Texting is defined as typing into or reading text from an electronic device (e.g. cellular phones, personal digital assistants (PDAs), pagers, computers, or any other device used to enter, write, send, receive, or read text). Examples of texting include the use of short message service, e-mail, instant messaging, Internet access or any other type of electronic text interaction, for the purpose of present or future communication.

After two or more state violations of texting regulations, your CDL will be deemed ineligible—sixty days for the second offense within three years and 120 days for three or more offenses within three years. After just the first violation (and each one after that) of this license ban, drivers may be fined up $2,750 in civil penalties. Motor carriers should not sanction or order a driver to text while driving. The only circumstance CMV drivers are permitted to text is to communicate with police officers or other emergency personnel in a crisis situation.

There are indications that texting while driving is even more dangerous than talking on a cell phone, because it is both mentally and physically distracting. To text, a driver must take his or her eyes off the road to look at a screen and hands off the wheel to type into the device.

As per recent research, CMV drivers who text while driving are 23.2 times more likely to cause a safety-critical event (e.g., accident, near-accident, unintentional lane change) than those who do not. When texting, drivers take their eyes off the road for an average of 4.6 seconds, which is roughly 371 feet of roadway if traveling 55 mph (or 80.7 feet per second).

## Don't Drive Distracted

You will need to clear all internal distractions prior to operating a CMV. Use these four steps to help:

- Look around the inside of your vehicle to pinpoint all possible distractions
- Map out a plan in advance to diminish/remove probable distractions
- Anticipate that distractions will happen
- Consider potential options prior to getting behind the wheel

Having a plan to prevent distractions is essential—statistics have shown that crashes can double if a driver's reaction time is a half-second slower. Follow these tips so you won't become distracted:

- Switch off all electronic devices.
- If you need to use your mobile phone, make sure it is nearby so that you can operate it without having to unhook your seat belt. Utilize an earpiece, speakerphone, or voice activated/hands-free dialing. Reaching for your cell phone (even to use the hands-free function) is a violation of regulations.
- Do not write or view text messages on a mobile device while driving.
- Make sure you are acquainted with your vehicle's features and mechanisms prior to getting behind the wheel.

- Before starting to drive, adjust all vehicle controls and mirrors to your liking.
- Make sure your music is set and programmed (radio stations, CDs, etc.).
- Secure cargo and make sure there are no superfluous items lying around.
- Plan your route prior to your trip by checking maps, and setting your GPS coordinates.
- Don't try to read or write while driving.
- Do not smoke, eat or drinking while driving. Depart early so you have enough time to take a break to eat.
- Do not participate in complicated or in-depth discussions with passengers.
- Ask passengers to agree to act sensibly and minimize distractions.

### Look Out for Other Distracted Drivers

Being able to identify drivers who are distracted can help you respond to and prevent an accident or other incident.

Look for the following:

- Drifting vehicles
- Vehicles driving at erratic speeds
- Preoccupied drivers
- Drivers talking to passengers and not paying attention to the road

If a driver appears distracted, stay clear of their vehicle and use caution if you need to pass.

## *Aggressive Drivers/Road Rage*

### What Is It?

Traffic gridlock coupled with today's stressful, fast-paced lifestyles has helped fuel aggressive driving (operating a vehicle in an unsafe, forceful way) and road rage (operating a vehicle with the objective of hurting other drivers or their vehicle). These drivers are often angry and hostile.

### Don't Be an Aggressive Driver

Your state of mind prior to operating your vehicle directly correlates to the stress you feel while driving.

- Decrease your stress level before and while driving.

- Stay focused on the road and don't give in to distractions such as your mobile phone, eating, etc. Play mellow music to help ease stress.

- Expect that you will run into delays due to traffic, construction, or bad weather and build in a travel time buffer for these unforeseen complications.

- Sometimes you can't help being late. If this is the case, just breathe deeply and acknowledge the delay.

- Have a sense of understanding for other drivers and why they may be driving a certain way. Do not take it personally.

- Lower your speed so you are not tailgating the vehicle ahead of you.
- Don't drive at a slow speed in the left lane.
- Keep your hands on the wheel at all times and do not make any motions that could irritate another driver, including shaking your head and signaling with your hands.
- Be thoughtful and considerate with your actions; for example, let other drivers in front of you.

### If You Are Confronted by an Aggressive Driver

- Try your best to stay clear of them.
- Do not try to defy them by increasing your speed or staying in your lane.
- Do not make eye contact.
- Pay no attention to their antagonistic actions and do not respond to them.
- Report aggressive drivers to law enforcement officials by specifying a vehicle description, license number, location and, if possible, the direction of the vehicle.
- Call the police if you have a mobile phone and can safely make the call.
- If you notice that an aggressive driver has been involved in an accident down the road, park your vehicle a safe distance away, wait for the police, and report the assertive behavior you saw.

## *Driving at Night*

### It's More Dangerous

Driving at night is more dangerous than during the daytime—driver, road, and vehicle hazards are not as noticeable, which decreases your reaction time.

### Driver Factors

#### Vision

In order to drive safely, it is essential for CMV drivers to maintain good vision. Get frequent eye exams, and if you are required to wear glasses or contact lenses for driving, remember to:

- Wear them at all times, even if only driving a short way. If your driver's license indicates that you must wear corrective lenses, it is illegal to drive without them.
- Make sure you always have an extra set of corrective lenses in your vehicle to use as a fallback in case your regular lenses are broken or lost.
- When driving at night, do not wear dark or tinted corrective lenses at night, even if you think they help reduce glare. Tinted lenses decrease the light you need in order to see clearly in the dark.

### Glare

Bright lights can be very dangerous—sometimes it takes several seconds for a driver to recover from this blinding glare.

### Fatigue and Lack of Alertness

Tiredness can be caused by physical or mental strain, repetition, sickness, or lack of sleep. It can hinder your vision and judgment, just like the effects of drugs and alcohol. If you are tired, you will not recognize and react as quickly to dangers, and your ability to make crucial decisions is compromised. If you fall asleep while driving, you could have an accident and end up hurting or killing yourself or others.

According to the National Highway Traffic Safety Administration (NHTSA), fatigued or drowsy driving causes about 100,000 police-reported accidents per year. And the "Sleep in America" poll taken by the National Sleep Foundation (NSF) found that 60 percent of Americans have driven while drowsy and more than a third (36 percent or 103 million people) said they have actually fallen asleep while driving. Drivers can doze for just a few seconds or actually fall asleep for longer periods of time. Either scenario considerably increases the chances of an accident.

### Those at Risk for Fatigue

Drowsiness is most common at night and in the mid-afternoon, which directly correlates to the times most crashes take place. People who drive at night are particularly at risk of falling asleep, especially after midnight and when driving for long periods of time. Commercial drivers (especially long-haul drivers and people with untreated sleep disorders or with short-term or chronic sleep deprivation) are one of the higher risk groups for driving accidents caused by fatigue, along with young men and shift workers. Drowsiness is a factor in at least 15 percent of all CMV crashes.

A study authorized by Congress that tracked 80 long-haul truck drivers in the United States and Canada found that each one got less than five hours of sleep per day on average (Federal Motor Carrier Safety Administration, 1996). Another report by the National Transportation Safety Board (NTSB) found that drowsy driving was the likely impetus for over half of the accidents involving the death of a truck driver (NTSB, 1990), and three or four additional individuals are killed for every truck driver casualty (NHTSA, 1994).

### Warning Signs of Fatigue

Even though the NSF's "Sleep in America" poll found that over half of Americans have driven while drowsy and one third said they actually fell asleep while driving, many people are unaware of the warning signs indicating they are at risk for falling asleep behind the wheel. You should stop and rest if you experience any of the following:

- Finding it hard to focus, recurrent blinking, or heavy eyelids
- Repetitive yawning or eye rubbing
- Daydreaming; loss of concentration/confused thoughts
- Difficulty recalling the past few miles driven; missing exits or traffic signs
- Nodding your head
- Straying from your lane, tailgating or drifting onto the shoulder rumble strip
- Feeling edgy and short-tempered

Attempting to drive when you are fatigued is considerably more hazardous than most drivers realize—it is a main cause of deadly accidents. If you notice any signs of tiredness, take a short nap or stop driving altogether and go to sleep for the night.

## Are You At Risk?

Before you begin to drive, determine if you:

- Are sleep-deprived or tired (your risk is tripled if you've had six hours of sleep or less)
- Have been experiencing sleeplessness (insomnia), sleep deprivation, or restless sleep
- Have been driving for a long time without resting
- Are driving during your typical sleep time (e.g. overnight or early morning). It is very common for CMV crashes to happen between the hours of midnight and 6 a.m.
- Are taking sedatives (antidepressants, cold tablets, antihistamines)
- Have been working over sixty hours per week, which increases your chances of falling asleep by 40 percent
- Are employed by more than one occupation, and your main job is comprised of shift work
- Will be driving by yourself or the route involves roads that are lengthy, isolated, dark, or monotonous
- Will be flying or dealing with time zone changes

## Tips to Prevent Drowsiness Before a Trip

- Get at least eight to nine hours of sleep
- Map out the entire trip in advance, determining the total distance and identifying rest stops and other operational issues
- Plan to drive during the hours you are typically awake, not overnight
- Bring a passenger with you
- Do not take medications that cause drowsiness
- See a doctor if you are sleepy during the day, have trouble sleeping at night or need to nap often
- Make exercise part to your routine to up your energy level

## To Stay Alert While Driving

- Use sunglasses to protect yourself from glare and eyestrain
- Open the window or use the air conditioner to circulate air
- Don't eat rich foods just before a trip
- Take time to relax during the day
- Drive and take turns with a partner
- Have a rest break about every 100 miles or two hours when driving long distances
- Take a break from driving to rest or take a nap
- Don't rely on caffeine, as it will make you alert at first—drowsiness will set in when it wears off.
- Drugs may cause you to stay awake, but not focused. Avoid taking them.

If you feel drowsy, you need to stop and sleep so you do not take chances with your life and the lives of others.

## Roadway Factors

### Poor Lighting

It is much more difficult to see clearly at night, particularly when driving on roads that are not well lit. Most of the time you will be solely relying on the light from your headlights. As a result, potential dangers will be much less obvious, especially those on or alongside the road who are not using lights or reflective gear. Be on the lookout for pedestrians, joggers, bicyclists, and animals.

Even when there is sufficient light to see, illuminated signs, buildings and traffic signals can impede your view of the road. Slow down when the light is reduced or obscuring your vision. If you need to brake suddenly, you should be able to stop in the distance you can see in front of you.

### Drunk Drivers

Drivers who are under the influence of alcohol or drugs are dangerous to themselves and others on the road. Beware of the times when bars and taverns are closing and look out for drivers who are drifting or driving erratically, stopping suddenly, or otherwise showing signs of drug or alcohol impairment.

## Vehicle Factors

### Headlights

When you drive at night, your headlights are typically the main light source you will use to see the road (and for others to spot you), so make sure they are clean, properly adjusted, and in good working order. It is important to keep in mind that you will not be able to see nearly as far with your headlights as you can during the day. Low beams allow you to see about 250 feet ahead and high beams about 350 to 500 feet. You will need to slow your speed so that you can stop within the distance you can see within the range of your headlights.

### Other Lights

The following lights on your vehicle must be clean and in good working order so that others on the road can clearly spot you:

- Reflectors
- Marker lights
- Clearance lights
- Taillights
- Identification lights

### Turn Signals and Brake Lights

It is even more important at night to have clear, properly working turn signals and brake lights at night so drivers are aware of your intentions.

### Windshield and Mirrors

Make sure both the interior and exterior of your windshield and mirrors are clear. Light from the setting sun or bright lights during evening hours can enhance glare, impairing your view.

## Night Driving Procedures

### Pre-Trip Procedures

Before starting out on your trip, make sure you are well rested and fully alert. If you feel tired, go to sleep or take a nap before you drive. Make sure any necessary eyewear is clean and free of scratches—do not attempt to wear sunglasses at night. Thoroughly inspect your vehicle according to pre-trip procedures. Give special care to lights and reflectors, ensuring they are clean and working properly. Wipe any that appear dirty.

### Avoid Blinding Others

Your headlights can blind drivers coming toward you and/or shine in the rearview mirrors of those traveling in the same direction. Set your lights so they are illuminated within 500 feet of an approaching vehicle and within 500 feet of a vehicle in front of you.

### Avoid Glare from Oncoming Vehicles

Avoid staring directly at the lights of approaching vehicles. Instead, avert your gaze slightly to the right of the right lane or shoulder. If other drivers fail to switch from high to low beams, don't try to flash them with your high beams. This could blind them and increase the possibilities of an accident.

### Use High Beams Whenever Possible

High beams enhance your night vision—make sure you use them whenever it is safe and permitted by law and you are not within 500 feet of an oncoming vehicle. Lights inside your vehicle can also be distracting to other drivers. Keep your interior lights turned off and your instrument lights on as low a setting as possible to clearly see the controls.

### If You Get Sleepy, Stop at the Nearest Safe Place

If you feel drowsy, check yourself in a mirror if you can safely do so. Even when people can barely keep their eyelids open, they often don't realize how close they are to the verge of sleep. It is imperative to stop driving if you look or feel sleepy in order to prevent an accident. Sleep is the only remedy.

# *Driving in Fog*

Fog is unpredictable and incredibly hazardous, particularly on highways, as it makes it very difficult to see the road ahead. If you encounter fog, be prepared to slow down—don't presume that the fog will disperse quickly. The safest thing to do in foggy conditions is stop altogether until visibility improves. If you can, pull over into a rest area or truck stop until visibility is better. If you need to drive, be sure to consider the following:

- Observe all fog-related warning signs.
- Reduce your speed before driving into fog.
- For the optimum visibility in foggy conditions, use fog lights and make sure your headlights are on the low-beam setting (even during the day), and be on the lookout for other drivers who did not switch on their lights.
- Use your 4-way flashers to make your vehicle more visible to drivers behind you.

- Be on the lookout for vehicles parked on the side of the road. Foggy conditions distort your view—the taillights/headlights of other vehicles up ahead may not be driving on the road at all.
- Utilize highway reflector lights located along the side of the road to guide you through turns in the road.
- Listen for traffic out of your viewing range.
- Do not pass other vehicles.
- Don't pull over to the shoulder and stop, unless you feel it is absolutely essential.

## *Winter Driving*

### Vehicle Checks

You will need to take precautions to ensure that your vehicle can handle winter driving conditions. When making your pre-trip inspection, give special consideration to the following:

#### Coolant Level and Antifreeze Amount

Use a coolant tester to confirm that the cooling system is full and there is enough antifreeze to prevent freezing.

#### Defrosting and Heating Equipment

Check to see that the defrosters are in good working order—they are essential to safe operation of your vehicle. Test the heater to make sure it works and you know how to use it properly. Check any other heaters located in the vehicle that you might need to use (e.g., mirror heaters, battery box heaters, fuel tank heaters).

#### Wipers and Washers

Check the condition of the windshield wiper blades, making sure they glide against the window with enough force to clean the windshield; if not, they might not clear off any snow correctly. Test the windshield washer controls and make sure there is enough washer fluid in the chamber. Utilize windshield washer antifreeze to stop the washer fluid from freezing. If the wipers don't work properly once you start driving, safely stop and park your vehicle to fix them.

#### Tires

Check the tread level on your vehicle's tires—it should be *at least* 4/32 inches deep in every major groove on the front tires and 2/32 inches deep on the other tires. These grooves provide the traction your vehicle needs to help you steer and navigate safely over wet roads and through snow, especially key during the winter. Use a gauge to verify if your vehicle's tread is deep enough to drive safely.

#### Tire Chains

Winter weather conditions may require using chains on your tires. Make sure you have enough chains and extra cross-links, and they are the proper size for your drive tires. Inspect the chains for broken hooks, worn or broken cross-links, and bent or broken side chains. Confirm that you know to properly fit the chains on your vehicle's tires before you need to in snowy/icy conditions.

### Lights and Reflectors

Ensure that the lights and reflectors are clear of any dirt or debris. It is particularly imperative that your lights and reflectors are clean during inclement weather conditions so your view is not compromised and others can see you. Re-check them when conditions are poor to ensure they are clean and in good working order.

### Windows and Mirrors

Prior to starting out, clear any obstructions from the windshield, windows, and mirrors such as ice, snow, etc. using a snow scraper, brush, and your defroster as needed.

### Hand Holds, Steps, and Deck Plates

Clear any ice and snow from the vehicle's handholds, steps, and deck plates to decrease your chances of slipping.

### Radiator Shutters and Winterfront

Clear any ice from the radiator shutters and make sure the winterfront is not too tightly closed. The engine could potentially overheat and stop working if the shutters freeze shut or the winterfront is too snug.

### Exhaust System

When there isn't much air circulating inside the vehicle's cab (such as when the windows are closed), any leaks in the exhaust system are particularly dangerous. If connections are loose, carbon monoxide can leak inside, making you drowsy or even killing you if amounts are large enough. Inspect the exhaust system for loose fittings and other indications of leaks, such as odd noises.

## Driving

### Slippery Surfaces

Drive slowly and cautiously when roads are slippery. When conditions are extremely slick, pull over and stop at the first safe location.

### Start Gently and Slowly

Use extreme care when starting out in wintry conditions—ease onto the road and do not rush.

### Check for Ice

Always be on the lookout for ice on the road surface, particularly bridges and overpasses, which often freeze first. If you do not see any water spraying up from other vehicles around you, this means the road is icy. Your mirrors and wiper blades are other indicators—if they are icy, then the road is probably slick as well.

### Adjust Turning and Braking to Conditions

Turn as slowly as you can and don't brake suddenly or use the engine brake or speed retarder—they can make the driving wheels skid on slippery surfaces.

### Adjust Speed to Conditions

Maintain a slow, steady speed so you don't have to repeatedly ease up and accelerate. Slow down and avoid braking when navigating a bend in the road and avoid passing slower vehicles unless absolutely necessary. Be aware that the road will become even more slippery if conditions warm and the ice begins melting.

#### Adjust Space to Conditions

Don't drive right next to or behind other vehicles. If you see traffic congestion in the distance, slow down or stop until it disperses. Concentrate on predicting when you will need to stop and slow down accordingly. Be on the lookout for snowplows and salt/sand trucks, and allow them a wide berth.

#### Wet Brakes

Your brakes will get wet if you are driving through heavy rain or road-flooding conditions, which can make the brakes weak, apply unevenly, or grab. This can decrease your braking power, cause your wheels to lockup, make your vehicle pull on one side or the other, and jackknife your vehicle if pulling a trailer. If possible, stay clear of deep puddles or flowing water.

If you cannot avoid standing water, heed to the following:

- Decrease your speed and shift into a low gear.
- Lightly apply the brakes in order to push the brake linings against the drums or discs to prevent mud, silt, sand, and water from getting in.
- Rev the engine and drive through the water while gently applying the brakes.
- Once you have driven through the water, keep pressing gently on the brakes for a short stretch to warm them up and dry them out.

Perform a safety check on the brakes when you can safely do so. Make sure there are no vehicles behind you and then check behind to make sure no one is following. Then, press on the brakes to make sure they are working properly. If not, follow the step above to dry them out more. IMPORTANT: Do not press the brakes and accelerator too much simultaneously or the brake drums and linings can overheat.

## *Driving in Very Hot Weather*

### Vehicle Checks

When outside temperatures are extremely hot, perform a regular pre-trip inspection, giving extra attention to the following items:

#### Tires

Inspect the tire mounting and air pressure, which will rise along with the temperature. As a result, you will need to check your vehicle's tires every two hours or 100 miles during exceptionally hot weather conditions. Do not release air from the tires, or the pressure will be too low when the tires cool down. If a tire is too hot to touch, wait to start driving again until it cools down, or it may catch on fire or have a blow out.

#### Engine Oil

Oil helps cool and lubricate the engine—make sure the vehicle has an ample supply. While you are driving, check the oil temperature gauge (if your vehicle is so equipped) to make sure the temperature stays within the proper range.

## Engine Coolant

Before you start driving, make sure the vehicle has the required levels of water and antifreeze as per the manufacturer's directions. Antifreeze helps regulate engine temperature in hot weather as well as cold. While you are driving, make sure the water/coolant temperature gauge is staying within the normal range. If it rises above the upper safe temperature range, pull off the road as soon as it is safe to do so and try to troubleshoot the problem. High temperatures are dangerous and could cause engine failure or even a fire.

Some vehicles allow you to inspect the coolant level while the engine is still hot via sight glasses, see-through coolant overflow containers, or coolant recovery containers. If the coolant reservoir is not pressurized, you can safely remove the cap and add coolant even when the engine is warm. If it is part of a pressurized system, do not remove the cap until the system has cooled. Pressure can cause the steam and boiling water to spew out, causing serious burns. If the radiator cap is cool enough to touch with your bare hand, it is likely safe to open.

If you need to add coolant to a system without a recovery or overflow tank, follow these steps:

- Shut the engine off.
- Wait until the engine has cooled down.
- Protect your hands with gloves or a thick cloth.
- Slowly turn the radiator cap to release the pressure seal (the first stop).
- Step away from the vehicle while the cooling system releases pressure.
- After the pressure has been released, push down on the cap and keep turning to remove it.
- Check the coolant level and add more if needed.
- Replace the cap; turn and tighten to the closed position.

## Engine Belts

Make sure belts are not cracked or worn. Learn how to check whether your vehicle's v-belts are tight enough by pressing on them. If they are too loose, the water pump and/or fan will not work properly, causing the vehicle to overheat.

## Hoses

Check that coolant hoses are in good working order—if a hose breaks while you are driving, the engine can fail or catch on fire.

# Driving

## Look Out for Bleeding Tar

During extremely hot weather conditions, tar often rises to the road surface, causing it to be slippery in spots.

## Go Slowly Enough to Prevent Overheating

Driving at a high speed in hot weather can generate more heat for the tires and engine. In desert regions, this heat build up can be hazardous, intensifying the chances of tire/engine failure or possibly even a fire.

## *Railroad-Highway Crossings*

Always dangerous, railroad-highway crossings are intersections where the roadway goes over train tracks. You should approach these types of crossings with the assumption that a train is coming. The distance and speed of an approaching train can be very difficult to determine.

### Types of Crossings

#### Passive Crossings

Since there are no traffic control mechanisms at passive crossings, you decide entirely on your own whether to stop or go ahead. You must acknowledge the crossing, look both ways for an approaching train, and determine if you can safely proceed.

#### Active Crossings

Active crossings are clearly marked with a traffic control mechanism such as flashing red lights (with or without bells) or flashing red lights combined with bells and gates to regulate traffic.

### Warning Signs and Devices

#### Advance Warning Signs

Prior to approaching a public railroad-highway crossing, you will see a round, black-on-yellow sign warning you to slow down, watch and listen for the train, and be prepared to stop at the tracks if a train is coming. It is a mandatory requirement for all passenger and hazmat carrying vehicles to stop.

See picture below for reference:

## Pavement Markings

Sometimes an advance warning sign is painted on the road. These are known as pavement markings and are in the shape of an "X" with the letters "RR" and a no passing marking on two-lane roads. See diagram below for reference.

**Pavement Markings**

Two-lane roads also have a no-passing zone sign. Right before the railroad tracks there could be a white stop line painted on the pavement. School buses must remain behind this line while stopped at these crossings.

## Crossbuck Signs

Signifying the grade crossing, crossbuck signs instruct you to give the train the right-of-way. If you do not see a white stop line painted on the road, this means vehicles that are required to stop must yield at a distance of fifteen feet or more than fifty feet from the rail of the nearest track. If the road crosses over more than one track, a sign below the crossbuck designates the number of tracks. See the diagram below for reference.

**Multiple tracks**

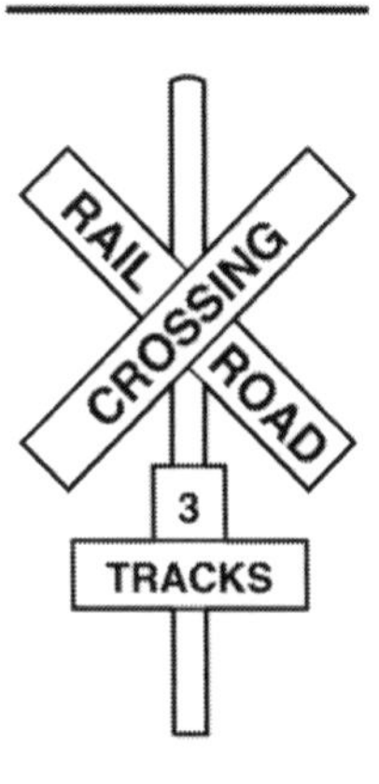

### Flashing Red Light Signals

Crossbuck signs at highway rail grade crossings often feature flashing red lights and bells to indicate that a train is coming. You must yield to the train—stop as soon as you see the lights begin to flash. If the crossing has more than one track, make sure all the tracks are clear before crossing. See the diagram below for reference.

### Gates

Railroad-highway crossings often feature safety gates with flashing red lights and bells. Stop as soon as the lights begin to flash and before the gate lowers across the road. Stay stopped until you see the gates go up and the lights have stopped flashing. Go ahead when it is safe. See the diagram below for reference.

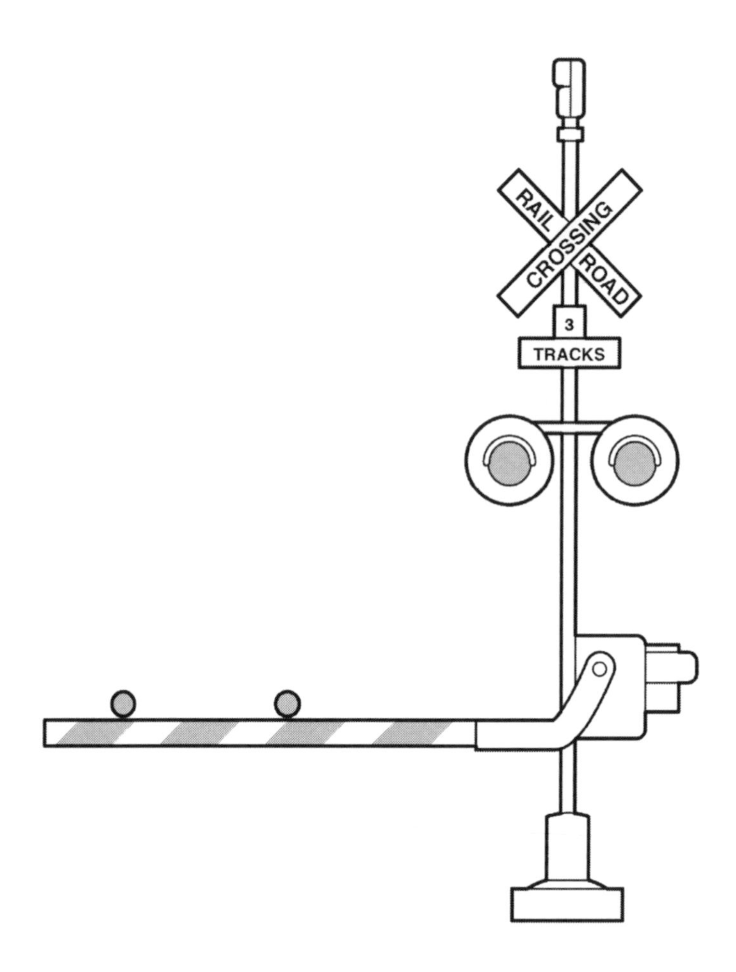


## Driving Procedures

### Never Race a Train to a Crossing

Do not try to beat a train to a crossing—it is incredibly dangerous and tough to gauge how fast a train is coming.

Reduce Speed

Slow your speed based on your capacity to see trains coming in both directions—you must be able to stop at tracks if needed.

Don't Expect to Hear a Train

Keep in mind that some crossings may not require or allow trains to use horns when approaching—these public crossings should have signs to indicate they are silent. You also may not hear the sound of a train coming due to noise inside your vehicle.

Don't Rely on Signals

Don't depend on signals, gates, or flagmen as your only source of caution regarding approaching trains. Make sure you are particularly aware at crossings without gates or flashing red light lights.

Double Tracks Require a Double Check

When approaching a crossing with double tracks, always look both ways before proceeding—a train on one track may conceal a train on the other track. Once one train has gone through the crossing, make absolutely certain no other trains are nearby before driving across the tracks.

Yard Areas and Grade Crossings in Cities and Towns

Use an equal amount of caution at yard areas and grade crossings located in cities and towns—they are just as hazardous as crossing in rural areas.

### Stopping Safely at Railroad-Highway Crossings

It is essential that you completely stop your vehicle at grade crossings under the following circumstances:

- You are hauling cargo that necessitates coming to a full stop under state or federal regulations.
- It is a legal requirement.

When stopping, make sure you:

- Look for traffic in back of you while slowing to a stop.
- Utilize a pullout lane, if one is available.
- Switch on your four-way emergency flashers.

### Crossing Railroad Tracks

Keep in mind that your vehicle can get hung up on railroad crossings with steep grades. Never get in a situation where you need to stop on the tracks. Make sure you'll be able to safely drive across before you attempt a crossing. Allow yourself at least fourteen seconds to clear a single track and fifteen or more to clear a double track, and do not shift gears while crossing.

### Special Situations

Use special caution when driving one of the following vehicles that can get stuck on raised crossings:

- Those with low clearance underneath (lowboy, car carrier, moving van, possum-belly livestock trailer).

- A single-axle tractor pulling a long trailer with its landing gear on the tandem-axle tractor setting.

If you do get hung up on the tracks, immediately exit the vehicle and get away from the tracks. Check signs posted at the crossing for emergency information. Call 911 or another emergency number and notify personnel of the crossing location using landmarks, signage and the DOT number, if posted.

## *Mountain Driving*

Gravity is a big factor when driving through mountainous areas—it will slow your vehicle when you are driving uphill, and increase your speed when driving down. If you are driving up a hill that is especially long or steep and/or you are hauling heavy cargo, you will have to shift into a lower gear in order to make it up the hill. When driving down a long, steep hill, make sure you slow down to a safe speed, stay in a low gear, and use correct braking methods. Plan your route ahead so you are aware of long, steep grades that might be difficult to navigate. If possible, consult other drivers who have traversed the hills to get an idea of a safe speed.

It is important to drive at a moderate enough speed so that the brakes work to slow your vehicle without getting too hot. Brakes that get too hot can begin to "fade," forcing you to press them harder and harder to make the vehicle stop. Continuously applying the brakes hard can cause them to keep fading until they do not work at all.

### Select a "Safe" Speed

It is important to select a speed that is not too fast for the:

- Combined weight of the vehicle and cargo.
- Length of the hill.
- Steepness of the hill.
- Road conditions.
- Weather.

Pay attention to speed and grade length/steepness warning signs. Never exceed the speed limit or "Maximum Safe Speed" posted. Use the engine's braking effect as the main method to control your speed. This is most pronounced when the engine is near the governed rpms and the vehicle is in a low gear. Don't wear out your brakes so that your vehicle will be able to safely slow or stop depending on road and traffic conditions.

### Select the Right Gear Before Starting Down the Grade

Before starting downhill, shift into a lower gear. Do not try to downshift after you have already begun the descent and your speed has increased. Trying to force an automatic transmission into a lower gear while accelerating downhill at high speed could damage the transmission and cause the vehicle to lose its engine braking effect.

If the vehicle is an older model, it's best to use the same gear traveling down a hill as you would need to drive up the hill. However, newer trucks are more streamlined and often feature low friction mechanisms and stronger, more efficient engines. As a result, they can climb hills in a higher gear and create less friction and air drag to impede them driving down hills. If you are driving a newer vehicle, you may have to use a lower gear driving down a hill than climbing it. Know ahead of time how your vehicle operates the best.

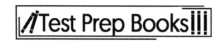

### Brake Fading or Failure

Brakes slow down a vehicle by using brake shoes or pads to create friction against the brake drum or disks. This causes the brakes to get very hot, but brakes are built to withstand high levels of heat. However, using the brakes excessively and/or not taking advantage of the engine braking effect can cause brakes to overheat and fade or fail as a result.

Improper brake adjustment can also cause brakes to fade. If the workload is not equal throughout the vehicle, the brakes out of adjustment will not perform to their capacity. As a result, the vehicle will not have enough braking power to stop properly. It doesn't take much for brakes to get out of adjustment, especially when they are used often. In addition, when brake linings are hot they can wear out much faster. It is important for your vehicle to have regular brake adjustment checks.

### Proper Braking Technique

When navigating a long and/or steep downgrade, the brakes should only be used to enhance the engine's braking effect. As soon as you shift the vehicle into the correct low gear, follow these braking techniques:

1. Depress the brake pedal with just enough pressure to feel the vehicle start to slow down.
2. Once your speed has decreased to about five mph lower than your "safe" speed, let up on the brakes. (This process should take about three minutes).
3. After your speed has risen to your "safe" speed, repeat steps 1 and 2.

As an example, if your "safe" speed is 40 mph, you should not use the brakes until you are going 40 mph. Once that happens, brake with enough pressure to slowly decrease your speed to 35 mph and then let up on the brakes. Keep repeating this procedure as many times as you need until you are at the bottom of the hill.

Many roads on steep mountains have escape ramps—these are exit areas for drivers who have lost control driving down a hill. They are made up of loose, soft material designed to slow a runaway vehicle, sometimes in tandem with an upgrade. Accompanied by signs marking their location, it is important to be aware where escape ramps are situated along your route. Escape ramps help prevent accidents on roads with steep grades.

## *Driving Emergencies*

There are two different types of driving emergencies:

- Traffic emergencies: when two vehicles are about to crash
- Vehicle emergencies: when tires, brakes, or other critical components fail.

You can help avoid emergencies by observing the safety procedures discussed throughout this guide. However, it is important to know how to react in case an emergency does occur.

## Steering to Avoid a Crash

In an emergency situation, stopping is not always the safest choice. If there is not enough room on the road to stop, you might need to turn your vehicle to avoid the hazard. It is almost always quicker to steer a vehicle away than it is to stop. However, top-heavy vehicles and tractors with multiple trailers can be prone to flipping over.

### Keep Both Hands on the Steering Wheel

You should have both hands on the steering wheel at all times. If you do need to turn quickly in response to an emergency, you'll need to grasp the steering wheel firmly in both hands.

### How to Turn Quickly and Safely

It is possible to safely execute a rapid turn if it's done the right way. Some safety tips to follow include:

- Do not brake at the same time you are turning—it can cause your wheels to lock and make you skid out of control.
- Only turn as much as you need to avoid danger—sharp turns increase the chances of a skid or rollover.
- Be ready to quickly "countersteer" (turn the wheel back in the other direction) as soon as you are clear of the obstacle. Emergency steering and countersteering go hand in hand.

### Where to Steer

If a driver coming towards you drifts into your lane, it is best to steer to the right. This could prompt the other driver to return to the correct lane if he or she recognizes what happened.

If there is an obstacle in your way, the circumstance will dictate the best direction to turn. Using your mirrors will help you determine which lane is clear and safe to use. If the shoulder is free, steering to the right might be the best decision—it is less likely for a vehicle to be on the shoulder, but there could be a vehicle passing on your left. If there are vehicles surrounding you on both sides, turning to the right might be best. This will prevent you from forcing another vehicle into oncoming traffic and the possibility of a head-on crash.

### Leaving the Road

Some emergencies may require you to drive off the road to avoid colliding with another vehicle. The shoulder is often a viable escape route as they are usually strong enough to support the weight of a CMV. Some tips to follow if you do need to leave the road:

- Avoid braking. If feasible, do not brake until your speed has decreased to about 20 mph. Then slowly use your brakes to prevent your vehicle from skidding on the loose gravel.
- Keep one set of wheels on the pavement if possible. It is easier to keep control if at least one set of wheels is left on the road.
- Stay on the shoulder. If there are no obstacles on the shoulder, stay until your vehicle completely stops. Use your signal lights and carefully check your mirrors before turning back onto the road.

- Returning to the road. If you must go back on the road before you can fully stop, use the following procedure:
- Hold onto the wheel firmly and make a sharp enough turn to return safely to the road.
- Don't try to slowly ease back onto the road—your tires might spin on the loose gravel and cause you to lose control.
- Countersteer as soon as your vehicle's front tires are on the road. These two turns should be executed as a one "steer-countersteer" action.

## How to Stop Quickly and Safely

You will most likely brake instinctively if another vehicle cuts in front of you. This is a good reflex to follow as long as you brake properly and have enough distance to safely stop. When braking, make sure to keep your vehicle in a straight line and have the ability to quickly turn if needed. There are two techniques—"controlled" or "stab" braking.

### Controlled Braking

To use this technique, hit the brakes as hard as you can without locking the wheels and keeping your steering very tight. If the wheels lock or you need to turn, let up on the brakes briefly, and then press down on them again as soon as you are able.

### Stab Braking

Stab braking involves the following steps:

- Fully apply the brakes.
- Let up on the brakes when the wheels lock up.
- As soon as the wheels start going, apply them again. The wheels can take up to a second to start going after the brakes are released. If you use the brakes again before the wheels start going, your vehicle won't straighten out.

### Don't Slam on the Brakes

Emergency braking does not mean slamming the brake pedal as hard as you can. That method will only lock the wheels and cause you to skid, which affects your control of the vehicle.

## Brake Failure

It is rare for brakes kept in good condition to fail. Most hydraulic brakes fail for one of two reasons: (1) Hydraulic pressure loss or (2) fading on long hills. Air brakes are discussed in another section.

### Loss of Hydraulic Pressure

The brake pedal will have a spongy feel or it will drop to the floor if the system doesn't get enough pressure. Some steps to follow:

- Downshift. Shifting down into a lower gear will help to slow the vehicle.

- Pump the brakes. Pumping the brake pedal can sometimes generate enough hydraulic pressure to bring the vehicle to a stop.
- Use the parking brake. Since the parking or emergency brake is unconnected to the hydraulic brake system, it can be utilized to slow the vehicle. But you must push the release button or pull the release lever at the same time you are using the emergency brake in order to regulate the brake pressure and prevent the wheels from locking up.
- Find an escape route. As you are trying to slow your vehicle, be on the lookout for a place to safely stop, such as an open field, side street, or escape ramp. Steering the vehicle uphill is also a viable method to help slow down and stop. When you do stop, keep the vehicle from rolling back by shifting into low gear, putting on the parking brake, and, if needed, rolling back into an obstruction that will help stop the vehicle.

### Brake Failure on Downgrades

Navigating hills slowly and using correct braking techniques will stop brakes from failing most of the time. If the brakes do happen to fail, you will have to use something external to your vehicle to help it stop.

Look first for signs indicating an escape ramp, as this will be your best choice. Escape ramps are typically situated a few miles from the top of the hill. Escape ramps help prevent injuries and vehicle damage for hundreds of drivers every year. Some types of escape ramps are lined with soft gravel that counterbalances the vehicle's movement to bring it to a stop. Other ramps feature an upturn, using the grade to stop the vehicle and soft gravel to keep it in place.

If your brakes fail while traveling downhill and there is an escape ramp available, use it. It will help decrease the possibilities of a serious accident. If there is no escape ramp, then look for the next best escape route, such as an open field or a flat or elevated side road. Make your decision as soon as you realized your brakes have failed. The more time that goes by, the more speed your vehicle will pick up, making it increasingly difficult to stop.

## Tire Failure

### Recognizing Tire Failure

If you are able to promptly determine that a tire is having an issue, you will have more time to respond to the situation. Taking just a few extra seconds to run through the following checklist will help:

#### *Sound*

A tire blowout is accompanied by a loud, distinguishable "bang." You might not feel the impact right away, causing you to think it was another vehicle. However, to be on the safe side, always presume the sound of a tire blowout is from your vehicle.

#### *Vibration*

If your vehicle is making a thumping sound or severely vibrating, it may have a flat tire. If it is one of the rear tires, this vibration may be our only indication of a flat.

*Feel*
If steering becomes difficult or feels "heavy," it could be an indicator that one of the front tires has failed. If a rear tire fails, the vehicle will sometimes sway or "fishtail," although dual rear tires typically stop this from occurring.

### Respond to Tire Failure
A tire failure places your vehicle in immediate danger. Respond by doing the following:

*Hold the Steering Wheel Firmly*
A front tire failure can cause you to loose your grip on the steering wheel. To avoid this from happening, always grasp the wheel firmly in both hands.

*Stay Off the Brake*
In an emergency situation, it's human nature to use the brakes. However, you could potentially lose control of the vehicle if you try to brake when a tire has failed. Unless you are in danger of hitting another object, do not brake until your vehicle has slowed down. Then slowly apply the brakes, pull over to the side of the road, and come to a complete stop.

*Check the Tires*
Once you have stopped and parked, get out and check all the tires, even if the vehicle appears to be driving ok. If the failure is in one of your dual tires, you may not be able to tell unless you do a visible inspection.

# *Antilock Braking Systems (ABS)*

ABS is a computerized system designed to prevent your wheels from locking when you apply them very hard. An add-on to your vehicle's regular braking system, it does not reduce or intensify the brakes' capability. Triggered when the wheels are about to lock up, ABS may not decrease the distance you will need to stop, but it will help you control your vehicle during hard braking.

## How Antilock Braking Systems Work

ABS is equipped with special instruments that sense situations that could cause the wheels to lock up. An electronic control unit (ECU) will then reduce and adjust pressure on the brakes to prevent the wheels from locking and provide the best possible braking capacity. In circumstances where your vehicle's wheels could lock up, ABS will react way quicker than you can. During all other situations, your brakes will function normally.

## Vehicles Required to Have Antilock Braking Systems

As per the Department of Transportation, the following types of vehicles must be ABS-equipped:

- Truck tractors with air brakes built on or after March 1, 1997.
- Other air brake vehicles (such as trucks, buses, trailers, and converter dollies) built on or after March 1, 1998.

- Trucks and buses with hydraulic brakes, a gross vehicle weight rating of 10,000 pounds or more, and manufactured on or after March 1, 1999. Many CMVs manufactured prior to these dates have been voluntarily outfitted with ABS.

### How to Know if Your Vehicle is Equipped with ABS

Tractors, trucks, and buses equipped with ABS feature yellow ABS malfunction lights on the instrument panel. On trailers, yellow ABS malfunction lights are located on the left side, either in the front section or on the rear corner. Dollies manufactured on or after March 1, 1998, have an ABS light on the left side.

On newer vehicles, the ABS malfunction light flashes briefly to check the bulb when the vehicle is turned on, and then quickly turns off. The light on some older systems might stay on until you reach a speed of 5 mph. If the light stays lit even after the bulb check, or turns on after you start driving, the ABS may not be working properly. It may be hard to determine if towed vehicles built prior to Department of Transportation requirements have ABS. To make sure, check under the vehicle for the ECU and wheel speed sensor wires protruding from the back of the brakes.

### How ABS Helps You

If your vehicle does not have ABS and you need to brake hard on a slippery surface, your wheels can lock up, causing you to lose control, skid, jackknife, or even spin around. ABS is designed to help prevent your wheels from locking up and enable you to remain in control. Even though ABS might not allow you to stop more quickly, it should enable you to avoid an obstacle while braking, and prevent skidding due to over braking.

### ABS on the Tractor Only or Only on the Trailer

When braking, you will have more control even if you only have ABS on the tractor, trailer, or only one axle. If the ABS is only on the tractor, you should have the ability to control your steering, and the possibility of jackknifing is decreased. However, if it starts to sway, watch the trailer and decrease pressure on the brakes (if you can do so safely). If just the trailer has ABS, the chances of it swaying out are decreased, but if you lose control of the steering control or begin to jackknife, decrease pressure on the brakes (if you can do so safely) until you regain control.

### Braking with ABS

If your vehicle is equipped with ABS, use your brakes as you normally would:

- Use only enough brake pressure as is required to safely stop and retain control.
- Use the brakes in the same manner, regardless if ABS is on the bus, tractor, the trailer, or both.
- As you slow your speed, watch your tractor and trailer and decrease brake pressure (if it is safe to do so) to maintain control.

This method has just one exception. If your vehicle is a straight truck or combination equipped with ABS on all axles, you can fully apply the brakes if you need to do an emergency stop.

### Braking if ABS is Not Working

Your brakes will still work fine even without ABS—drive and brake just as you normally would. A yellow malfunction light on the dash will turn on if something isn't functioning properly. On newer vehicles, the

ABS malfunction light will briefly flash when the vehicle is started up. On some older systems, the light might stay on until you reach a speed of 5 mph. If the light stays lit even after the bulb check, or turns on after you start driving, you may have lost ABS functionality on one or more wheels. It is important to keep in mind that you still have your standard brakes even if the ABS isn't working properly. You can continue to drive, but make sure to get the system checked soon.

### Safety Reminders

Keep the following in mind when driving an ABS equipped vehicle:

- You won't be able to drive faster, follow behind another vehicle more closely, or drive more recklessly.
- You won't be able to avoid power or turning skids—ABS is designed to prevent brake-induced skids or jackknifes, but not those triggered by spinning the drive wheels or taking a turn too fast.
- Don't assume the distance you need to stop will be shorter—ABS will help you retain control of your vehicle, but it doesn't necessarily decrease stopping distance.
- Your maximum stopping power won't be boosted or reduced—ABS is a supplement for your normal brakes, not a substitute.
- The way you typically brake will not be any different—in normal brake conditions, your vehicle will stop as usual. ABS will only be a factor if one of your wheels would have become locked due to braking too much.
- ABS can't take the place of bad brakes or improper brake maintenance.
- Remember: A safe driver is still the best safety feature on your vehicle.
- Remember: Drive in a manner that you will never need to use your ABS.
- Remember: ABS could help to prevent a serious crash if you need to use it.

## *Skid Control and Recovery*

Your vehicle will skid if its tires stop gripping the road, the result of one of the following conditions:

- Over-braking. If you brake too hard, the wheels can lock up. In slippery conditions, use of the speed retarder can also cause your vehicle to skid.
- Over-steering. Executing a sharper turn than the vehicle can handle.
- Over-acceleration. Making the drive wheels spin by giving them too much power.
- Driving Too Fast. Driving faster than the road conditions allow is the most common cause of serious skids. By modifying your driving to your surroundings, you won't be traveling too fast and therefore over-brake or make a sharper turn than your vehicle can handle.

## Drive-Wheel Skids

The types of skids that happen most often are when the rear wheels lose traction through braking or accelerating too much. Those caused by accelerating typically occur in ice or snow conditions. If you find yourself skidding when conditions are slippery, take your foot off the accelerator. If the road is very slick, push in the clutch. Otherwise, the engine might prevent the wheels from moving freely and regaining traction.

Rear wheel braking skids happen when the rear drive wheels lock up. Since wheels that are locked have less traction than those that are moving, rear wheels typically slide sideways to try to match the front wheels. A bus or straight truck will slide sideways, or "spin out." In vehicles towing trailers, a drive-wheel skid can cause the trailer to push the towing vehicle sideways, causing a sudden jackknife.

See the diagram below for reference:

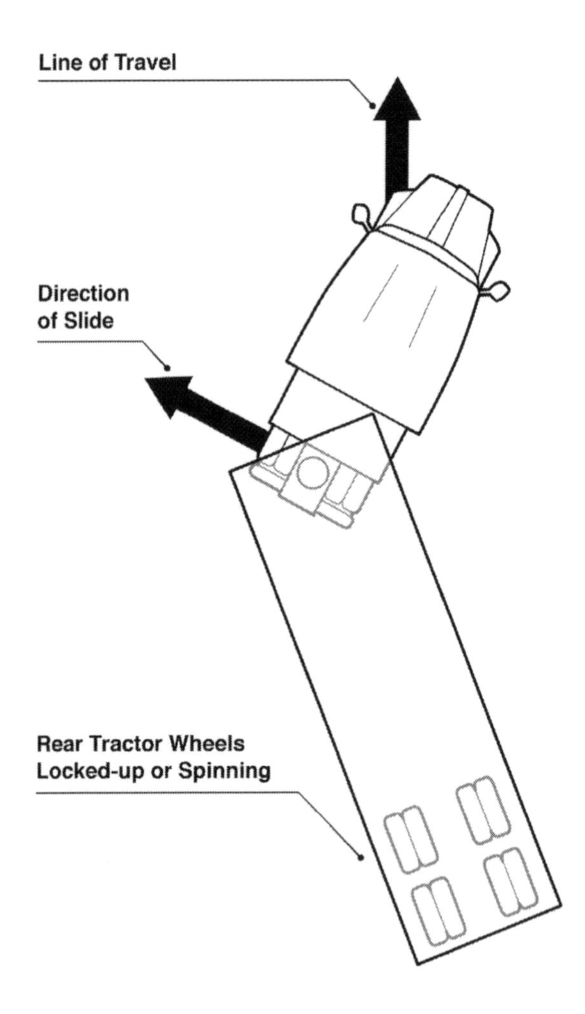


## Correcting a Drive-Wheel Braking Skid

The following steps will help correct a drive-wheel braking skid:

1. Stop Braking. Taking pressure off the brakes will allow the rear wheels to move and help prevent them from sliding.
2. Countersteer. As a vehicle re-rights itself, it may continue to turn. By quickly turning the steering wheel in the other direction, you can prevent skidding the opposite way.

While in a skid, it requires quite a bit of practice to lay off the brake, quickly turn the wheel, press in the clutch and countersteer. Make sure to practice these skills on a large driving range or "skid pad."

### Front-Wheel Skids

Most front wheel skids are caused when vehicles travel faster than the road conditions allow. Front-wheel skids can also be caused by a not having enough tread on the front tires and hauling cargo that is distributed without enough weight on the front axle. In a front-wheel skid, the front end of the vehicle has the tendency to move in a straight line no matter how far you turn the steering wheel. If the road is very slippery, you may not be able to navigate a curve or turn. If you experience a front-wheel skid, the only way to stop is by slowing your vehicle as fast as you can without turning or braking hard.

## *Accident Procedures*

If you have an accident and aren't critically injured, you must take steps to stop any additional harm. The procedure to follow at the scene of an accident includes:

- Protecting the area.
- Notifying authorities.
- Caring for the injured.

### Protect the Area

You will first need to make sure another accident does not occur in the same location.

Protect the area by doing the following:

- If your vehicle was involved in the accident, do your best to move it over to the shoulder. This will let other vehicles get around the scene and help avoid another accident.
- If you pull over to help, park your vehicle away from the accident. Emergency vehicles will need to have a clear amount of space surrounding the accident.
- Turn your flashers on.
- Place reflective triangles on the road as a warning to other vehicles. Make sure they are visible so that drivers can see them in plenty of time to get around the accident.

### Notify Authorities

If you have a mobile phone or CB radio, call for help before leaving your vehicle. If not, wait until the accident scene is protected, then call or send someone to alert the authorities. Try to pinpoint your location via landmarks or road signs so you can tell the dispatcher where to find you.

### Care for the Injured

If someone at the scene has emergency experience and is assisting those with injuries, stay clear unless asked to help. Otherwise, do your best to help anyone who is hurt, making sure to follow these steps:

- Don't move someone who is seriously injured unless it is essential to move them away from heavy traffic or a fire hazard.
- Stop heavy bleeding by applying direct pressure on the wound.
- Make sure the injured person is kept warm.

## *Fires*

Truck fires are very dangerous. Make sure you know what causes fires, how to prevent them, and the procedure for putting them out.

### Causes of Fire

Some causes of vehicle fires include:

- The scene of an accident. Leaking fuel, incorrect use of flares.
- Tires. Tires that are under-inflated and dual tires that make contact.
- Electrical system. Short circuits caused by damaged insulation and loose connections.
- Fuel. Ignited by a driver who is smoking, incorrect fuel procedures, or loose fuel connections.
- Cargo. Freight that is flammable or inadequately closed or loaded, bad ventilation.

### Fire Prevention

In order to prevent fires from happening, go through the following checklist:

- Pre-trip inspection. Thoroughly check the electrical, fuel, exhaust systems, tires, and freight. Make sure the fire extinguisher is fully charged.

- En route inspection. Whenever you stop during a trip, inspect the tires, wheels, and truck body to make sure they are not too hot.

- Follow safe procedures. Heed proper safety procedures for fueling, braking, using flares, and other activities that can trigger a fire.

- Monitoring. Glance periodically at the vehicle's instruments and gauges to make sure none of the systems are overheating, and utilize your mirrors to check for signs of smoke from the vehicle or tires.

- Caution. Handle anything flammable with special care.

### Fighting Fires

It is imperative that you are aware of how to fight fires. Drivers without this knowledge have made a fire situation worse. Make sure you read and understand the instructions printed on the fire extinguisher located in your vehicle so that you know how to operate it before you need to in an emergency. If a fire does occur, follow these procedures:

## Pull Off the Road

First and foremost, get your vehicle off the road and come to a complete stop. Make sure you park in an open area, away from buildings, trees, brush, other vehicles, or anything that could catch on fire. Do not pull into a gas station! Call the authorities to alert them of your situation and location.

## Keep the Fire from Spreading

You will need to make sure the fire doesn't spread before you attempt to extinguish it. If the fire is in the engine, turn off the ignition as soon as possible and avoid opening the hood if you can. Spray the extinguisher through the vehicle's louvers, radiator, or underneath. If your freight is on fire and your vehicle is a van or box trailer, do not open the doors, particularly if the cargo contains hazardous substances. Opening the doors will "feed" the fire with oxygen, possibly increasing its intensity.

## Extinguish the Fire

When using a fire extinguisher, make sure you stand as far away from the fire as you can. Aim the nozzle at the source or bottom of the fire, not higher up near the flames.

## Use the Right Fire Extinguisher

The diagrams below explain which fire extinguisher works best for each type of fire. B:C extinguishers are intended for electrical fires and burning liquids. A:B:C types can be used for wood, paper, and cloth fires as well.

| **Class/Type of Fires** | |
|---|---|
| Class | Type |
| A | Wood, paper, ordinary combustibles. Extinguish by cooling and quenching using water or dry chemicals |
| B | Gasoline, oil, grease, greasy liquids. Extinguish by smothering, cooling, or heat shielding using carbon dioxide or dry chemicals. |
| C | Electrical equipment fires. Extinguish with non-conducting agents such as carbon dioxide or dry chemicals. Do not use water. |
| D | Fires in combustible metals. Extinguish by using specialized extinguishing powders. |

| **Class of Fire** | **Type of Extinguisher** |
|---|---|
| B or C | Regular dry chemical |
| A, B, C, or D | Multipurpose dry chemical |
| D | Purple K dry chemical |
| B or C | KCL dry chemical |
| D | Dry powder special compound |
| B or C | Carbon dioxide (dry) |
| B or C | Halogenated Agent (gas) |
| A | Water |
| A | Water with anti-freeze |
| A or B | Water, loaded steam style |
| B, on some A | Foam |

Other Tips:

- Water can be used on wood, paper, or cloth, never try to use water to extinguish an electrical fire (it can cause shock) or a gasoline fire (it will make the flames spread).
- A burning tire should be cooled. May require a good deal of water.
- Wait for the firefighters to arrive if you are not positive what type of extinguisher to use, particularly if it is a hazardous materials fire.
- Allow the wind to carry the extinguisher to the fire by standing upwind.
- Continue to put out the fire until the burning material is cooled. The fire can restart even if you don't see smoke or flames.

# *Alcohol, Other Drugs, and Driving*

## Alcohol and Driving

It is a very hazardous to drive after drinking alcohol. Drinking and driving is the cause of over 20,000 deaths every year. Alcohol affects muscle coordination, reaction time, depth perception, night vision, judgment and inhibition—all necessary for safe driving. Some drivers can be affected by just one drink.

### How Alcohol Works

When you have an alcoholic beverage, the alcohol enters your blood stream, where it first travels to your brain. Your body will emit a small amount through your urine, perspiration, and via breathing, but the rest goes to your liver. But the liver is only able to process a third of an ounce of alcohol per hour, much less than the alcohol contained in a standard drink. As a result, only time will help remove the effects of alcohol. If you drink more quickly than your body can process the alcohol, more alcohol will remain in your bloodstream, impairing your driving even more. Blood Alcohol Concentration (BAC) is used to measure the level of alcohol in the body.

The following drinks all contain the same amount of alcohol:

- A 12-ounce glass of 5% beer.
- A 5-ounce glass of 12% wine.
- A 1 1/2-ounce shot of 80 proof liquor

### What Determines Blood Alcohol Concentration?

A number of factors determine BAC:

- The quantity of alcohol (more alcohol equals a higher BAC)
- How quickly the alcohol is consumed (drinking more rapidly equals a higher BAC)
- Weight (Smaller people don't have to drink as much to reach the same BAC)

### Alcohol and the Brain

As BAC builds up in the body, the alcohol increasingly affects your brain and the various body functions it controls. Judgment and self-control are the first to be influenced, which can prevent you from realizing you are getting drunk. This is particularly dangerous for someone who plans to drive, as good judgment and self-control are absolutely essential to drive safely.

As BAC increases, other body functions that are affected include muscle control, vision, and coordination. Effects on driving may include:

- Drifting into another lane.
- Rapid, jerky starts.
- Not using signals or lights.
- Going through stop signs and red lights.
- Passing incorrectly.

All of these effects increase the possibilities of an accident and loss of your driver's license.

According to statistics, it is much more likely for drivers who have been drinking to get into an accident than those who have not.

### How Alcohol Affects Driving

Drinking alcohol affects the judgment, vision, coordination, and reaction time of all drivers. This results in dangerous driving mistakes, such as:

- Slower reaction time
- Driving too fast or too slow
- Driving in the wrong lane
- Hitting the curb
- Weaving

## Other Drugs

In addition to alcohol, other drugs (both legal and illegal) may also impair driving performance. As a commercial driver, many of these are illegal to use or have in your possession while on a work assignment. These include any type of "controlled substance" that could influence your ability to drive safely, such as amphetamines ("pep pills," “uppers,” and "bennies"), narcotics, prescription and over-the-counter drugs (cold medicines), which may cause drowsiness or other impairments. Medicines given to a driver by a doctor are allowed if the doctor has stated that the drug will not affect driving capability.

It is important to check the warning labels on medicines and to heed a doctor's recommendations about potential side effects. Avoid using any illegal drugs and any drug that masks tiredness – rest is the only remedy for exhaustion. Alcohol or drugs (even those that are over-the-counter) used in tandem with other drugs can exacerbate their effects. The best rule of thumb is to avoid mixing drugs and driving. Driving under the influence of drugs can cause a crash resulting in death, injury, and property damage. It can also cause you to be arrested, fined and/or jailed, not to mention the end of your driving career.

## Illness

Occasionally you might be too sick to drive safely. If this is the case, you should not operate your CMV under any circumstances. If you fall ill while driving, navigate to the closest location where you can safely stop.

# *Hazardous Materials Rules for All Commercial Drivers*

As a commercial driver, you need to be able to identify hazardous cargo and be aware if you need a hazardous materials endorsement on your CDL license to haul it.

## What Are Hazardous Materials?

Hazardous materials are goods that are risky to transport. See the diagram below for reference:

| Hazard Class Definitions | | |
|---|---|---|
| **Class** | **Class Name** | **Example** |
| 1 | Explosives | Ammunition, dynamite, fireworks |
| 2 | Gases | Propane, oxygen, helium |
| 3 | Flammable | Gasoline, fuel, acetone |
| 4 | Flammable solids | Matches, fuses |
| 5 | Oxidizers | Ammonium nitrate, hydrogen peroxide |
| 6 | Poisons | Pesticides, arsenic |
| 7 | Radioactive | Uranium, plutonium |
| 8 | Corrosives | Hydrochloric acid, battery acid |
| 9 | Miscellaneous Hazardous Materials | Formaldehyde, asbestos |
| None | ORM-D (other regulated material-domestic) | Hairspray or charcoal |
| None | Combustible liquids | Fuel oils, lighter fluid |

## Why Are There Rules?

The safety rules regarding hauling hazardous materials are intended to:

- Contain the product.
- Communicate risk.
- Ensure that drivers and equipment remain safe.

### To Contain the Product

Many hazardous goods are so dangerous that they can cause bodily harm or death on contact. To protect drivers and other people, the companies shipping these products follow regulations regarding how to package them safely for transport. Similar containment rules are in place to guide drivers about how to load, transport, and unload bulk tanks.

### To Communicate the Risk

To alert dockworkers and drivers of risky cargo, shippers are required to utilize special documentation and diamond shaped hazard labels.

If you have an accident or experience a leak or spill while hauling hazardous cargo, you might not be able to alert emergency personnel about the dangerous goods you are transporting. To help alleviate this problem, keep your hazardous material documentation in an easily accessible spot on top of your other shipping papers:

- In a pouch on the driver's door, or
- In clear view within reach while you are driving, or
- On the driver's seat when you need to leave the vehicle.

## Lists of Regulated Products

Placards are designed to alert others that you are hauling hazardous cargo. They are signs placed on the exterior of a vehicle identifying the cargo's hazard classification. Vehicles with placard identification must have at least four placards that are exactly the same, located on the front, rear, and both sides and clearly displayed from all four directions. They must be at least 10 3/4 inches square, in a diamond shape that is turned upright on a point. Cargo tanks and other bulk packaging vehicles show the identification number of their materials on placards or orange panels.

Identification Numbers are a four-digit code used by emergency personnel to classify hazardous materials for transport purposes. An identification number may signify more than one chemical shipping documentation. Each identification number begins with the letters "NA" or "UN." A list of chemicals and their corresponding identification numbers can be found in the US DOT Emergency Response Guidebook (ERG).

Most (but not all) vehicles hauling hazardous materials are required to have placards. Specific regulations regarding the use of placards are listed in a later section of this guide. You are permitted to operate a vehicle carrying hazardous cargo if placards are not required. If the materials do require placards, you are not allowed to carry them unless you have the hazardous materials endorsement on your driver's license.

See diagram below for more information:

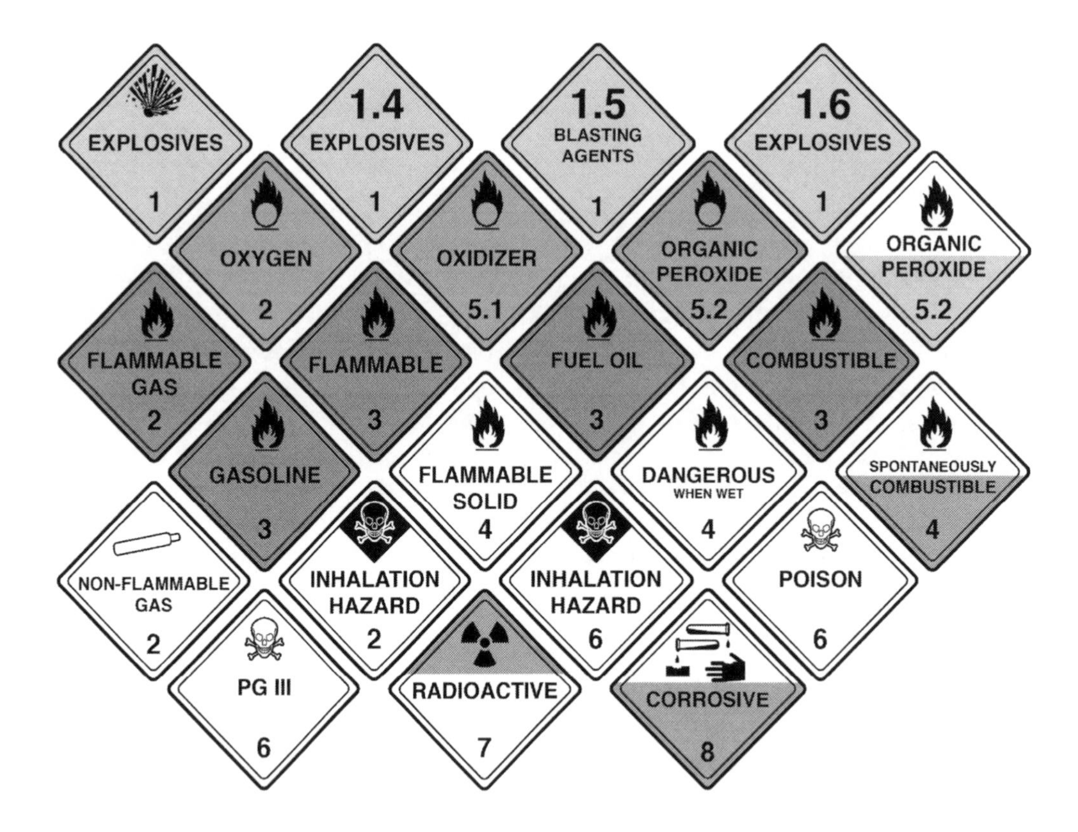


If you drive a placarded vehicle, you must have the hazardous materials endorsement on your driver's license and know how to load and transport hazardous materials safely. This requires passing a written test on hazardous cargo.

Some vehicles carrying liquid or gases (they don't necessarily have to be hazardous) require a tank endorsement. These include:

- Vehicles that are Class A or B CDL with permanently mounted cargo tanks of any capacity; or
- Vehicles hauling portable tanks with capacities of 1,000 gallons or greater

You must have a working knowledge of placard regulations if you plan on having a hazardous materials endorsement. Ask your employer if you are not sure whether your vehicle requires placards. If you do not have the hazardous materials endorsement, you should never drive a vehicle that requires placards. This is a criminal offense—if you are pulled over, you will receive a citation and no longer be able to drive your vehicle, costing you time and money. If you fail to display a placard when carrying hazardous materials, you are risking your own life and the life of others in the event of an accident. First responders will have no idea you are hauling dangerous materials.

Drivers of hazardous cargo must also be aware which materials can be combined together in a load and which cannot. The list of regulations is available in a later section of this guide. If you are unsure, refer to this list and consult your employer.

# Transporting Cargo Safely

In order to get a CDL, you must know fundamental cargo safety rules. If the material you are carrying is loaded incorrectly or improperly secured, it can be dangerous to yourself and others. Cargo that falls off of your vehicle while you are driving can impact traffic or injure or kill others on the road. It could also injure or kill if you need to stop quickly or get into an accident. Overloading could also damage your vehicle or make it more difficult to steer.

Regardless of whether you pack and safeguard the cargo yourself, you are responsible for:

- Inspecting your cargo.
- Identifying overloaded materials and improperly balanced weight.
- Being aware that the cargo you are carrying is correctly secured and does not block your view in any way.
- Being aware that your cargo does not limit your access to emergency equipment.

If you are hauling hazardous cargo requiring placards, you must also have a hazardous materials endorsement on your license. The information needed to pass the hazardous materials test can be found in a later section of this guide.

## *Inspecting Cargo*

Ensuring that your vehicle is not overloaded and the cargo is correctly distributed and secured is part of your pre-trip inspection procedure.

### After Starting

Within the first fifty miles of starting out on a trip, stop to check that the cargo is secured, making any necessary adjustments.

### Re-Check

Inspect the cargo and the devices used to secure it as often as needed during a trip to make sure the materials are properly in place. Do a re-check:

- After driving for three hours or 150 miles.
- After every break during your trip.

Federal, state, and local laws vary by location regarding CMV weight, securing and covering cargo, and where it is legal to drive large vehicles. Before heading out on a trip, be aware of the regulations on your route.

# *Weight and Balance*

It is your responsibility to make sure the cargo you are carrying is not overloaded. Here is a list of important weight definitions:

- Gross Vehicle Weight Rating (GVWR): The loaded weight of a single vehicle as stipulated by the manufacturer.
- Gross Combination Weight Rating (GCWR): The loaded weight of a combination (articulated) vehicle as stipulated by the manufacturer. If the manufacturer does not specify a GCWR, the figure is determined by adding the GVWR of the powered vehicle together with the total weight of the unit being towed and any cargo.
- Axle Weight: The weight transferred to the ground by one axle or one set of axles.
- Tire Load: The maximum weight a tire can safely bear as defined by the pressure rating listed on the side of each tire.
- Suspension Systems: The capacity rating as specified by the manufacturer.
- Coupling Device Capacity: The maximum weight rating specified for that device.

## Legal Weight Limits

The weight of the cargo you are hauling must not be higher than the maximum GVWR, GCWR, and axle weight for the state(s) on your route. The maximum axle weight is often determined via a bridge formula, which allows a lower maximum axle weight for axles that are situated closer together. This is designed to avoid carrying too much weight over bridges and roadways.

If your vehicle is overloaded, it can also affect your steering, braking, and speed control. Trucks that are overloaded travel uphill very slowly, and too fast when going down hills. It takes longer for overloaded vehicles to stop, and brakes are more likely to fail if forced to work too hard.

It might not be safe for you to drive in inclement weather or a mountainous region even if your cargo is within the legal maximum weight limit. Make sure to take this into consideration before starting out.

## Don't Be Top-Heavy

It is imperative that your cargo is not piled too high or too heavy. If the vehicle's center of gravity is too high, you are more likely to tip over, particularly when driving around a bend or if you need to veer quickly to avoid an obstacle. Make sure the materials you are hauling are loaded as low as possible and the lighter cargo is stacked on top of heavier items.

## Balance the Weight

It is also important that the cargo you are hauling is properly balanced. If the steering axle is bearing too much weight, it can be difficult to steer and damage the steering axle and tires. The vehicle may also not steer correctly if the front axles aren't bearing enough weight (the result of cargo shifting to the back). If the driving axles are under-loaded, the vehicle may not get enough traction. This can cause the drive wheels to spin, making it difficult for the vehicle to operate when weather conditions are poor. There is an increased possibility of rollover if there is too much weight in the center of the hauled unit. If your towed unit is a flatbed, the cargo is also more likely to shift or fall off if it is loaded too heavy.

See diagram below for reference:

## *Securing Cargo*

### Blocking and Bracing

Blocking is secured to the cargo deck and placed tightly against the material being hauled to prevent it from sliding. Cargo is also held in place with bracing, which extends from the upper section of the cargo to the floor and/or walls of the cargo compartment.

## Cargo Tiedown

Cargo on flatbed trailers or trailers without sides must be securely tied down to prevent it from shifting around or falling off. Tiedowns can also be used in closed vans to stop materials from moving around. You must be sure to use tiedowns that are the correct kind and strength for the cargo being hauled. According to federal regulations, the collective limit of any securement system used to prevent cargo from shifting must be at least one-half times the weight of the cargo. Appropriate tiedown equipment is required, including ropes, straps, chains, and tensioning devices (winches, ratchets, clinching components). These tiedowns must be properly attached to the vehicle with fasteners such as hooks, bolts, rails, and rings. See diagram below for reference:

Tie - Down Devices

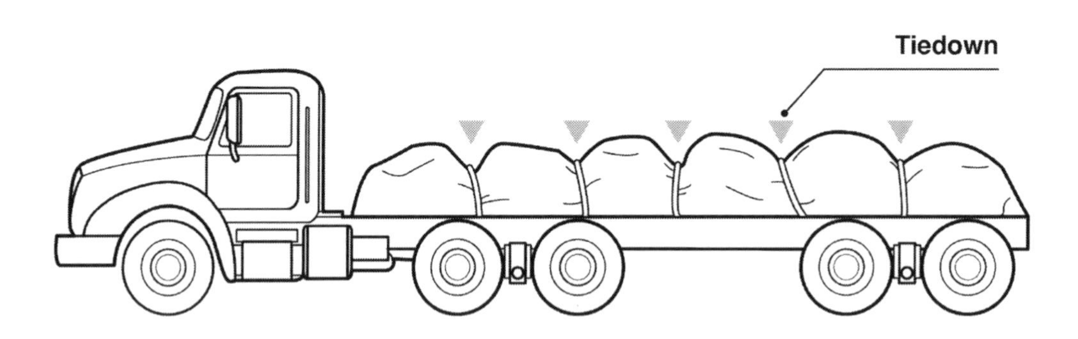


The material you are hauling should have at least a minimum of two tiedowns, with at least one tiedown for each ten feet of cargo. There should be at least two tie-downs holding the cargo, no matter how small it is. Make sure your cargo has enough tiedowns to meet these requirements. If you need to secure various heavy pieces of metal, there are special regulations to follow. You will need to determine what these requirements are if you are hauling this type of load.

## Header Boards

Front-end header boards (also called "headache racks") are designed to prevent the cargo from hitting the driver in case of an accident or sudden stop. Check that the front-end structure is in good working condition so that it will be able to block any cargo being hauled from pitching forward.

## Covering Cargo

Why cargo needs to be covered:

- To protect people from spilled cargo.
- To protect cargo from weather conditions.

Many states require spill protection for safety reasons. You need to be aware of the regulations for the states on your route.

As you are driving, check your mirrors to ensure your cargo covers are secure. If a cover appears to be flapping, it could indicate it is about to tear away, which could expose the cargo, potentially blocking your view or another driver's.

### Sealed and Containerized Loads

Cargo is loaded into containers for situations where freight is transported by rail or ship for part of its journey. The container is moved to a truck either at the beginning and/or end of the trip. Some container units have their own devices to tie them down or latches that connect the unit directly to a special frame. Other containers are placed on flat bed trailers. All containers need to be correctly secured the same as other cargo.

Containers are typically already sealed, so you won't be able to check the contents, but you should make sure gross weight and axle weight limits are within the proper range.

## *Cargo Needing Special Attention*

### Dry Bulk

If you are carrying a dry bulk tank, pay special attention when navigating bends and sharp turns, as these loads have a high center of gravity, which can cause materials to shift.

### Hanging Meat

If you are hauling a refrigerated vehicle containing hanging meat (such as suspended beef, pork, lamb), drive slowly and pay special attention when navigating bends and off/on ramps, as these loads are often unstable with a high center of gravity.

### Livestock

Livestock is basically moving cargo and requires special care. If you are carrying less than a full load, use false bulkheads to prevent livestock from moving around. But keep in mind that even when livestock are grouped together, they can lean on turns, shifting the center of gravity and increasing the possibility of a rollover.

### Oversized Loads

Oversized loads are typically only allowed on the road at particular times and usually require special transit permits. Specific equipment may be required such as "wide load" signs, flashing lights, flags, etc. A police escort or accompanying vehicles carrying warning signs and/or flashing lights may be necessary. Use extra caution when hauling these types of oversized loads.

# Transporting Passengers Safely

If you wish to drive a bus, you will most likely need a CDL and must have a passenger endorsement. The number of multiple passengers, (including the driver) requiring a CDL varies from state to state, so check with your local state DMV to make sure. To get the endorsement you must pass a knowledge test on the "Driving Safely" and "Transporting Passengers Safely" sections of this guide. (If the bus has air brakes, you will also need to pass a knowledge test on Air Brakes). In addition, you will be required to pass the skills tests for your vehicle class.

## *Vehicle Inspection*

Prior to driving your bus, ensure it is safe by reviewing the inspection report written up by the previous driver. Sign this report only if issues reported earlier have repaired or deemed not necessary for repair. This certifies that previous issues have been repaired.

### Vehicle Systems

Before you begin driving your bus, make sure the following items are working properly:

- Service brakes, including air hose couplings (if your bus is equipped with a trailer or semitrailer)
- Parking brake
- Steering unit
- Lights and reflectors
- Tires (those on the front should not be recapped or regrooved)
- Horn
- Windshield wiper(s)
- Rear-view mirror(s)
- Coupling devices (if so equipped)
- Wheels and rims
- Emergency gear

### Access Doors and Panels

Walk around and inspect the exterior of the bus, closing any open emergency exits and access panels (for luggage, restrooms, engine, etc.) prior to driving.

### Bus Interior

Since buses left unattended are sometimes vandalized, inspect the inside prior to driving to ensure the safety of your passengers. The aisle and steps leading up to the bus should be clear of any debris and the following sections should be in safe and proper working order:

- Handholds and railings
- Carpeting
- Signal/warning devices, including the restroom emergency button, if so equipped
- Emergency exit grips
- Seats (must be securely fastened)

Do not drive with an open emergency exit door or window. The "Emergency Exit" sign must be clear and/or lit if the bus has lights. Make sure it is on in the evening and any other time outside lights are used.

### Roof Hatches

If needed, some of the emergency roof hatches can be left partially open to allow fresh air to circulate. However, make sure they are not left open all the time, and pay special attention to the fact that your bus will have a higher clearance while they are open. Your bus must have legally required fire extinguisher and emergency reflectors, and spare electrical fuses (unless it has built-in circuit breakers). Make sure all these items are present and in good working order.

### Use Your Seatbelt!

Check that the driver's seatbelt is in good working order and make sure you always use it for safety reasons.

## *Loading and Trip Start*

The aisle should be completely free of luggage and other items so that passengers have a clear pathway. Make sure your passengers stow their baggage and other belongings in a secure place in order to:

- Prevent damage
- Allow you (the driver) to move freely without restrictions
- Allow passengers to exit through a window or door in the event of an emergency
- Protect passengers from injury if any belongings fall out of the overhead compartment or jostle about

### Hazardous Materials

Be on the lookout for any passenger luggage or belongings that may contain hazardous materials. Most hazardous materials are not allowed on buses. The Federal Hazardous Materials Table lists the types of items that are considered hazardous and risky to public health, safety, and property during transport. These items must be clearly marked with one of the nine four-inch, diamond-shaped hazard labels, listing the name, identification number, and hazard classification of the substance. Check passenger baggage and belongings for these diamond shaped labels. Do not allow any hazardous material on your bus unless you are absolutely certain it is within the proper legal regulations.

See table below for reference:

| Hazard Class Definitions | | |
|---|---|---|
| **Class** | **Class Name** | **Example** |
| 1 | Explosives | Ammunition, dynamite, fireworks |
| 2 | Gases | Propane, oxygen, helium |
| 3 | Flammable | Gasoline, fuel, acetone |
| 4 | Flammable solids | Matches, fuses |
| 5 | Oxidizers | Ammonium nitrate, hydrogen peroxide |
| 6 | Poisons | Pesticides, arsenic |
| 7 | Radioactive | Uranium, plutonium |
| 8 | Corrosives | Hydrochloric acid, battery acid |
| 9 | Miscellaneous Hazardous Materials | Formaldehyde, asbestos |
| None | ORM-D (other regulated material-domestic) | Hairspray or charcoal |
| None | Combustible liquids | Fuel oils, lighter fluid |

## Forbidden Hazardous Materials

Small-arms ammunition labeled ORM-D, emergency hospital supplies, and drugs are permitted on buses. Small amounts of other hazardous materials are also allowed if the shipper cannot transport them any other way.

Buses must never carry:

- Division 2.3 poison gas, liquid Class 6 poison, tear gas, irritating material.
- More than 100 pounds of solid Class 6 poisons.
- Explosives in the same area people are situated, except small arms ammunition.
- Substances considered radioactive in same area people are situated.
- Over 500 pounds of legally permitted hazardous materials, and no more than 100 pounds of any one class of hazardous materials.

Passengers may try to get on your bus with a hazardous substance that is not labeled. Do not permit everyday hazards such as car batteries or gasoline on your bus.

## Standee Line

Passengers must stand behind the driver's seat. Buses that have an area for standing room must be clearly marked with a two-inch line on the floor (called the standee line) or some other indicator communicating the standing area to passengers. All standing passengers must stay behind this line.

### At Your Destination

Once you arrive at the designated or intermediate stop(s), you should announce:

- The location
- Reason for stopping
- Next departure time
- Bus number

Remind disembarking passengers to take all belongings with them. If the aisle is located on a lower level than some of the seats, remind these passengers to watch their step prior to coming to a complete stop. If you are driving a charter bus, do not permit passengers to get on the bus until the slated departure time in order to help prevent theft and/or vandalism of the bus or passenger belongings.

## *On the Road*

### Passenger Supervision

Most charter and intercity bus companies have specific regulations pertaining to the comfort and safety of passengers. Before you begin driving, make sure you clarify any rules regarding smoking, drinking, or the use of electronic devices that might disturb others. Spelling out the rules at the beginning will help prevent issues from happening down the road. While driving, use your mirrors to check the inside of the bus as well as the road ahead, the sides, and the rear. You may have to repeat the rules to passengers and/or ask them to refrain from placing their arms or heads outside the window.

### At Stops

Make sure to warn passengers to watch their step when exiting the bus, as they may trip when stepping on or off, or when the bus starts or stops. Wait for them to take their seat or hold onto something before starting. Make sure to start up and come to a stop as smoothly as you can to prevent passengers from getting hurt.

On occasion, you may have a passenger who is drunk or unruly. Take care to keep this passenger as safe as the others. Don't let them get off in an unsafe location—it might be best to wait to the next stop that is better lit with more people. Many bus companies have guidelines for handling unruly passengers.

### Common Accidents

Most bus accidents occur at intersections. It's best to approach them carefully, even if the traffic flow is a directed via signal or stop sign. Sometimes school and commuter buses bump their mirrors or run into passing vehicles when disembarking from a bus stop. Be aware of the clearance area required by the bus you are driving and look out for poles and tree limbs at stops. Have a thorough understanding of the space your bus needs to accelerate and merge into traffic. Wait until a large enough space opens up before pulling away from a stop. Do not presume that other drivers will slow down to allow you to merge in front of them.

### Speed on Curves

Accidents are often the result of navigating a bend too fast, often when the road is slippery due to poor weather conditions such as rain or snow. Banked curves feature a safe "design speed." The speed posted is typically safe for cars during decent weather conditions, but it may be too high for many buses. The bus could roll over or skid off the road, depending on the traction level. Make sure you slow your speed on curves—if you are navigating a banked curve and the bus is leaning toward the outside, you are driving too fast.

### Railroad-Highway Crossing/Stops

#### Stop at RR Crossings

- Stop your bus between 15 and 50 feet before approaching a railroad crossing.
- Look and listen in both directions for trains. Open your front door to check if it improves your ability to see or hear an approaching train.
- After a train has gone by, make sure another train is not coming in the other direction before crossing.
- If your bus has manual transmission, never switch gears while driving across the tracks.
- For these circumstances, you are not required to stop, but you must slow down and carefully check for other vehicles:
- At streetcar crossings
- Sites where a policeman or flagman is directing traffic
- At a green traffic signal
- At "exempt" or "abandoned" crossings

### Drawbridges

Come to a complete stop at drawbridges lacking a signal light or someone to monitor traffic control. Stop the bus at least 50 feet ahead of where the bridge rises up and make sure the bridge is completely closed before proceeding to cross.

It is not necessary to stop, but you need to slow down and check that the bridge is safe to cross, when:

- The traffic light is green.
- The bridge has someone monitoring traffic when the bridge is open.

## *After-Trip Vehicle Inspection*

Check your bus following each shift. If you drive for an interstate bus company, you will be required to fill out a written inspection report for each bus you operate. Indicate any issues that could lead to crash safety or repair. If there are no problems, mark this on the report.

Sometimes safety-related items such as handholds, seats, emergency exits, and windows need repair. If this damage is reported at the end of a shift, the parts can be fixed before the next trip. If you drive a commuter bus, make sure passenger signaling devices and brake door interlocks are in good working order.

## Prohibited Practices

Do not stop to get gas while passengers are on board unless absolutely essential. Never add fuel in a closed building while carrying passengers.

While you are driving, refrain from having conversations with or participating in any activity that could divert your attention.

Do not tow or push a bus that is disabled while passengers are inside, unless it would be dangerous for them to exit the bus. Make sure the bus is only towed or pushed to a nearest safe spot to allow passengers to get off. Follow the guidelines of your bus company regarding towing or pushing disabled buses.

## Use of Brake-Door Interlocks

City commuter buses may be equipped with a brake and accelerator interlock system. The interlock engages the brakes and puts the throttle in idle position when the back door is open. When the back door is closed, the interlock releases. Make sure you do not use this safety feature instead of the parking brake.

# Air Brakes

This section is essential if you want to drive a truck or bus with air brakes, or pull a trailer with air brakes. If you want to pull a trailer with air brakes, you also need to read the next section covering Combination Vehicles.

Air brakes utilize compressed air to operate the brakes. Although they are a useful and safe method of stopping big, heavy vehicles, it is essential that they are used correctly and have regularly maintenance. Air brakes are comprised of three different types of braking systems:

- Service brake: employs and releases the brakes when the brake pedal is utilized during normal driving.
- Parking brake: employs and releases the parking brakes when the parking brake control is engaged.
- Emergency brake: uses components of both the service and parking brake systems to stop the vehicle in case the brake system fails.

These systems are discussed in greater detail below.

## *The Parts of an Air Brake System*

An air brake system has many different components. Make sure you have knowledge of the parts reviewed below.

### Air Compressor

Attached to the engine through gears or a v-belt, the air compressor pumps air into the air storage reservoirs. Either air or the engine cooling system may cool the compressor. It might have its own oil supply or get its lubrication from engine oil. If it has its own oil supply, check the oil level prior to driving.

### Air Compressor Governor

The air compressor's governor regulates the air pumped into the air storage tanks. When the air tank pressure reaches its maximum level (around 125 pounds per-square-inch or "psi"), the governor will prevent the compressor from pumping air. When the air tank pressure goes back to a normal level (around 100 psi), the compressor will start pumping air again.

### Air Storage Tanks

Compressed air is stored in air storage tanks. Although the amount and size of air tanks vary among commercial vehicles, the stored air is enough to supply the brakes for several uses, even if the compressor stops working.

### Air Tank Drains

Compressed air often contains small quantities of water and compressor oil, which can be detrimental to the air brake system. In cold weather conditions, the water can freeze, causing the brakes to fail. The water and oil have the tendency to drip to the bottom of the air tank. It is very important to make sure the air tanks in your vehicle are completely drained via the drain valve in the bottom. There are two types of drain valves:

- Manual: operated by turning the valve a quarter turn or pulling a cable. These tanks must be drained manually at the end of each day of driving or trip.
- Automatic: water and oil are automatically ejected. These tanks may also have manual drains. Some automatic air tanks are equipped with electric heating devices, which help prevent the automatic drain from freezing in cold weather.

### Alcohol Evaporator

Some air brake systems are equipped with an alcohol evaporator. This deposits alcohol into the air system, helping to prevent ice from building up in the air brake valves and other parts during cold weather. If ice gets inside the air brake system, the brakes can freeze up and stop working. Check the alcohol reservoir level and refill every day during cold weather or as needed. It is still necessary to drain the air tanks every day to expel water and oil. (Unless the vehicle is equipped with automatic drain valves.)

### Safety Valve

The first tank in the air compressor system has a safety relief valve, which is designed to protect the tank and the rest of the system from becoming too pressurized. The open setting for this valve is typically 150 psi. If the safety valve is releasing air, it needs to be checked by a mechanic.

### The Brake Pedal

The brakes are engaged by pressing on the brake pedal (also known as the foot valve or treadle valve). The harder the pedal is pressed, the more air pressure is released. Taking your foot off of the brake pedal disengages the brakes, decreasing air pressure. This causes some compressed air to escape, reducing air pressure in the tanks and requiring the air compressor to kick in. Needlessly pushing in and letting up on the pedal can release air faster than the compressor can replenish it. If the air pressure level is too low, the brakes will not function properly.

### Foundation Brakes

Each wheel has foundation brakes, with the s-cam drum brake being the most common. The various brake components are listed below.

#### Brake Drums, Shoes, and Linings

Located on each end of the vehicle's axles, the brake drums are bolted to the wheels and house the braking mechanism. The vehicle stops by pressing the brake shoes and linings up against the inside of the drum. This pressure causes friction, slowing the vehicle (and generating heat). The degree of heat a drum can handle before getting damaged depends on how hard and how long the brakes are used. The brakes can stop working if they get too hot.

## S-cam Brakes

Pressing the brake pedal releases air into each brake chamber. The air pressure pushes the rod out, engaging the slack adjuster and twisting the brake camshaft. This causes the s-cam to turn (named as such because of its "S" shape).

The s-cam pushes the brake shoes away from each other, pressing them against the inside of the brake drum. When the brake pedal is released, the s-cam falls back and a spring forces the brake shoes away from the drum, allowing the wheels to move. See diagram below:

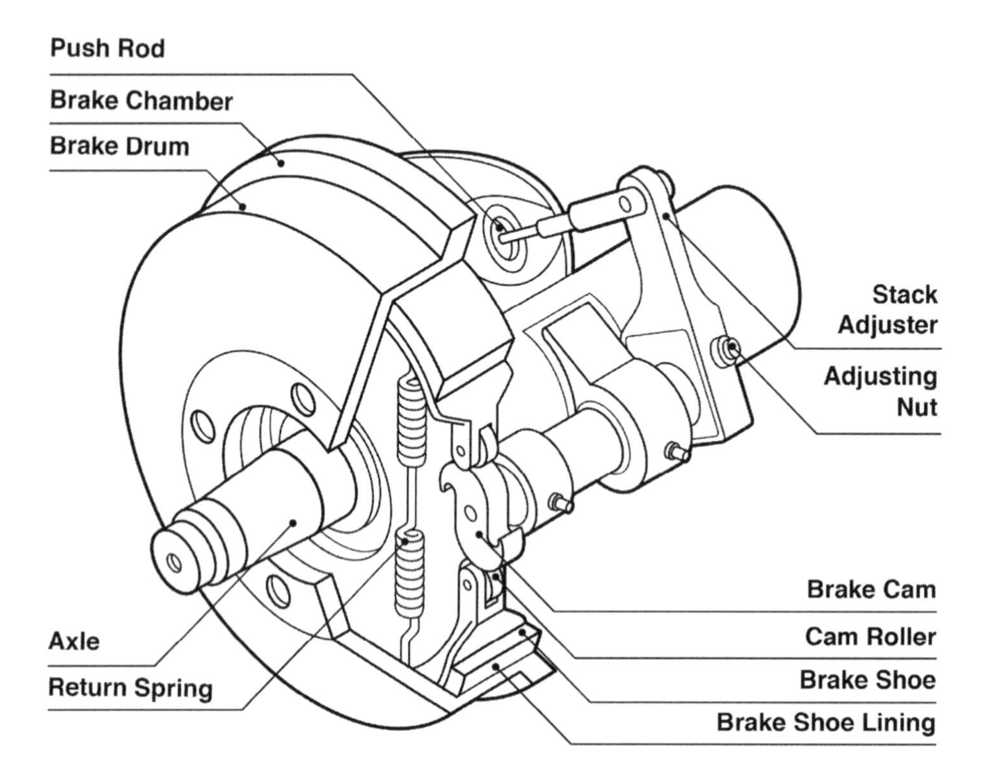


## Wedge Brakes

Wedge brakes feature a brake chamber push rod that ejects a wedge directly between two brake shoes, forcing them apart and pushing them against the inside of the brake drum. These types of brakes can contain just one brake chamber, or they might have two chambers that force the wedges in at both ends of the brake shoes. Wedge brakes may need manual adjustment or they could be self-adjusting.

## Disc Brakes

Air-operated disc brakes use air pressure to operate a brake chamber and slack adjuster, like s-cam brakes. However, a "power screw" is used rather than a s-cam. The power screw is turned as a result of the pressure placed on the slack adjuster by the brake chamber. Similar to a large c-clamp, the power screw clamps onto the disc or rotor located between the brake lining pads of a caliper. S-cam brakes are more common than wedge or disc brakes.

### Supply Pressure Gauges

All vehicles with air brakes have a pressure gauge to indicate the amount of pressure in the air tanks. If the system has dual air brakes, each will have its own gauge, or one gauge with two pressure needles. (Dual systems are covered later in this guide).

### Application Pressure Gauge

The application pressure gauge indicates the level of air pressure being applied to the brakes. (Not all vehicles are equipped with this feature). If you need to increase the application pressure to maintain your speed, this is an indicator that the brakes are starting to fade, need adjusting, have air leaks, or mechanical problems. Decrease your speed and downshift into a lower gear.

### Low Air Pressure Warning

Vehicles equipped with air brakes must have a low air pressure indicator to signal a warning when there's a chance the air pressure could fall below 60 psi. On older vehicles it could be one half the amount of the compressor governor cutout pressure. The warning is typically a red light, and may feature a buzzer as well.

Some vehicles have a type of warning called a "wig wag"—a device that releases a mechanical arm when the system pressure falls below 60 psi. This arm will then automatically rise back up when the system pressure increases above 60 psi, although some devices need to be reset manually and will not remain in the up position until the pressure rises above 60 psi. On large buses it is not unusual for signals on low-pressure warning devices to buzz at 80-85 psi.

### Stop Light Switch

When you brake, you must be able to warn drivers behind you. The air brake system has an electric switch that illuminates the brake lights when the air brakes are engaged.

### Front Brake Limiting Valve

A front brake limiting valve and a control knob can be found in the cab area of some older vehicles (manufactured prior to 1975). The knob is typically labeled "normal" and "slippery." When the knob is placed in the "slippery" position, the limiting valve reduces "normal" air pressure to the front brakes by half. Although limiting valves were designed to prevent the front wheels from skidding on slick roads, they decrease a vehicle's braking power. Front wheel braking is sufficient to use in all circumstances. According to braking tests, it is unlikely to experience a front wheel skid as a result of using the brakes, even during icy conditions. If this knob is present, make sure it stays in the "normal" position.

Automatic front wheel limiting valves decrease the air applied to the front brakes, except in hard braking situations (60 psi or more application pressure). Since they are engaged automatically, they are not driver-operated.

### Spring Brakes

Every commercial vehicle is required to have both emergency and parking brakes held in place mechanically (since air pressure can leak). Most CMVs use spring brakes for this purpose, held in place by air pressure when driving. If there is no air pressure, the brakes are engaged via the springs. The driver releases the air from the spring brakes through a parking brake mechanism located in the cab that signals the springs to engage the brakes. The springs will also apply the brakes if all the air is leaked from the air brake system.

The spring brakes on tractor and straight trucks will completely engage when air pressure drops to a level of 20 to 45 psi (typically 20 to 30 psi). It is important to safely stop the vehicle as soon as you see the low air pressure warning light and hear the buzzer go off. Do not wait for the brakes to automatically engage, apply the brakes yourself while you still have control. Spring brakes must be adjusted properly in order to retain the required level of braking power and to ensure both the regular brakes and emergency/parking brakes function correctly.

## Parking Brake Controls

Newer vehicles with air brakes are equipped with a yellow, diamond-shaped control knob to operate the parking brakes. To apply the parking brakes (spring brakes), the knob is pulled out; when the brakes need to be released, it is pushed in. Older vehicles often have a lever to operate the parking brakes, which must be utilized whenever the vehicle is parked.

### Caution

The brake pedal should never be pressed when the spring brakes are on, as the combined forces of the springs and the air pressure could damage the brakes. Although most brake systems have a built-in failsafe to prevent this from occurring, not all feature this type of design, and those that do may not always work. As a general rule, it is best to make sure you always press down on the brake pedal down when the spring brakes are on.

### Modulating Control Valves

Some vehicles feature a control mechanism called a modulating valve to steadily engage the spring brakes. It is spring-loaded to give drivers a feel for the braking action. The more pressure that is placed on the mechanism, the more difficult it is to apply the spring brakes. This is designed so the driver can control the spring brakes in the event of a failure to the service brakes. If you need to place a vehicle in park that has a modulating control valve, make sure you pull the lever as far as it will go and make sure the locking device snaps it in place.

### Dual Parking Control Valves

The spring brakes are applied when the main air pressure is diminished. Certain vehicles, such as buses, are equipped with air tanks specifically designed to release the spring brakes so the vehicle can be operated in case of an emergency. A push-pull valve is utilized to engage the spring brakes for parking purposes. The other valve is spring loaded in the "out" position; when it is pressed in, air from this separate tank releases the spring brakes so the vehicle can move. Letting go of the control engages the spring brakes again. Since this separate tank only has enough air to do this procedure a few times, it is important to plan carefully before operating the vehicle, or else you might end up in an unsafe place when the separate air supply is out.

## Antilock Braking Systems (ABS)

A computerized system designed to prevent your wheels from locking up during hard braking situations, antilock brakes are required on the following types of vehicles:

- Truck tractors equipped with air brakes manufactured on or after March 1, 1997

- Other vehicles equipped with air brakes (trucks, buses, trailers, and converter dollies) manufactured on or after March 1, 1998

Many CMVs manufactured prior to these dates have also been updated with ABS. In order to determine whether your vehicle has ABS, check the manufacture date on the vehicle's certification label.

If there is an issue with a vehicle's ABS, a yellow malfunction light will illuminate. These are located:

- On the instrument panel if it is a tractor, truck, or bus
- On the left side (either on the front or rear corner) if it is a trailer
- On the left side if it is a dolly manufactured on or after March 1, 1998

If the vehicle is newer, the malfunction light will illuminate briefly when the vehicle is first turned on for a bulb check, and then turn off. If the vehicle is older, the light may stay lit until you are traveling at a speed higher than five mph. If the light remains on after the bulb check, or lights up as you are driving, the ABS might not be working on one or more wheels.

It might be difficult to discern whether a towed unit built prior to DOT requirements is equipped with ABS. To check, inspect the electronic control unit (ECU) located under the unit and the wheel speed sensor wires in the back of the brakes.

Supplementary to the normal brakes, it is important to note that ABS not diminish or increase the brake's normal proficiency. ABS is only activated when wheels are about to lock up. It does not necessarily lessen the vehicle's stopping distance, but it does help control the vehicle during hard braking.

## *Dual Air Brake*

Most CMVs utilize a dual air brake system—two separate air brake systems, each with its own air tanks, hoses, lines, etc., that share a single set of brake controls. The "primary system" is designed to control the regular brakes on the rear axle(s), and the "secondary system" controls the regular brakes on the front axle (and sometimes one rear axle). Both systems deliver air to the trailer (if the vehicle is so equipped).

Prior to operating a vehicle with a dual air system, you will need to let the air compressor rise to a pressure of at least 100 psi in both systems. Check the gauges for both the primary and secondary air pressure (or needles, if the system has two needles in one gauge), keeping an eye on the low air pressure warning light and buzzer. When air pressure in both systems rises to the pre-set level determined by the manufacturer (must be greater than 60 psi), they should turn off.

A drop in air pressure (just prior to dipping below 60 psi in either system) will trigger the warning light and buzzer. If you are driving when this occurs, stop as soon as possible and safely park the vehicle. If just one air system is experiencing very low pressure, either the front or rear brakes will not be working properly, taking you longer to stop. Safely stop the vehicle and have the air brakes repaired.

## *Inspecting Air Brake Systems*

When inspecting a vehicle with air brakes, follow the same basic seven-step inspection procedure described earlier in this guide, with the addition of the following items listed below in the order they fit into the seven-step method:

## During Step 2 Engine Compartment Checks

If the air compressor is belt-driven, check to make sure the air compressor drive belt is snugly in place and in good condition.

## During Step 5 Walkaround Inspection

Check the slack adjusters on the S-cam brakes. Make sure the vehicle is parked on level ground and the wheels are chocked to prevent it from moving. Release the parking brakes so you can manually manipulate the slack adjusters. Wearing gloves, pull hard on each slack adjuster within reach. If one of them shifts more than an inch from where it is connected to the push rod, adjust it or have it realigned. You may have difficulty stopping your vehicle if there is too much brake slack. Brakes that are out-of-adjustment are the most common issue spotted during roadside inspections. Check the slack adjusters to ensure safety.

Automatic slack adjustors are available on all vehicles manufactured after 1994. Even though they are self-adjusting when the brakes are fully applied, they still need to be inspected. They do not require manual adjusting except when the brakes are undergoing maintenance and the slack adjusters are being installed. When the pushrod stroke exceeds the legal brake adjustment limit in a vehicle with automatic adjusters, it indicates one of the following:

- There is a mechanical problem in the adjuster
- There is an issue with the related foundation brake parts
- The adjuster was incorrectly installed

If manual adjustment of an automatic adjuster is needed in order to place the brake pushrod stroke within legal limits, it is likely concealing a mechanical problem. In addition, adjusting most automatic adjusters too often can prematurely wear them out. When brakes with automatic adjusters are out of adjustment, it is best to take the vehicle to a repair shop to safely fix the problem. Manually adjusting automatic slack adjusters can be a risky undertaking, since it can mask the effectiveness of the braking system.

It is best to view the manual adjustment of an automatic adjuster as a temporary fix used only in emergency situations—the brake will typically revert back to being out of adjustment anyway since this method does not correct the underlying adjustment problem. (Note: Because different companies manufacture automatic slack adjusters, operation methods vary between systems. You will need to consult the manufacturer's Service Manual before attempting to determine a brake adjustment problem.)

### Check Brake Drums (or Discs), Linings, and Hoses

The brake drums (or discs) should not contain cracks greater than half the width of the friction area. Linings (friction material) need to be tight and clean (not drenched with oil or grease) and not extremely thin. All mechanical parts should be snugly in place, with no broken or missing components. The air hoses attached to the brake chambers should not be cut or worn from excessive rubbing.

## Step 7 Final Air Brake Check

Perform the following inspections instead of the hydraulic brake check shown in the earlier section: Check Brake System.

## Test Low Pressure Warning Signal

Turn the engine off once the air pressure level is sufficient and the low pressure warning light is not on. Turn on the electrical power and press up and down on the brake pedal to reduce pressure in the air tanks. The low air pressure warning light should illuminate prior to the pressure dropping below 60 psi in the air tank (or in dual air systems, the tank with the lowest air pressure). See diagram below for reference. If the warning light does not go on, you could unknowingly lose air pressure, causing abrupt emergency braking in a single tank system, or increased stopping distance in a dual system. Until the spring brakes engage, braking would be limited.

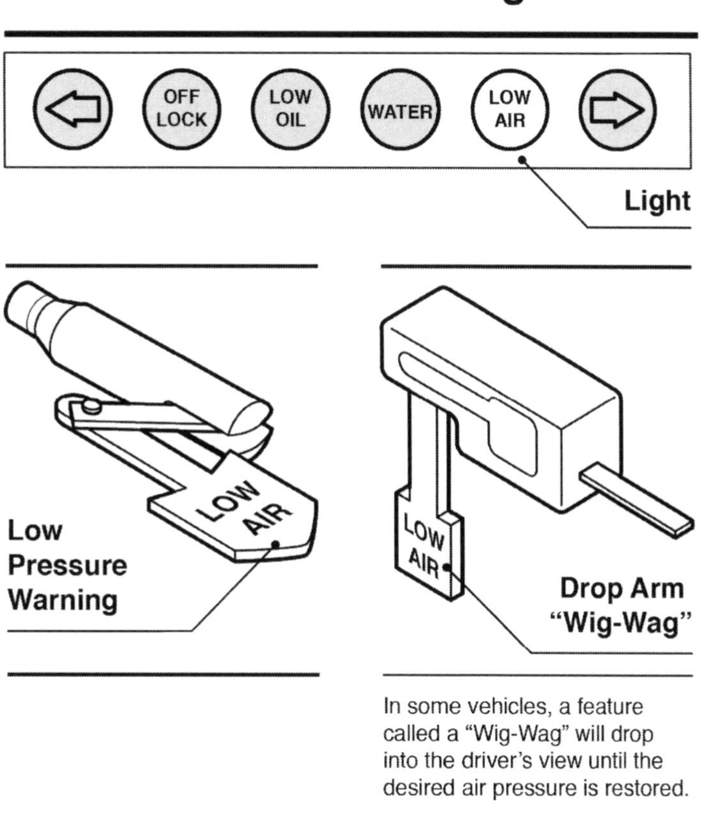


In some vehicles, a feature called a "Wig-Wag" will drop into the driver's view until the desired air pressure is restored.

## Check That Spring Brakes Come On Automatically

Continue to step up and down on the brake pedal to reduce tank pressure. When the air pressure falls to the manufacturer's specification level (20 to 45 psi), the tractor protection valve and parking brake valve should close (pop out) if the vehicle is a tractor-trailer combination. On other types of vehicles, the parking brake valve should close (pop out). This action should prompt the spring brakes to engage.

## Check Rate of Air Pressure Buildup

In vehicles with dual air systems, the pressure should rise from 85 to 100 psi within 45 seconds when the engine is operating at a normal rpm. (If the vehicle's air tanks are larger than the minimum required, it could take longer, but still within the safe range—check the manufacturer's specifications.) In single air systems (built before 1975), the pressure typically rises from 50 to 90 psi within three minutes with the engine idling at a speed of 600 to 900 rpms. If your vehicle takes too long to build up air pressure, the level might fall too much while you are driving, forcing you to make an emergency stop. Get the issue repaired prior to driving the vehicle.

#### Test Air Leakage Rate

Check the air leakage rate by following these steps:

- Make sure the air system is completely charged (around 125 psi)
- Turn the engine off
- Chock the wheels
- Release the tractor protection valve (if necessary)
- Push in the parking brake
- Fully apply the foot brake and hold it for one minute

Look at the air gauge—if the air pressure falls more than three pounds in one minute (for a single vehicle) or four pounds in one minute (for a combination vehicle), the vehicle is losing air too quickly. Before driving the vehicle, check for air leaks. If any leaks are discovered, get them repaired right away or the brakes could fail while you are driving.

#### Check Air Compressor Governor Cut-in and Cut-out Pressures

The air compressor should begin pumping air around 100 psi and stop around 125 psi. (Check the manufacturer's specifications to be sure.) Operate the engine at a fast idle. The air governor should cut-out the air compressor while in the manufacturer's specified pressure range and the air pressure on your vehicle's gauge(s) should stop increasing. While the engine is still idling, press up and down on the brake in order to reduce pressure in the air tank(s). The compressor should cut-in around the manufacturer's specified pressure range and the pressure should start rising. If the air governor is not working as described above, it might not retain enough air pressure to ensure safe driving and require repair.

#### Test Parking Brake

Stop the vehicle, engage the parking brake, and gently pull against it while in a low gear to check that it will hold.

#### Test Service Brakes

Once at a normal air pressure, release the parking brake, drive the vehicle slowly forward (going about five mph), and firmly step on the brake pedal. If the vehicle "pulls" to one side, has an unusual feel, or a delayed stopping action, this could indicate an issue requiring repair.

## *Using Air Brakes*

### Normal Stops

For normal stops, press down on the brake pedal, regulating the pressure so that the vehicle comes to a smooth, safe stop. If the vehicle has a manual transmission, don't press in the clutch until the engine rpm is near idling. When you are stopped, select a gear to start up again.

## Braking with Antilock Brakes

If your vehicle lacks ABS, your wheels may lock up if you need to brake suddenly on a slick surface. This may cause you to lose control of your vehicle's steering if the steering wheels lock up, or make you skid, jackknife or spin. ABS computer sensors help you avoid wheel lockup and retain control by decreasing brake pressure to a safe level. Although ABS might not help you stop more quickly, it should help you steer around an obstacle while braking and prevent skids due to over braking.

Even if your vehicle only has ABS on the tractor, the trailer, or one axle, you will still have more control over the vehicle when braking. Use the brakes as you normally would.

When only the tractor has ABS, you should still be able to steer, and your chances of jackknifing are decreased. However, you will need to watch the trailer—if it starts to swing out, decrease pressure on the brakes (if you can safely do so).

When only the trailer has ABS, the chances of the trailer swinging out are less likely, but you may have difficulties controlling your steering. If you lose steering control or the tractor starts jackknifing, decrease pressure on the brakes (if you can safely do so), until you gain control.

When you drive a tractor-trailer combination with ABS, use your brakes as you normally would, i.e. brake with only the amount of force required to stop safely and maintain control.

Whether you have ABS on the tractor, the trailer, or both, use the brakes in the same manner. As you slow your speed down, check your vehicle's tractor and trailer and let up off the brakes (if it is safe to do so) to maintain control. The one exception: if you always drive a straight truck or combination with working ABS on all axles, you can use the brakes to their full capacity if you need to stop suddenly.

You still have normal brake functionality, even if your vehicle is not equipped with ABS or your vehicle has it, but it fails. Drive and use your brakes as usual, but make an appointment to get the system serviced promptly.

## Emergency Stops

It is typical to react by slamming on the brakes if another vehicle pulls or swerves in front of you. This is fine, as long as there's enough distance to stop, and you properly use the brakes. When you brake, make sure your vehicle stays in a straight line and you can safely turn if needed. There are two braking methods you can use, "controlled braking" or "stab braking."

### Controlled Braking

This technique involves using the brakes with as much force as you can without causing the wheels to lock up, while keeping your steering wheel movements very small. Let up off the brakes if you need to widen your steering or if the wheels lock up, then go back to applying the brakes as soon as you can.

### Stab Braking

This style involves fully using your brakes, and then quickly letting up once the wheels lock. As soon as the wheels move again, once more completely use the brakes. (At least a second might go by before the wheels begin rolling after the brakes are released. If you engage the brakes before the wheels move, the vehicle won't stay straight.)

## Stopping Distance

Stopping distance was previously described in the section on "Speed and Stopping Distance." However, if you drive a vehicle with air brakes, you will have to factor in "brake lag," which will cause an additional delay when stopping. Brake lag is the amount of time it takes the brakes to engage after the brake pedal is pushed. Hydraulic brakes (the type used on cars and light/medium trucks), work right away, but air brakes need time (at least one half second) for the air to pass through the lines and reach the brakes.

As a result, there are four different factors that need to be added together to determine the total stopping distance for vehicles with air brake systems: Perception Distance + Reaction Distance + Brake Lag Distance + Braking Distance = Total Stopping Distance. A vehicle traveling at a speed of 55 mph on decent road conditions will have an air brake lag distance of about 32 feet, or a total stopping distance of over 450 feet.

## Brake Fading or Failure

Brakes slow down a vehicle by using brake shoes or pads to create friction against the brake drum or disks. This causes the brakes to get very hot, but brakes are built to withstand high levels of heat. However, using the brakes excessively and/or not taking advantage of the engine braking effect can cause brakes to overheat and fade or fail as a result.

Extreme use of the service brakes can cause them to fade and overheat. The intense heat causes chemical changes in the brake lining, reducing friction and causing the brake drums to expand. As the overheated drums swell, the distance the brake shoes and linings have to move to touch the drums increases, reducing the intensity of this interaction. If the brakes continue to be stressed, brake fade could increase enough that you may not be able to slow or stop the vehicle.

Improper brake adjustment can also cause brakes to fade. If the workload is not equal throughout the vehicle, the brakes out of adjustment will not be performing to their capacity. As a result, the vehicle will not have enough braking power to stop properly. It doesn't take much for brakes to get out of adjustment, especially when they are used often. In addition, when brake linings are hot, they can wear out much faster. It is important for your vehicle to have regular brake adjustment checks.

## Low Air Pressure

If your vehicle's low air pressure warning light illuminates, this could indicate an air leak in the system. You need to find a safe place to stop and park immediately—if there is not enough air in the air tanks, controlled braking will be impossible. If the air pressure falls between 20 to 45 psi, the spring brakes will engage. If the vehicle is carrying a large load, it will take longer to stop since the spring brakes are not available on all axles. A vehicle traveling on a slick road or carrying a light load can potentially skid out of control when the spring brakes engage. Play it safe and stop the vehicle while it still contains enough air in the tanks to use the foot brakes.

## Parking Brakes

The parking brakes should be used every time you need to park, (except as indicated below.) If the vehicle is a newer model, the parking brake control knob is typically a yellow, diamond shaped knob marked "parking brakes"; on older vehicles, the knob might be blue and round or some other shape (including a lever that swings from side to side or up and down). To engage the parking brake, pull the knob out. When you start up again, push it in to release.

Exceptions:

Do not use the brakes if they are:

- Excessively hot (e.g. if you just drove down a steep hill)—the heat can damage them
- Extremely wet in freezing conditions—the brakes can freeze up and make the vehicle impossible to move

In these situations, park on level ground and use wheel chocks to hold the vehicle in place. If the brakes are too hot, allow them to cool down before using the parking brakes. If the brakes are wet, heat and dry them gently while driving in a low gear.

If automatic air tank drains are not present on your vehicle, drain the air tanks at the end of each shift to remove moisture and oil to prevent the brakes from failing.

You should never leave your vehicle unattended without first applying the parking brakes or chocking the wheels. The vehicle could roll, causing injury and damage.

# Combination Vehicles

This section details the basic information required to pass the knowledge tests for combination vehicles (tractor-trailer, doubles, triples, straight truck with trailer). If you need to take the knowledge exam for doubles and triples, you should also study the next section.

## *Driving Combination Vehicles Safely*

Driving a combination commercial vehicle is more complicated and demanding than a single CMV, as these vehicles are typically heavier, longer, and require more complex skill set. This section highlights essential safety issues that pertain expressly to combination vehicles.

### Rollover Risks

Truck rollovers cause over half of all CMV driver crash fatalities. Towed units that are heavily loaded are ten times more likely to tip over in an accident than those that are empty. These units have a higher center of gravity, making them easier to tip over.

To help prevent your vehicle from turning over, make sure the cargo is loaded as low to the ground as possible, and navigate around turns very slowly. When driving a combination vehicle, it is even more imperative to load the cargo low and properly centered than when driving a straight truck. If the cargo is located on one side of the truck bed, it can make the trailer lean to that side, increasing the chances of a rollover. It should be positioned in the center and distributed as much as possible.

Since a rollover is most likely to occur when a CMV takes a turn too quickly, make sure to navigate corners and exit/on ramps at a slow pace, and do not attempt quick lane changes, especially when your vehicle is fully loaded.

### Steer Gently

Because CMV trailers have the tendency to sway back and forth, quick lane changes can cause them to tip easily. It is not uncommon for accidents to occur where only the trailer has turns over.

This swaying motion is caused by "rearward amplification." Vehicles with a rearward amplification of 2.0 are twice as likely to have their trailer tip over than the tractor. Triples have a rearward amplification of 3.5, which means the chances of tipping the last vehicle on a triple unit are 3.5 times more likely than a five-axle tractor.

When operating a vehicle that is hauling a trailer, you should drive gently and smoothly. Any quick movement with the steering wheel could cause the trailer to turn over. Maintain a safe following distance behind other vehicles (at least one second for each ten feet of the vehicle's length, plus another second if traveling over 40 mph). Make sure to scan far enough ahead so you won't need to change lanes quickly. At night, drive at a slow enough pace to ensure you can spot any road obstructions before it is too late to make a lane change or stop. Shift down in to a low gear in order to take turns safely.

## Brake Early

Whether the load you are hauling is empty or full of cargo, make sure to maintain and control your speed. When a large combination vehicle is empty, it takes longer to stop than when it is fully loaded. In addition, the stiff suspension springs and robust braking system provide poor traction, causing the wheels to lock up easily and increasing the chances of the trailer swaying out and hitting other vehicles. It doesn't take much for the tractor to jackknife.

"Bobtail" tractors (tractors without semitrailers) require special caution, as they have been shown to be very difficult to stop smoothly and quickly. They often require a longer stopping time than a fully loaded tractor-semitrailer. When driving any combination vehicle, leave ample distance ahead so you can brake safely without being caught off-guard and needing to stop suddenly.

## Railroad-Highway Crossings

Railroad-highway crossings can be problematic for combination vehicles, as they can get easily hung up on raised crossings. The following types are most likely:

- Low clearance units (e.g. lowboy, car carrier, moving van, possum-belly livestock trailer).
- Single-axle tractors hauling a long trailer with its landing gear formulated to handle a tandem-axle tractor.

If you get stuck on the tracks, exit the vehicle immediately and get away from the tracks. Check nearby signage for an emergency number to contact. Call 911 or some other emergency number, giving the operator the crossing location and all identifiable landmarks, particularly the DOT number, if indicated.

## Prevent Trailer Skids

When a trailer's wheels lock up, it has the tendency to sway and swing, particularly when carrying very little or no cargo. This is referred to as a "trailer jackknife."

The procedure for stopping a trailer skid is:

### Recognize the Skid

Checking your mirrors is the best first course of action if you think your trailer has started to skid. Any time you need to brake hard, scan the mirrors to ensure the trailer is staying in place. It is very tough to avoid a jackknife situation once the trailer sways into another lane.

### Stop Using the Brake

Let up off the brakes to regain traction and refrain from using the trailer hand brake (if the vehicle is so equipped) to "straighten out the rig." This will only make the situation worse, as the trailer wheel brakes were the initial cause of the skid. When the trailer wheels are able to regain firm contact with the road, the trailer will realign behind the tractor.

## Turn Wide

When navigating a bend in a CMV, keep in mind that the rear wheels will not be in line with the front wheels. This is called offtracking or "cheating."

The diagram below demonstrates how offtracking creates a wider route than the rig itself, with longer vehicles offtracking even more. The rear wheels of the CMV offtrack a little, but the trailer's rear wheels offtrack even more. If the vehicle has more than one trailer, the rear wheels of the last one will offtrack the most.

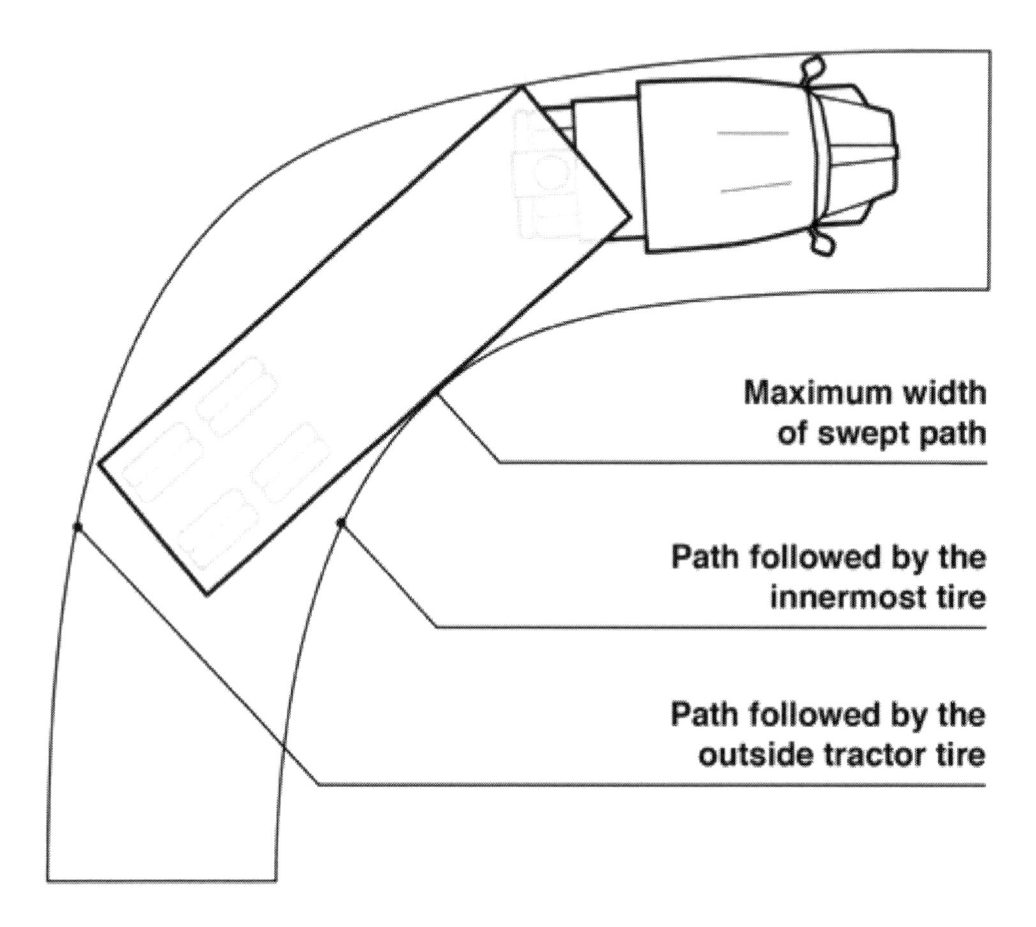


You will need to steer the front end of the vehicle in a wide enough turn when rounding a corner so that rear end does not hit the curb, pedestrians, or anything else on the side of the road or sidewalk. At the same time, you will need to keep the rear of the vehicle close to the curb in order to prevent other drivers from passing you on the right side. If you find you cannot make the turn without entering into another traffic lane, turn wide as you complete the turn. This is a more effective strategy than curving wide to the left before starting the turn because it stops other drivers from passing on your right side.

See the diagram below for reference.

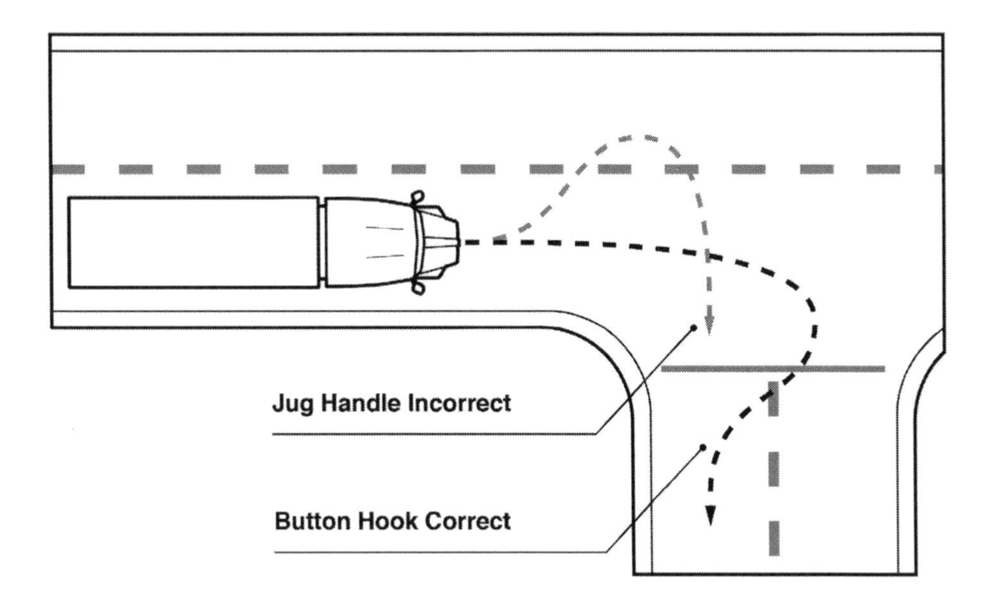


## Backing with a Trailer

Backing up with a trailer attached is very different from backing in a car, straight truck, or bus, where you turn the top part of the steering wheel in same direction you wish to move. Backing with a trailer requires turning the steering wheel in the opposite direction. Once the trailer begins to turn, rotate the steering wheel in the other direction to follow the direction of the trailer. Whenever you need to back up while pulling a trailer, try to make sure your vehicle is situated so you can back up straight. If it is absolutely necessary to back up on a curved trajectory, back to the driver's side so you can see clearly.

See the diagram below for reference.

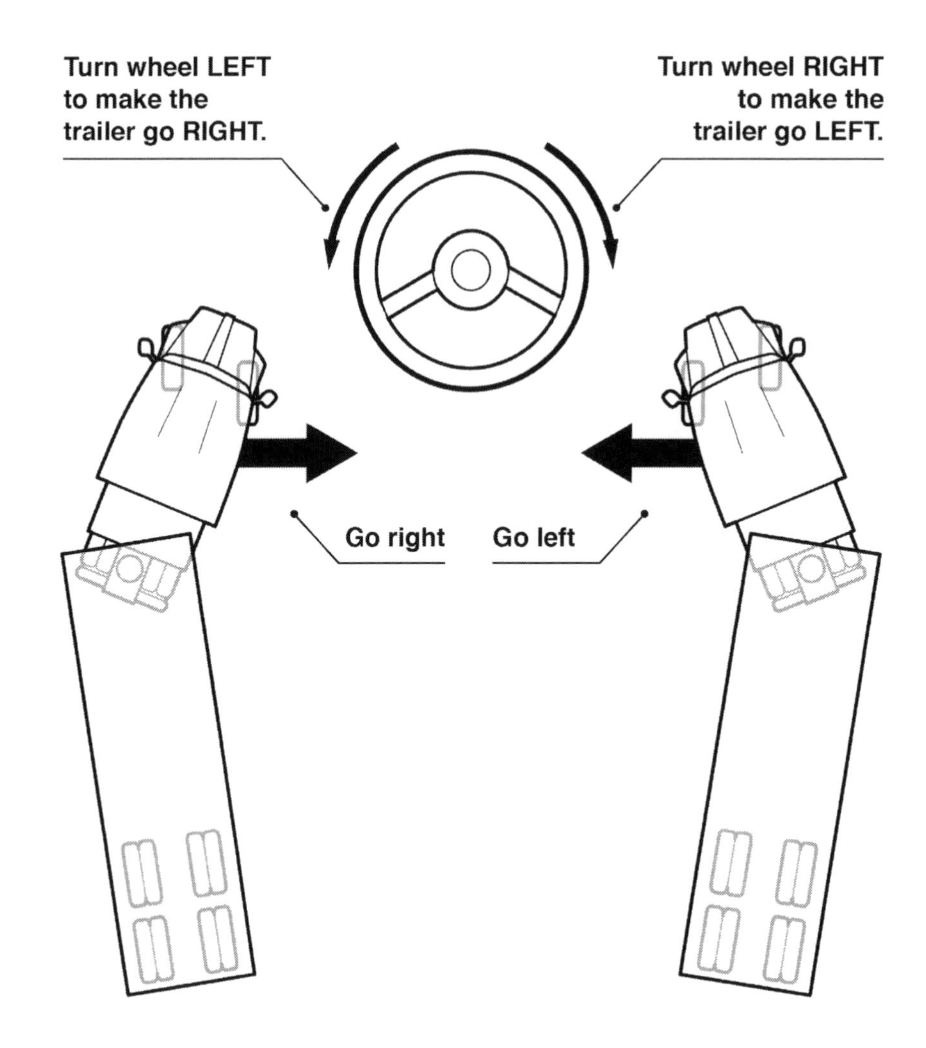
Turn wheel LEFT
to make the
trailer go RIGHT.
Turn wheel RIGHT
to make the
trailer go LEFT.
Go right
Go left

Look at Your Path

Before you attempt to back up, get out of your vehicle and walk all around, scanning the path you will travel. Make sure the path behind the vehicle is clear and there is enough room around the sides and top of the vehicle.

Use Mirrors on Both Sides

Repeatedly scan the outside mirrors on both sides of the vehicle. If you are not sure whether there is enough clearance, get out and re-check your route.

Back Slowly

This will allow you to make any necessary modifications before getting too far off track.

Correct Drift Immediately

As soon as you notice the trailer deviating too much from the correct course, adjust its path by turning the top of the steering wheel in the direction the trailer is moving.

Pull Forward
When backing a trailer, pull the vehicle forward as necessary to make re-alignments.

# *Combination Vehicle Air Brakes*

Prior to reading the information below on combination vehicle air brakes, re-read the prior section on air brakes. The braking system in combination vehicles involves controlling the trailer brakes, in addition to the air brake parts explained previously. These parts are listed below.

## Trailer Hand Valve

The trailer brakes are controlled via the trailer hand valve (also called the trolley valve or Johnson bar). You should only use this valve to test the trailer brakes, not while driving as it can cause the trailer to skid. The foot brake distributes air to all of a vehicle's brakes, including the trailer(s), and is much less likely to cause the vehicle to skid or jackknife.

Do not use the hand valve when you park, as the air might leak out and cause the brakes to unlock (in trailers without spring brakes). When parking, always use the parking brakes. If the trailer is lacking spring brakes, use wheel chocks to prevent the trailer from rolling.

## Tractor Protection Valve

Regulated by a "trailer air supply" control valve located in the cab, the tractor protection valve is designed to retain air within the vehicle's brake system in the event the trailer disengages or the air brakes start leaking. You can manually open and shut the tractor protection valve via this control valve. If air pressure gets too low (20 to 45 psi), the tractor protection valve will close automatically, preventing the release of air from the tractor. It also releases air from the trailer emergency line, prompting the trailer emergency brakes to engage, which could cause you to lose control of the vehicle. (Emergency brakes are covered in a later section.)

## Trailer Air Supply Control

On most newly manufactured vehicles, the trailer air supply control used to regulate the tractor protection valve is a red, eight-sided knob. Push it in to provide air to the trailer, and pull it out to stop the airflow and engage the trailer emergency brakes. When the air pressure falls to 20 to 45 psi, the valve will automatically pop out, which causes tractor protection valve to close.

Older vehicles may have a different design for the "emergency" or tractor protection valve control. It might not work spontaneously and could feature a lever instead of a knob. If you are pulling a trailer, the lever will be set in the "normal" position. Move the lever into the "emergency" position if you need to turn off the air and use the trailer emergency brakes.

## Trailer Air Lines

Every combination vehicle contains two lines to carry air: (1) the service line and (2) the emergency line. These lines run between the vehicle components (from tractor to trailer, trailer to dolly, dolly to second trailer, etc.)

### Service Air Line

The service line (also called the control line or signal line) transports the air that is regulated by the foot brake or the trailer hand brake. The level of pressure applied to the foot brake or hand valve determines the force of air in the service line, which is attached to a series of relay valves. These valves help the trailer brakes work more quickly.

### Emergency Air Line

The emergency line (also called the supply line) has two objectives:

- To transport air to the trailer air tanks.
- To regulate the emergency brakes on combination vehicles

If the emergency line loses air pressure, the trailer emergency brakes will turn on and the tractor protection valve will close (causing the air supply knob to pop out). This loss of pressure could be due to the trailer coming loose from the tractor, causing the emergency air hose to tear, or the breakdown of a hose, metal tubing, or some other part.

Emergency line components (hose, couplers, etc.) are often red in color to avoid confusion with the blue service line.

## Hose Couplers (Glad Hands)

The coupling devices used to join the service and emergency air lines between the vehicle components are called glad hands. Featuring a rubber seal, the couplers prevent air from escaping. Make sure the couplers and rubber seals are clean before attaching them to the glad hands. To make the connection, press the two rubber seals together with the couplers facing each other at a 90-degree angle. Turn the glad hand connected to the hose to attach and lock the couplers. It is important to make sure that you couple the correct glad hands together. The components are sometimes color-coded to distinguish the various parts that fit together; typically blue for the service lines and red for the emergency (supply) lines. Some vehicles may have metal tags that are attached to the lines labeled with the words "service" and "emergency."

See the diagram below for reference.

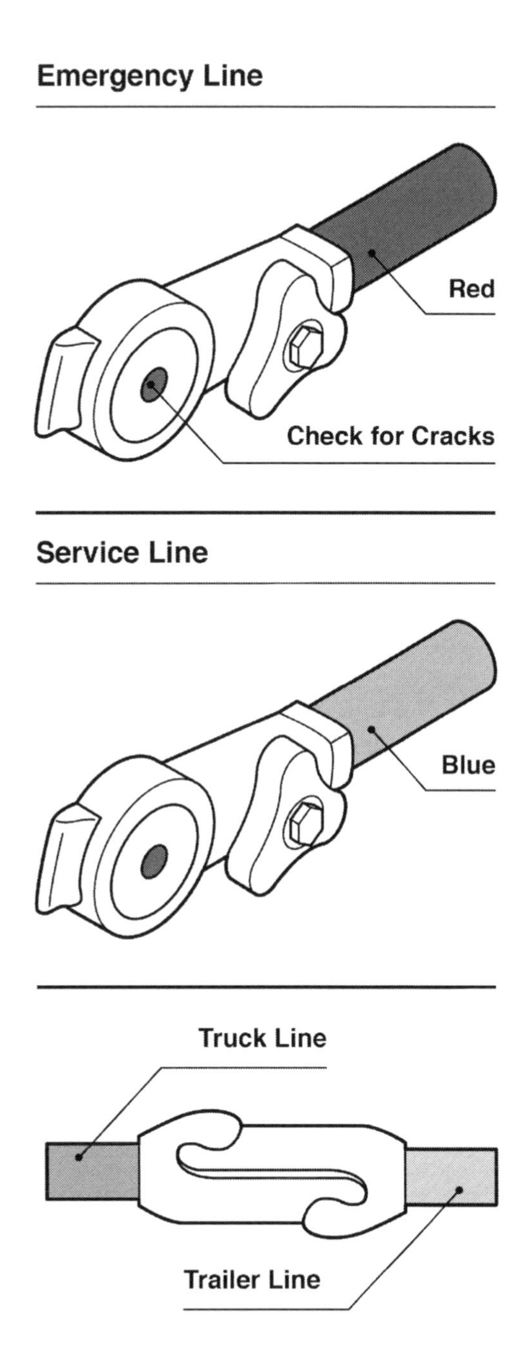


If the air lines are crossed, supply air will be carried through the service line instead of the trailer air tanks. As a result, the trailer spring brakes (parking brakes) won't have the ability to release. Make sure to check the air line connections if the spring brakes aren't releasing when you press the trailer air supply control, as they could be improperly connected.

Since older trailers lack spring brakes, the trailer wheels will spin and the emergency brakes will not function if the air supply in the trailer air tank leaks out. Before you drive, make sure you always test the trailer brakes by using the hand valve or pulling the air supply (tractor protection valve) control. While in a low gear, pull against them lightly to ensure the brakes are working.

The air supply needs to be kept clean and clear. Some vehicles have "dead end" or dummy couplers in order to keep water and dirt from clogging the components. Attach the hoses to these dummy couplers when the air lines are not connected to a trailer. On some vehicles, the glad hands can be locked together (depending on the couplings) in lieu of dummy couplers.

### Trailer Air Tanks

One or more air tanks supply the air pressure for the trailer brakes on every trailer and converter dolly. The air comes the tractor's emergency (supply) line. The air tanks carry pressure to the brakes via relay valves.

The brake pedal (and the trailer hand brake) regulates the service line pressure. The pressure in the service line indicates of the amount of pressure that should be transported to the trailer brakes by the relay valves.

The air tanks need to be checked frequently for water and oil accumulation; if they get clogged, the brakes might not work properly. Open the drain valve on each tank daily to extract any debris, even if the tanks on your vehicle feature automatic drains.

### Shut-Off Valves

The service and supply air lines located in the rear of trailers designed to tow other trailers feature shut-off valves (also called cut-out cocks). These valves close the air lines when the trailer is not towing another unit. To make sure they will function as intended, check that all the shut-off valves are open except the ones in the rear of the last trailer, which must remain closed.

### Trailer Service, Parking and Emergency Brakes

Newer model trailers feature spring brakes just like trucks and truck tractors. However, on converter dollies and trailers that were manufactured prior to 1975, spring brakes were not a requirement. Those lacking spring brakes have emergency brakes, which are supplied by the air stored in the trailer air tank. The emergency brakes will come on whenever the emergency line loses air pressure, which could be the result of the following:

- The air supply knob being pulled out or the trailer is disconnected.
- A major leak in the emergency line, causing the tractor protection valve to close.

As long as there is air pressure in the trailer air tank, the brakes will work. However, when all the air leaks out, the brakes will fail. Since these trailers have no parking brake, it is very important to use wheel chocks when parking a trailer without spring brakes.

A major leak in the service line may not be detected until you attempt to use the brakes. The leak will cause the air tank pressure to drop rapidly and the trailer emergency brakes to come on if the pressure plunges low enough.

# *Antilock Brake Systems*

## Trailers Required to Have ABS

ABS is a requirement on trailers and converter dollies manufactured on or after March 1, 1998. However, for those manufactured before this date, ABS was a voluntary requirement. Trailers equipped with ABS feature yellow malfunction lights on the front or rear corner on the left side. Dollies built on or after March 1, 1998, are required to have an ABS light on the left side.

It may be hard to discern whether a vehicle built prior the required date is equipped with ABS. To make sure, check under the vehicle for the ECU and wheel speed sensor wires projecting out of the back of the brakes.

ABS is a computerized system that is supplemental to your vehicle's regular brakes. It is designed to prevent your wheels from locking when you apply them very hard. An add-on to your vehicle's regular braking system, it does not reduce or intensify the brakes' capability. Triggered when the wheels are about to lock up, ABS may not decrease the distance you will need to stop, but it will help you control your vehicle during hard braking.

## Braking with ABS

The system's computer can detect when the wheels are about to lockup, reducing the braking pressure to a safe level and enabling you to remain in control. Even if the ABS is only present on the trailer, or just one axle, you will still have more control when braking. The changes of the trailer swinging out are lower when only the trailer features ABS. However, if you lose control of the steering or start to jackknife, decrease pressure on the brakes (if you can do so safely) until you regain control.

Brake as you normally would when operating a tractor-trailer combination featuring ABS, i.e. use the minimum level of braking power that is absolutely necessary to stop safely and maintain control. This holds true whether you have ABS just on the tractor, just on the trailer, or on both units. As you decrease your speed, pay close attention to the various vehicle components. Step off the brakes (if you can safely do so) to maintain control.

It is important to keep in mind that you still have your standard brakes even if the ABS fails. You can continue to drive, but make sure to get the system checked soon. ABS is strictly supplementary—it won't enable you drive faster, follow behind other vehicles more closely, or drive less cautiously.

# *Coupling and Uncoupling*

In order to safely operate a combination vehicle, it is imperative that you know how to couple and uncouple properly. It is very dangerous if the vehicle is not coupled and uncoupled correctly. Common steps regarding coupling and uncoupling are listed below. However, you will need to be aware of the coupling and uncoupling instructions specific to your CMV, as there are variances between different vehicles.

## Coupling Tractor-Semitrailers

### Step 1. Inspect Fifth Wheel

Inspect for parts that may be damaged/missing and make sure the fifth wheel is firmly mounted to the tractor, with no cracks in the frame, etc. Check that the plate for this wheel is well greased. If the fifth wheel plate is not lubricated enough, friction between the tractor and trailer could cause steering problems. Make sure the fifth wheel is correctly positioned for coupling:

- The wheel should be tilted down toward the back of the tractor.
- The jaws should be open.
- The safety-unlocking handle is in the automatic lock position.
- Make sure the sliding fifth wheel is locked (if the vehicle is so equipped)
- Check that the trailer kingpin is not bent or broken.

### Step 2. Inspect Area and Chock Wheels

Check that the area surrounding the vehicle is clear and the trailer wheels are chocked or the spring brakes are on. Make sure any cargo is snugly in place to guard against movement from the tractor/trailer combination.

### Step 3. Position Tractor

Move the tractor so that it is positioned directly in front of the trailer without backing under the trailer at an angle. (This can thrust the trailer sideways, breaking the landing gear.) Check the position by scanning all along both sides of the trailer using both mirrors.

### Step 4. Back Slowly

Back up slowly just until the fifth wheel is touching the trailer—do not hit it with any force.

### Step 5. Secure Tractor

Engage the parking brake and move the transmission into neutral.

### Step 6. Check Trailer Height

The trailer height should be low enough so that it rises up a bit when the tractor is backed underneath. If it is too low, the tractor could collide with the trailer nose, causing damage; if the trailer is positioned too high, it might not couple correctly. Raise or lower the trailer as necessary and make sure the kingpin and fifth wheel are aligned.

### Step 7. Connect Air Lines to Trailer

Inspect the seals on the glad hands. Connect the tractor emergency air line to trailer emergency glad hand and the tractor service air line to the trailer service glad hand. Make sure air lines are positioned so they aren't crushed or wedged in when you back the tractor under the trailer.

## Step 8. Supply Air to Trailer

Check the air supply to the trailer brake system by pressing the "air supply" knob located inside the cab or shift the tractor protection valve control from the "emergency" to the "normal" position. Wait until the air pressure reaches a normal level.

Check the brake system for any crossed air lines:

- Shut off the engine so you can hear the brakes working.
- Step on and off the trailer brakes, listening for the sound of the trailer brakes being applied and released. You should hear the sound of the brakes being pressed and the escape of air when the brakes are released.
- Check the air brake system pressure gauge for indications of major air loss.
- Once you are positive the trailer brakes are in good working order, start engine. Check that the air pressure level is in the normal range.

## Step 9. Lock Trailer Brakes

Pull the "air supply" knob out or shift the tractor protection valve control from "normal" to "emergency."

## Step 10. Back Under Trailer

To prevent striking the kingpin too hard, back the tractor slowly under the trailer using the lowest reverse gear. Come to a complete stop once the kingpin is locked into the fifth wheel.

## Step 11. Check Connection for Security

Slightly lift the trailer landing gear off the ground. Slowly move the tractor ahead while the trailer brakes are still in a locked position to make sure the two units are still connected.

## Step 12. Secure Vehicle

Shift the transmission into neutral and turn on the parking brakes. Turn off the engine and make sure you have the key to prevent someone from moving the truck while you are underneath.

## Step 13. Inspect Coupling

You may need to get a flashlight in order to do a thorough inspection of the coupling. Check that the area between the upper and lower fifth wheel is snug. Space between the two indicates some kind of issue—if the kingpin is wedged on top of the closed fifth wheel jaws, the trailer could easily detach from the tractor. Crawl underneath the trailer and scan the rear of the fifth wheel to ensure that the fifth wheel jaws are firmly closed around the shank of the kingpin and the locking lever is in the "lock" position. Make sure the safety latch is positioned over the locking lever. (The catch on some fifth wheels needs to be positioned manually). Do not operate the coupled vehicle if the coupling is incorrect—take it in for repair.

## Step 14. Connect the Electrical Cord and Check Air Lines

Plug the electrical cord into the trailer and secure the safety catch. Make sure the air and electrical lines are in good working order and are out of the way of any of the vehicle's moving components.

### Step 15. Raise Front Trailer Supports (Landing Gear)

Raise the landing gear using a low gear range (if the vehicle is so equipped). Switch to a higher gear and raise the landing up all the way once the vehicle is no longer bearing any weight. Do not operate the vehicle with landing gear partially in the up position—it could snag on railroad tracks or other obstructions. Once the landing gear is up, make sure the crank handle is safely secured.

When the full weight of the trailer is resting on the tractor:

- Make sure there is enough space between the back of the tractor frame and the landing gear. The tractor should not strike the landing gear when making sharp turns.
- Make sure there is sufficient space between the upper part of the tractor tires and the trailer's nose.

### Step 16. Remove Trailer Wheel Chocks

Remove and safely stow wheel chocks.

## Uncoupling Tractor-Semitrailers

The following steps will help you safely uncouple your vehicle units.

### Step 1. Position the Rig

Check that the parking area pavement is strong enough to support the weight of the trailer.

Move the tractor in line with the trailer. The landing gear can be damaged if you attempt to pull out at an angle.

### Step 2. Ease Pressure on the Locking Jaws

Lock the trailer brakes by turning off the trailer air supply and then back up slowly to reduce pressure on the fifth wheel locking jaws. While the tractor is pressing against the kingpin, engage the parking brakes. This holds the vehicle in place while keeping pressure off the locking jaws.

### Step 3. Chock the Trailer Wheels

If the trailer lacks spring brakes, or if it is unclear whether it does, make sure to chock the trailer wheels. If air leaks out of the trailer air tank, the emergency brakes will release, causing the trailer to roll if chocks are not in place.

### Step 4. Lower the Landing Gear

If the trailer does not contain any cargo, lower the landing gear until it solidly touches the ground. If trailer is full of cargo, turn the crank a few extra turns in a low gear once the landing gear makes solid contact with the ground to relieve the tractor of some of the load. However, make sure you do not lift the trailer off the fifth wheel. Following these steps will:

- Make it easier to unhook the fifth wheel.
- Make it easier to couple the units when you resume driving.

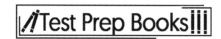

### Step 5. Disconnect the Air Lines and Electrical Cable

Detach the air lines from the trailer and join the air line glad hands to the dummy couplers in the rear of the cab or couple them together. Make sure the electrical cable is hung up with the plug facing downward to keep moisture out. Check that the lines are out of the way of any obstructions so the tractor does not damage them.

### Step 6. Unlock the Fifth Wheel

Elevate the release handle lock and move the release handle to the "open" position while making sure your legs and feet are out of the way of the rear tractor wheels in the event the vehicle rolls backward.

### Step 7. Pull the Tractor Partially Clear of Trailer

Move the tractor forward until fifth wheel comes free from under the trailer. Stop the vehicle once the tractor frame is positioned under the trailer (this will prevent the trailer from crashing to ground if the landing gear drops or gives way).

### Step 8. Secure Tractor

Put the transmission in neutral and put on the parking brake.

### Step 9. Inspect Trailer Supports

Check that the pavement is able to support the trailer weight and the landing gear is undamaged.

### Step 10. Pull Tractor Clear of Trailer

Release the parking brakes, make sure the area ahead is clear, and drive tractor forward until it is free of the trailer.

# *Inspecting a Combination Vehicle*

Follow the seven-step inspection directions outlined in Section 2 to check your combination vehicle. However, keep in mind a combination vehicle has more of the same items to inspect (e.g. tires, wheels, lights, reflectors, etc.), as well as some new components, which are listed below:

## Additional Things to Check During a Walkaround Inspection

Do these checks in addition to those already listed in Section 2.

### Coupling System Areas

Check the fifth wheel (lower section).

- Make sure the coupling system is firmly mounted to the frame.
- Check for any missing or damaged parts.
- Make sure components are well greased.
- Make sure there is no space between the upper and lower fifth wheel.
- Check that the locking jaws are positioned around the shank, not the kingpin head. (See diagram on the next page)

- Make sure the release arm is positioned correctly and the safety latch/lock is on.

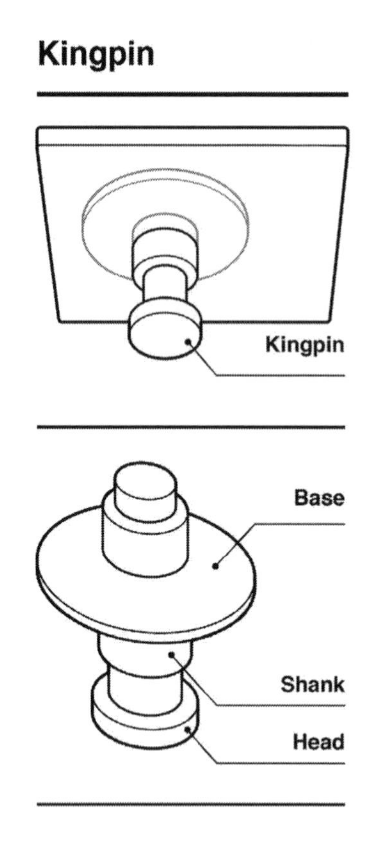


Check the fifth wheel (upper section).

- Make sure the glide plate is firmly mounted to the trailer frame.
- Check for any damage to the kingpin.

Air and electric lines to trailer.

- Check that the electrical cord is securely in place and plugged in.
- Make sure the air lines are free of leaks, attached correctly to the glad hands, and suitably positioned, allowing enough slack for turns.
- Make sure all lines are undamaged.

Sliding fifth wheel.

- Check to see that there is no damage or missing parts to the slide.
- Make sure it is well greased.
- Check for all the locking pins and make sure they are securely locked.
- Make sure no air is leaking if the vehicle is air powered.
- Make sure the fifth wheel is properly positioned—it needs to be back far enough so that the tractor frame won't strike the landing gear, or the cab won't come in contact with the trailer, when you are navigating turns.

### Landing Gear

- Make sure the landing gear is in the up position, and none of the components are missing, bent or broken.
- Check that the crank handle is properly positioned and secured.
- If the system is power operated, make sure there are no air or hydraulic leaks.

## Combination Vehicle Brake Check

Do the following checks in addition to those listed in the section covering the inspection of air brake systems. The brakes on a double or triple trailer should be checked in the same manner as those on any combination vehicle.

### Check That Air Flows to All Trailers

Keep the vehicle in place by engaging the tractor parking brake and/or chocking the wheels. Wait for air pressure to drop within the normal range, and then press the red "trailer air supply" control to transport air to the emergency (supply) lines. Operate the trailer handbrake to carry air to the service line. Go around to the back of the unit and open the emergency line shut-off valve in the back of the last trailer. Listen for the sound of air coming out, which means the system is properly charged. Close the emergency line valve. Open the service line valve to make sure you can hear service pressure air carried through all the trailers, and then shut the valve. This test is conducted under the assumption that neither the trailer handbrake nor the service brake pedal is on. If you do NOT hear air coming out of both lines, check to see that the shut-off valves on the trailer(s) and dolly(ies) are in the OPEN position. Air must be transported all the way to the back in order for all brakes to work.

### Test Tractor Protection Valve

Charge the trailer air brake system by bringing the air pressure to a normal level and pressing the "air supply" knob. Turn off the engine and press the brake pedal up and down several times to decrease air pressure in the tanks. Make sure the trailer air supply control (also called the tractor protection valve control) pops out (or changes from a "normal" to "emergency" position) when the air pressure drops to the pressure range stipulated by the manufacturer. (Typically 20 to 45 psi.)

If the tractor protection valve is not working properly, a leaking air hose or trailer brake could drain all the air out of the tractor, causing the emergency brakes to come on and making the vehicle difficult to control.

### Test Trailer Emergency Brakes

Charge the trailer air brake system as directed in the previous step (testing the tractor protection valve) and make sure the trailer wheels are rolling freely. Then stop and pull out the trailer air supply knob (also called the tractor protection valve or trailer emergency valve), or put it in the "emergency" position. Move the trailer slowly forward using the tractor to make sure the trailer emergency brakes are on.

### Test Trailer Service Brakes

Check that air pressure is flowing normally, release the parking brakes, gently pull the vehicle forward, and engage the trailer brakes using the hand control (trolley valve), if so equipped. You should be able to detect the brakes coming on, letting you know that the trailer brakes are attached and working properly. Although the trailer brakes should be tested with the hand valve, the foot pedal should be used to operate them normally—this will carry air to the service brakes located at all the wheels.

# Doubles and Triples

This section lists the information found on the CDL knowledge test for safe operation of double and triple trailers. It explains the importance of driving cautiously when operating a CMV pulling more than one trailer, how to properly couple and uncouple the vehicle units, and how to thoroughly inspect doubles and triples.

## *Pulling Double/Triple Trailers*

Enhanced awareness is required when pulling double/triple trailers, as they are typically less steady than other CMVs, increasing the chances of issues arising. Some areas of concern are discussed below.

### Prevent Trailer from Rolling Over

Steering steadily and navigating turns and on/off ramps slowly is necessary when pulling multiple trailers in order to avoid them from turning over. Do not assume you can take a curve at the same speed when hauling a double or triple as you would in a straight truck or a single trailer combination vehicle.

### Beware of the Crack-the-Whip Effect

The "crack-the-whip" effect is even more pronounced in double/triple trailers, making them even more likely to flip over than other combination vehicles, particularly the last trailer in a combination.

### Inspect Completely

Vehicles with two or three trailers contain a greater number of components that need inspecting. Make sure to check all of them by following the procedures listed later in this section.

### Look Far Ahead

Double and triple combination vehicles require steady and smooth operation to prevent them from flipping over or jackknifing. Make sure to always scan the road far enough in the distance so you can slow the vehicle or make a gradual lane change if needed.

### Manage Space

Keep in mind the extra distance that is required around double and triple combinations. Not only is their length more extensive, but they also need more room for turning and stopping. As a result, make sure to keep more space between the vehicle in front of you and your vehicle has enough clearance when entering or crossing traffic and making lane changes.

### Adverse Conditions

Harsh driving conditions, including inclement weather, slick roads, and driving in mountainous areas, require even more caution when pulling doubles and triples. Keep in mind that the longer vehicle length and greater number of axles increase the possibility of skids and the loss of traction.

### Parking the Vehicle

Park in a location where you'll be able pull straight ahead. Make sure you know parking lot configurations so that you can get out quickly and easily when you need to resume driving.

### Antilock Braking Systems on Converter Dollies

Converter dollies built on or after March 1, 1998, must have antilock brakes—they will feature a yellow light on the left side of the dolly.

## *Coupling and Uncoupling*

Incorrectly coupling and uncoupling of double and triple trailers is very dangerous. Proper steps are listed below.

### Coupling Twin Trailers

#### Secure Second (Rear) Trailer

If the second trailer is lacking spring brakes, pull the tractor near the trailer, attach the emergency line, charge the trailer air tank, and disconnect the emergency line. This will make sure that the trailer emergency brakes are firmly in place (as long as the slack adjusters are properly adjusted). If you think the brakes are not holding, make sure to chock the wheels.

For safety reasons, the trailer with the heaviest cargo should be right behind the tractor, and the trailer carrying lighter weight should be in the last position. Some dollies have a coupling device called a converter gear designed to couple a semitrailer to the rear of a tractor-trailer combination, making a double bottom rig.

See the diagram below for reference.

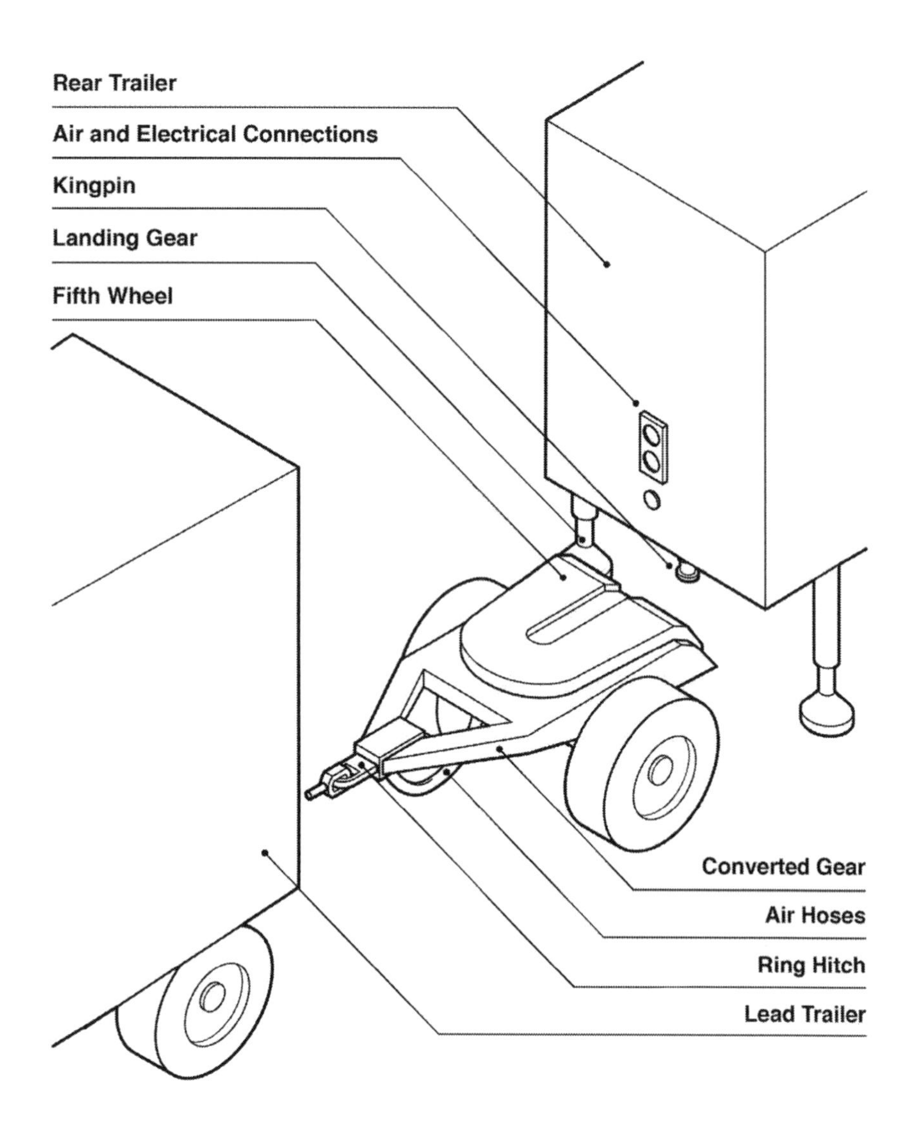


## Position Converter Dolly in Front of Second (Rear) Trailer

Open the air tank petcock to release the dolly brakes (or engage the dolly parking brake control if the dolly has spring brakes.) If the two units are not situated too far apart, manually move the dolly so it is aligned with the kingpin. Or, pick up the converter dolly using the tractor and first semitrailer:

- Place the two units as close as you can to the converter dolly.
- Wheel the dolly to the back of the first semitrailer and couple it to the trailer.
- Lock the pintle hook.
- Raise and secure the dolly support.
- Wheel the dolly as close as you can to the nose of the second semitrailer.
- Lower the dolly support.
- Unfasten the dolly from the first trailer.
- Move the dolly so it is aligned with the kingpin in front of the second trailer.

### Connect Converter Dolly to Front Trailer

- Back up the first semitrailer into place so it is in front of the dolly tongue.
- Fasten the dolly to the front trailer.
- Lock the pintle hook.
- Raise and secure the converter gear support.

### Connect Converter Dolly to Rear Trailer

- Make sure the trailer brakes are firmly locked and/or the wheels chocked.
- Make sure the trailer is the correct height. (It needs to be a little lower than the center of the fifth wheel, so trailer is raised up a bit when the dolly is pushed under.)
- Back the converter dolly underneath the rear trailer.
- Raise the landing gear a little bit to prevent damage in the event the trailer rolls.
- Pull against the pin of the second semitrailer to make sure the coupling is secure.
- Visually inspect the coupling, checking that there is no space between the upper and lower fifth wheel and the locking jaws are firmly closed around the kingpin.
- Attach all the safety chains, air hoses, and light cords.
- Shut the converter dolly air tank petcock and shut-off valves at the back of the second trailer (service and emergency shut-offs).
- Open the shut-off valves located at the back of the first trailer (and on the dolly if it has them).
- Completely raise the landing gear.
- Charge trailer brakes by pressing in the "air supply" knob, and open the emergency line shut-off at the back of the second trailer to check for air. If you are unable to detect any air pressure, this indicates there is some kind of issue and the brakes are not in working order.

## Uncoupling Twin Trailers

### Uncouple Rear Trailer

- Park the vehicle in a straight line on a stable level surface.
- Engage the parking brakes so the vehicle won't roll.
- If the second trailer vehicle is lacking spring brakes, chock the wheels.
- Lower the landing gear of the second semitrailer enough to take some weight off the dolly.
- Close the air shut-offs in the back of the first semitrailer (and on the dolly if it has them).
- Disconnect and secure all dolly air and electric lines.
- Release the dolly brakes.
- Release the converter dolly fifth wheel latch.
- Gently move the tractor, first semitrailer, and dolly forward to bring the dolly out from under the rear semitrailer.

### Uncouple Converter Dolly

- Lower the dolly landing gear.
- Unfasten the safety chains.
- Engage the converter gear spring brakes or chock the wheels.
- Unfasten the pintle hook on the first semi-trailer.
- Slowly move ahead clear of the dolly.

Never unfasten the pintle hook while the dolly is positioned under the rear trailer, as the dolly tow bar could spring up, potentially causing damage, and making it hard to re-couple.

### Coupling and Uncoupling Triple Trailers

Couple Tractor/First Semitrailer to Second/Third Trailers

- Couple the tractor to the first trailer.
- Use the procedure for coupling tractor-semitrailers listed previously.
- Move the converter dolly into place and couple the first trailer to the second trailer using the procedure for coupling doubles.
- The triples vehicle is now properly coupled.

Uncouple Triple-Trailer Rig

- Uncouple the third trailer by moving the dolly out, then unfastening the dolly via the uncoupling procedure used for doubles.
- Uncouple the rest of the unit as you would any double-bottom rig using the previously listed procedure.

### Coupling and Uncoupling Triple Trailers

Couple Tractor/First Semitrailer to Second/Third Trailers

Couple the tractor to the first trailer using the previously explained procedure for coupling tractor-semitrailers. Slide the converter dolly into place and couple the first trailer to second trailer via the same procedure used to couple doubles.

Uncouple Triple-Trailer Rig

Uncouple the rear trailer by pulling the dolly out and unlatching the dolly via the procedure used to uncouple doubles. Then uncouple the rest of the vehicle following the same method previously described for uncoupling double-bottom rigs.

### Coupling and Uncoupling Other Combinations

The coupling and uncoupling procedures listed above pertain to the more typical tractor-trailer combinations. However, it is important to keep in mind that there are many other methods depending on the type of rig. As a result, you will need to know the coupling and uncoupling procedure specific to your vehicle(s).

## *Inspecting Doubles and Triples*

Combination vehicles have more parts that need to be checked than on a single vehicle. When inspecting doubles and triples, you will use the seven-step inspection procedure described previously, but some components will require multiple checks since there are more of them (e.g. tires, wheels, lights, reflectors, etc.). There are also some new items that will need inspecting, which are listed below.

## Additional Checks

Do the following checks in addition to the Walkaround inspection discussed earlier in this guide:

### Coupling System Areas

Check fifth wheel (lower)

- Make sure it is securely mounted to the frame.
- Check for missing or damaged parts.
- Make sure it is well greased.
- Check that there is no gap between the upper and lower fifth wheel.
- Make sure the locking jaws are positioned around the shank, not the kingpin head.
- Check that the release arm is correctly in place and the safety latch/lock is on.

Check fifth wheel (upper)

- Make sure the glide plate is firmly mounted to the trailer frame.
- Check that the kingpin is undamaged.

Air and electric lines to trailer

- Make sure the electrical cord is securely plugged in and tightly in place.
- Check that the air lines are correctly attached to the glad hands, there are no air leaks, and they are positioned to allow enough slack for turns.
- Make sure none of the lines show signs of damage.

Sliding fifth wheel

- Make sure there are no missing components or signs of damage on the slide.
- Check that the fifth wheel is well greased.
- Do a check for all locking pins and make sure they are firmly latched.
- If the vehicle is air powered, make sure there are no air leaks.
- Make sure the fifth wheel is positioned far enough back so that the tractor frame will not strike the landing gear, or the cab will come in contact with the trailer, when turning the vehicle.

### Landing Gear

- Make sure the landing gear is in the up position and there are no missing components or visible damage.
- Check that the crank handle is firmly secured.
- If the vehicle is power operated, make sure there are no air or hydraulic leaks.

### Double and Triple Trailers

- Check that the shut-off valves (located at the back of each trailer and in the service and emergency lines) are in the proper positions:
- Rear of front trailers: OPEN.
- Rear of last trailer: CLOSED.
- Converter dolly air tank drain valve: CLOSED.
- Make sure the air lines are secured and the glad hands are correctly attached.
- If your vehicle has a spare tire on the converter gear (dolly), make sure it is properly in place.

- Make sure the pintle-eye of the dolly is correctly positioned in the pintle hook of the trailer(s).
- Check that the pintle hook is locked in place.
- Make sure the safety chains are fastened to the trailer(s).
- Check that the light cords are securely locked in the trailer(s) sockets.

### Additional Things to Check During a Walkaround Inspection

Do the checks listed below in addition to the checks listed in the section on "Inspecting Air Brake Systems."

## *Doubles/Triples Air Brake Check*

Check the brakes on a double or triple trailer as you would any combination vehicle, following the instructions discussed in the previous section of this guide. In addition, you will need to perform the following checks that pertain to double or triple trailers:

### Additional Air Brake Checks

#### Check That Air Flows to All Trailers (Double and Triple Trailers)

Securely stop the vehicle via the tractor parking brake and/or chocking the wheels. Once the air pressure is at a normal level, press the red "trailer air supply" knob in order to supply air to the emergency (supply) lines. Use the trailer handbrake to transport air to the service line. Walk around to the back of the last trailer and open the emergency line shutoff valve. Listen for the sound of air escaping, which indicates that the entire system is charged. Shut the emergency line valve and open the service line valve to make sure the air pressure is carried through all the trailers, and then shut the valve. (Keep in mind that the trailer handbrake or service brake pedal must be on while performing this test). If you do NOT hear the sound of air escaping from both lines, make sure the trailer and dolly shut-off valves are in the OPEN position. The brakes will not work unless air is carried all the way through the unit.

#### Test Tractor Protection Valve

Charge the trailer air brake system by bringing the air pressure to a normal level and pressing the "air supply" knob. Turn off the engine and then step up and down on the brake pedal several times to decrease the air pressure in the tanks. When the air pressure drops into the pressure range specified by the manufacturer (typically 20 to 45 psi), the trailer air supply control (also known as the tractor protection valve control) should pop out (or move from "normal" or "emergency" mode). If the tractor protection valve is not working correctly, the air could drain out of the tractor via an air hose or trailer brake leak, causing the emergency brakes to come on, and you to lose control of the rig.

#### Test Trailer Emergency Brakes

Charge the trailer air brake system and make sure the trailer wheels can move freely. Then come to a stop and pull out the trailer air supply control (also called tractor protection valve control or trailer emergency valve) or move it into the "emergency" position. Using the tractor, pull the trailer slowly ahead to make sure the trailer emergency brakes are working.

#### Test Trailer Service Brakes

After checking that air pressure is in the normal range, release the parking brakes, gently pull the vehicle forward, and apply the trailer brakes with the hand control (trolley valve), if the vehicle has one. You should feel the brakes engage, indicating that the trailer brakes are correctly attached and in good working order. You should test the trailer brakes with the hand valve, but operate them with the foot pedal, in order to carry air to the service brakes located at all wheels.

# Tank Vehicles

You will need a tank endorsement for some vehicles carrying liquids or gases. These include:

- Those requiring a Class A or B CDL, and the material being transported has an individual rated capacity of more than 119 gallons and an aggregate rated capacity of at least 1000 gallons that is either permanently or temporarily attached to the vehicle or the chassis.

- Class C vehicles when the vehicle is used to haul hazardous liquid or gas cargo in the type of tanks described above.

You must inspect the tanker prior to loading, unloading, or driving a tanker in order to ensure that the vehicle is in good working order and can safely transport the liquid or gas.

## *Inspecting Tank Vehicles*

When inspecting your tank vehicle, keep in mind that there are numerous types and sizes, each with components specific to that unit. Refer to the vehicle's operator manual so you know the particulars of inspecting the tank vehicle you will be driving.

### Leaks

Since you are transporting a gas or liquid, leaks are the most important detail to look for when checking all tank vehicles. It is against the law to transport liquids or gases in a leaking tank. If caught, you will receive a citation, be banned from driving, and might be held responsible for the clean up of any spilled materials. You will need to look underneath and all around the vehicle for any indications of leaks, checking the following in particular:

- Make sure the body or shell of the tank is free of dents or leaks.
- Check the intake, discharge, and cut-off valves.
- Make sure all valves are properly positioned prior to loading, unloading, or operating the vehicle.
- Inspect all pipes, connections, and hoses for leaks, especially around the joints.
- Check the manhole covers and vents to ensure that the covers contain gaskets, close properly, and the vents are clear.

### Check Special Purpose Equipment

If your vehicle is equipped with any of the following items, make sure they are in good working order:

- Vapor recovery kits.
- Grounding and bonding cables.
- Emergency shut-off systems.
- Built in fire extinguisher.

Never attempt to operate a tank vehicle with open valves or manhole covers.

### Special Equipment

Inspect the emergency equipment specific to your vehicle. Determine which items are required and make sure you they are present and in good working order.

## *Driving Tank Vehicles*

Transporting liquids in tank containers requires a specific skill set due to the high center of gravity and movement of the material.

### High Center of Gravity

Tank vehicles carry the bulk of the cargo weight high off road, which makes the vehicle top-heavy and more likely to tip over, particularly liquid tankers. Because tests have indicated that tank vehicles can roll over while traveling the normal speed limits posted for curves, you will need to navigate bends and on ramps/off ramps well below the posted speeds.

### Danger of Surge

If the tank you are hauling is partially full, the liquid can slosh around inside, disrupting your driving. For example, when you stop, the wave of liquid from the surge can strike the end of the tank, causing the vehicle to move in the same direction as the wave. If you are driving on a slick road when this happens, the wave can push the tanker out into the middle of an intersection. It is important to know how the vehicle you are operating handles.

### Bulkheads

Some liquid tanks use bulkheads to break the tank into several smaller units. Carefully distribute these smaller tanks during the loading and unloading process, making sure not to place too much weight in the front or back of the vehicle.

### Baffled Tanks

Baffled liquid tanks contain bulkheads with holes to allow the liquid to flow through and help control forward and backward liquid surge. However, side-to-side surge is still a possibility and can cause the vehicle to tip over.

### Un-Baffled Tanks

Forward-and-back surge is very prevalent in un-baffled liquid tankers (sometimes called "smooth bore" tanks), since they have nothing inside to slow down the liquid movement. These types of tankers typically carry food products such as milk. Sanitation requirements prohibit the use of baffles since they make cleaning out the inside of the tank much more difficult. Use extra caution when operating smooth bore tanks, particularly when starting and stopping.

### Outage

Because heat causes liquids to expand, make sure you always leave a little extra room when loading a tanker—this is called "outage." Since the degree of expansion varies according to each liquid, know the outage requirement of the liquid you are hauling.

### How Much to Load?

Some liquids are very dense (such as some acids) and may exceed legal weight limits. If you are transporting a liquid of this type, you may need to only partially fill the tank. The amount of liquid you will need to load depends on:

- How much the liquid will expand in transit.
- The weight of the liquid.
- Legal weight limits.

## *Safe Driving Rules*

Safe driving rules regarding tank vehicles include:

### Driving Smoothly

The high center of gravity and liquid surge of a tank vehicle require smooth driving, particularly starting, slowing, navigating curves, and lane changes and stopping.

### Controlling Surge

In order to control liquid surge, make sure you steadily work the brakes and do not release too quickly when stopping. Use your brakes well ahead of the time you need to stop and increase the distance you are following behind the vehicle ahead of you. Use controlled or stab braking if you need to stop quickly to avoid an accident. These methods are covered in a previous section—review if necessary. Keep in mind that the tanker could tip over if you veer suddenly while braking.

### Curves

Slow down when approaching a curve, and then increase your speed slightly as you navigate the curve, keeping in mind that the posted speed may be too fast for your vehicle.

### Stopping Distance

Be aware of the distance required to stop your vehicle. Keep in mind that wet roads double the typical distance needed to stop and an empty tanker may take longer to stop than one that is fully loaded.

### Skids

To avoid skids, refrain from over steering, driving too fast and braking too hard. If the drive or trailer wheels on a tanker begin to skid, the vehicle could jackknife. When driving any vehicle that begins to skid, work quickly to regain wheel traction.

# Hazardous Materials

Cargo that is risky to health, safety, and property during transport is called hazardous materials. These include items such as explosives, gases, solids, flammable and combustible liquid, and other substances. They are often referred to on road signs as HAZMAT, or HM in government regulations. Since these materials are very dangerous and have such a high potential to cause harm, all levels of government regulate the management of hazardous materials.

Parts 100 – 185 of title 49 of the Code of Federal Regulations contains information about Hazardous Materials Regulations (HMR). The common reference for these regulations is 49 CFR 100 – 185.

These regulations include a Hazardous Materials Table. However, because regulation definitions can vary, the list does not include all items. The type of cargo and the shipper's decision regarding whether or not the material falls under the hazardous material definition determine which items will be labeled as hazardous materials. Vehicles carrying certain kinds or amounts of hazardous materials are required to display diamond-shaped, square on point, warning signs called placards.

This section will help you understand your role and responsibilities when transporting hazardous materials. However, bear in mind that because government regulations are continually changing, it is essential to always refer to the most current copy of the complete regulations, which includes a comprehensive glossary of terms.

You will need to have a commercial driver's license (CDL) with a hazardous materials endorsement prior to operating any vehicle hauling hazardous material as defined in 49 CFR 383.5. In order to obtain this endorsement, you will need to pass a written test about the regulations and requirements for hazardous materials.

This section outlines the information required to pass this exam. However, keep in mind that in order to be aware of the most up-to-date regulations, you will also need to read and understand the federal and state rules that pertain to hazardous materials, and attend hazardous materials training courses. These classes are typically provided by your employer, colleges/universities, and related associations. Copies of the Federal Regulations (49 CFR) are available through your local Government Printing Office bookstore and industry publishers. In addition, union and/or company offices often have copies on hand.

The regulations stipulate that all drivers carrying hazardous materials must undergo training and testing provided by your employer or a designated representative. Employers are required to maintain training records for every driver who transports hazardous materials for a period of ninety days. Drivers who transport hazardous materials must be trained and tested at least once every three years.

This includes training regarding the security risks of carrying hazardous materials, particularly how to identify and react to potential security threats.

Specialized training is required for drivers who:

- Transport some types of flammable gas or radioactive materials.
- Transport cargo tanks and portable tanks.

The driver's employer or his or her designated representative must provide this training.

In some regions, permits are required to carry particular explosives or bulk hazardous wastes, and drivers may need to follow specific hazardous materials routes. In addition, especially dangerous material (such as rocket fuel) may need a federal permit or exemption. You will need to be aware of permits, exemptions, and special routes for the locations in which you will be operating.

## *The Intent of the Regulations*

### Containing the Material

Because hauling hazardous materials is a potentially dangerous matter, regulations are designed to protect the driver, anyone nearby, and the environment. These "containment rules" specify how to safely prepare the materials for transport and outline the proper methods for loading, carrying and unloading this type of cargo.

### Communicating the Risk

It is the responsibility of the shipper to alert drivers and others involved regarding the hazardous nature of the cargo by marking items with hazard warning labels and including the required shipping papers, emergency response information, and placards. By following these steps, the shipper, carrier, and the driver are all aware of the potential risks.

### Assuring Safe Drivers and Equipment

You will be required to pass a written exam outlining the procedures for transporting hazardous materials prior to receiving a hazardous materials endorsement on your CDL. In order to pass the exam, you will need to know how to:

- Identify various hazardous materials.
- Safely load cargo.
- Properly placard your vehicle as per regulations.
- Safely transport cargo.

Study and follow the hazardous materials regulations in order to reduce the possibility of damage and injury. Failure to abide by the rules is not only dangerous, but it can result in fines and time in prison. It is important to inspect your vehicle before and during each trip, as you could be pulled over by a police officer for a spot check. This could involve an inspection of your shipping papers, vehicle placards, and the hazardous materials endorsement on your CDL, as well as your understanding of hazardous materials.

## *Hazardous Materials Transportation—Who Does What*

### The Shipper

Prior to sending the cargo to its proper destination via truck, rail, vessel, or airplane, the shipper refers to the hazardous materials regulations in order to determine the cargo's:

- Identification number
- Proper shipping name.
- Hazard class.

- Packing group.
- Proper packaging.
- Proper label and markings.
- Proper placards.

The shipper is responsible for:

- Packaging, marking, and labeling the hazardous items.
- Preparing the shipping papers.
- Supplying emergency response information.
- Providing placards.
- Verifying that the shipment has been prepared according to the rules (unless the cargo tanks have been supplied by another source).

### The Carrier

The carrier transports the material from the shipper to its destination. Before taking the cargo, the carrier makes sure the shipper has properly described, marked, labeled, and organized the items, rejecting any that are incorrectly prepared. The carrier is also responsible for informing the appropriate government agency of any hazardous materials accidents and/or incidents.

### The Driver

The driver is responsible for:

- Making sure the shipper has correctly classified, marked, and labeled the hazardous materials.
- Refusing any packages and cargo that is leaking.
- Placarding the vehicle while loading the cargo, if so required.
- Safely transporting the material in a timely manner.
- Following the regulations specific to transporting hazardous materials.
- Maintaining the proper hazardous materials shipping papers and emergency response information.

## *Communication Rules*

### Definitions

Many terms used to classify hazardous materials vary from the typical term definitions you may have seen in the past. There are nine different hazard classes used to describe the potential dangers correlated with each item.

The types of materials included in these nine classes are listed in the table below; definitions of other significant hazardous materials terms can be found in the glossary at the end of this section.

| Hazardous Materials Table | | | |
|---|---|---|---|
| **Class** | **Division** | **Name of Class or Division** | **Examples** |
| 1 | 1.1<br>1.2<br>1.3<br>1.4<br>1.5 | Mass explosives<br>Projection hazards<br>Mass fire hazards<br>Very insensitive<br>Extreme insensitive | Dynamite<br>Flares<br>Display fireworks<br>Ammunition<br>Blasting Agents<br>Explosive devices |
| 2 | 2.1<br>2.2<br>2.3 | Flammable gases<br>Non-flammable gases<br>Poisonous/toxic gases | Propane<br>Helium<br>Fluorine, compressed |
| 3 | - | Flammable liquids | Gasoline |
| 4 | 4.1<br>4.2<br>4.3 | Flammable gases<br>Spontaneously combustible<br>Spontaneously combustible when wet | Ammonium Picrate,<br>Wetted white<br>phosphorous sodium |
| 5 | 5.1<br>5.2 | Oxidizers<br>Organic peroxides | Ammonium nitrate<br>Methyl ethyl ketone<br>Peroxide |
| 6 | 6.1<br>6.2 | Poison (toxic material)<br>Infectious substances | Potassium cyanide<br>Anthrax virus |
| 7 | - | Radioactive | Uranium |
| 8 | - | Corrosives | Battery fluid |
| 9 | - | Miscellaneous<br>Hazardous materials | Polychlorinated<br>Biphenyls (PCB) |
| e | - | ORM-D (other regulated material-domestic) | Food flavorings,<br>medicine |
| | - | Combustible liquids | Fuel oil |

Shipping papers (including shipping orders, bills of lading, and manifests), list and specify the hazardous cargo being transported.

Shippers must properly list all hazardous materials and include an emergency response number on shipping papers. Carriers and drivers are required to make sure they have quick access to these papers and the necessary emergency response information is clearly indicated. To make sure the papers are handy, drivers should keep them in one of the following places:

- In a pouch on the driver's door
- Within immediate reach while driving—in clear view while the seat belt is on
- On the driver's seat when exiting the vehicle

If you get into an accident or the hazardous materials you are carrying spill or leak, you could be unable to let first responders know that you are hauling dangerous cargo. These shipping papers can help make emergency personnel aware of the hazardous material you are transporting.

## Package Labels

Most cargo containing hazardous materials will be marked with a diamond-shaped hazard-warning label to make others aware of the potential danger. If the label won't fit on the package, the shipper might firmly attach a tag with the label to the package. For example, it can be difficult to affix labels to compressed gas cylinders, so they will often have tags or decals.

## Lists of Regulated Products

### Placards

Placards are warning signs placed on the outside of a vehicle and bulk packages used to identify the cargo hazard classification and notify others of the hazardous materials located inside. There must be at least four identical placards on a placarded vehicle, placed on the front, rear, and both sides so that they are visible from all four directions. At least 10 3/4 inches square, placards are square-on-point, in a diamond shape. Cargo tanks and other bulk packaging will show the cargo identification number on placards, orange panels or white square-on-point signs that are the same size as placards. See the diagram below for reference:

Emergency personnel use these identification numbers to identify hazardous materials (some numbers may be used to classify more than one chemical). The letters "NA" or "UN" precede each four-digit number. The United States Department of Transportation's Emergency Response Guidebook (ERG) has a listing of hazardous chemicals and their designated identification numbers. There are three major lists that shippers, carriers, and drivers refer to when classifying hazardous materials. A driver should always check a material's name against all three lists before transporting it, since some items are found on all lists, but others just one. Always check the following lists:

- Section 172.101, the Hazardous Materials Table.
- Appendix A to Section 172.101, the List of Hazardous Substances and Reportable Quantities. Appendix B to Section 172.101, the List of Marine Pollutants.

### The Hazardous Materials Table

The diagram below displays a section of the Hazardous Materials Table. Column 1 lists the shipping mode(s) affected by each hazardous item and other data regarding the shipping description. The next five columns show the shipping name, hazard class or division, identification number, packaging group, and required labels. Column 1 may contain up to six different symbols:

- (+) Signifies the correct shipping name, hazard class, and packing group, even if the material isn't technically defined as hazardous.

- (A) Indicates that the hazardous material listed in the second column falls under the Hazardous Materials Regulation (HMR) only when slated for air transport unless it is considered a hazardous substance or waste material.

- (W) Means the hazardous material displayed in the second column falls under HMR only when slated for water transport unless it is considered a marine pollutant, or hazardous substance or waste material.

- (D) Signifies that the shipping name can be used to describe cargo hauled domestically, but may not be suitable for international transport.

- (I) Indicates a shipping name appropriate for materials transported internationally; a different shipping name may be assigned when the transport is domestic.
- (G) Means the hazardous material described in the second column has been assigned a generic shipping name and must be accompanied by a technical name (a specific chemical that defines the product as hazardous) on the shipping paper.

The second column shows the correct shipping names and descriptions of hazardous substances that are regulated. They are listed alphabetically to make finding the correct entry easier. The shipping paper must list the proper shipping names for each item, which should be displayed in regular typeface. Those listed in italics are not the proper shipping names.

| **49 CFR 172.101 Hazardous Materials Table** | | | | | | | | | |
|---|---|---|---|---|---|---|---|---|---|
| Symbols | Hazardous materials description and proper shipping names | Hazard class or division | Identification numbers | PG | Label Codes | Special provisions (172.102) | Packaging (173. ***) | | |
| | | | | | | | Exceptions | Non bulk | Bulk |
| (1) | (2) | (3) | (4) | (5) | (6) | (7) | (8A) | (8B) | (8C) |
| A | Acetaldehyde ammonia | 9 | UN1841 | III | 9 | IB8, IP6 | 155 | 204 | 240 |

The third column lists the class or division of the hazardous material. Sometimes a "forbidden" status is listed—these items are strictly prohibited from transport. Hazardous cargo shipments should be placarded based on the quantity and hazard class of the item(s). You should be able to determine the proper placard based on the following:

- The hazard class of the material
- The amount of the item(s) being shipped.
- The total amount of the hazardous material(s) you will be carrying

The fourth column displays the identification number for each proper shipping name. Each identification number begins with the letters "UN" or "NA"—"NA" numbers are used to designate shipments within the United States and to and from Canada. The identification number must be prominently located on the outside packaging of the hazardous material, including cargo tanks and other bulk packaging, as well as the shipping paper. In the event of an accident or other incident, emergency personnel can use this number to quickly identify the hazardous materials.

The fifth column lists the hazardous material's packing group (displayed in Roman numeral format).

The sixth column lists the hazard warning label(s) required by shippers of hazardous materials. Some cargo may need more than just one label if there is more than one type of hazard present.

The seventh column displays any additional stipulations. Refer to the federal regulations for special information if there is an entry in this column. If it is a number between one and six, the hazardous material is a poison inhalation hazard (PIH). PIH materials require specific instructions regarding shipping papers, marking, and placards.

The eighth column is compromised of three parts reflecting the section numbers and packaging requirements for each hazardous material listed.

Note: The ninth and tenth columns do not apply to transportation by highway.

## Appendix A to 49 CFR 172.101: The List of Hazardous Substances and Reportable Quantities

Any spills of a reportable quantity of the hazardous items listed in the chart below must be reported to the DOT and the EPA by either you or your employer.

The column on the right lists the reportable quantity (RQ) for each item. When any of these items are being carried in one package in a reportable quantity or greater, the shipper is required to display the letters RQ on the shipping paper and package, which may appear before or after the description.

If the shipping paper or package contains the words INHALATION HAZARD, the corresponding POISON INHALATION HAZARD or POISON GAS placards must be displayed in addition to any other placards required by the product's hazard class. Make sure the hazard class placard and the POISON INHALATION HAZARD placard are always in clear view, even if you are transporting small quantities.

| **Hazardous Substances and Reportable Quantities** | |
|---|---|
| Hazardous Substance | Reportable Quantity (RQ) Pounds (Kilograms) |
| Phenyl mercaptan @ | 100 (45.4) |
| Phenylmercury acetate | 100 (45.4) |
| N-Phenylthiourea | 100 (45.4) |
| Phorate | 10 (4.54) |
| Phosgene | 10 (4.54) |
| Phosphine | 100 (45.4)* |
| Phosphoric acid | 5,000 (2270) |
| Phosphoric acid, diethyl 4-nitrophenyl ester | 100 (45.4) |
| Phosphoric acid, lead salt | 10 (.454) |
| *Spills of 10 pounds or more must be reported. | |

## Appendix B to 49 CFR 172.101: List of Marine Pollutants

Appendix B lists those chemicals deemed toxic to marine life. This list is only used for chemicals in a container with a capacity of 119 gallons or more without a placard or label as specified by the HMR when transported via highways. Any bulk packages of a Marine Pollutant must display the Marine Pollutant marking (white triangle with a fish and an "X" through the fish). This marking (it is not a placard) must also be displayed on the outside of the vehicle. In addition, a notation must be made on the shipping papers near the description of the material: "Marine Pollutant."

### The Shipping Paper

A shipping paper for hazardous materials must include:

- Page numbers (if more than one page is included). The total number of pages must be listed on the first page (i.e. "Page 1 of 4").
- The correct shipping description for each hazardous material.
- Proper certification signed by the shipper stating that the shipment was prepared as per regulations.

## The Item Description

If both hazardous and non-hazardous materials are listed on a shipping paper, the hazardous items must be:

- Listed first.

- Highlighted with a contrasting color, OR

- Identified by an "X" in the "HM" column located in front of the shipping description (ID#, Shipping Name, Hazard Class, Packing Group). The letters "RQ" may be used in place of "X" if a reportable quantity needs to be identified.

The correct order and listing of hazardous materials is as follows:

- Identification number
- Proper shipping name
- Hazard class or division
- Packing group, if any (displayed in Roman numerals and may be preceded by "PG")

The identification number, shipping name, and hazard class are not abbreviated unless specifically authorized by hazardous materials regulations.

The description must also show:

- The total amount and unit of measure of the cargo.
- The total number and item type (e.g.: "6 Drums").
- The letters RQ, if the cargo is a reportable quantity.
- The name of the hazardous substance if the letters RQ are present (if not included in the shipping name).
- The technical name of the hazardous material for all items classified with the letter "G" (Generic) in Column 1.

Shipping papers are also required to list an emergency response telephone number designated by the shipper (unless excepted). In the event of an accident or emergency, first responders can use this number to retrieve information about any hazardous materials involved in a spill or fire. The telephone number must belong to:

- The person submitting the hazardous material for transport (if the shipper/submitter is the emergency response information (ERI) provider); or

- An agency or organization able to accept responsibility for providing the detailed information listed in paragraph (a)(2) of this section. The person who is registered with the ERI provider must be identified by name, contract number or some other unique identifier assigned by the ERI provider.

Shippers are required to submit emergency response information for each hazardous material being shipped to the transport carrier. The emergency response information must be obtainable outside the

CMV and must explain how to safely handle incidents concerning the hazardous cargo. The following information is required:

- The basic description of the material and its technical name
- Immediate health hazards
- Fire or explosive dangers
- Precautions to be taken in case of an accident or incident
- Procedures for dealing with fires
- Instructions for handling spills or leaks without a fire
- Initial first aid procedures

This information can be listed on the shipping paper, as part of a separate document that includes the hazardous cargo's technical name and basic description, or in a guidebook such as the Emergency Response Guidebook (ERG). Some transport carriers include an ERG inside each vehicle hauling hazardous items. It is up to the driver to submit emergency response information to any federal, state, or local authority that responds to or investigates a hazardous materials incident.

The total quantity, number and type of cargo must be listed before or after the basic description. The package type and measurement unit may be shown in an abbreviated format. For example: 10 ctns. UN1263, Paint, 3, PG II, 500 lbs.

If the material is hazardous waste, the shipper must include the word WASTE in front of the correct shipping name on the shipping paper (hazardous waste manifest). For example: UN1090, Waste Acetone, 3, PG II.

If the material is non-hazardous, it must not be identified with a hazard class or an identification number.

Shippers are required to keep a hard copy of shipping papers (or an electronic image) for two years (three years for hazardous waste) after the initial carrier accepts the material. If the company provides carrier service only and does not initiate the shipment, the required timeframe for retaining the shipping paper (or electronic image) is one year.

Important Note: Complete regulatory requirements for the transportation of hazardous materials are available in the Code of Federal Regulations, Title 49, Parts 100-185.

## Shipper's Certification

The certification (signature) of the shipper should be present on the original shipping paper, indicating the shipper's guarantee that the material has been prepared as per regulations. Exceptions include:

- The shipper is a private carrier transporting their own cargo
- The package is provided by the carrier (for example, a cargo tank)

Unless a package is obviously dangerous or does not conform to the HMR, you can assume that the shipper's certification concerning proper packaging is correct. Some carriers may have additional requirements regarding the transport of hazardous materials. When accepting shipments, make sure you adhere to the rules imposed by your employer.

## Package Markings and Labels

The shipper provides the required classification for the hazardous cargo, which varies according to the material size and type. It is typically printed directly on the package, an attached label, or tag. The name of the hazardous material must match the one listed on the shipping paper. When required, the shipper will put the following on the package:

- The name and address of shipper or consignee.
- The name and identification number of the hazardous material.
- The necessary labels.

Make sure you compare the shipping paper with the labels/markings on the hazardous cargo. The shipper must list the proper basic description on the shipping paper, and verify that the correct labels are displayed on the packaging. If you do not recognize the material, ask the shipper to contact the office of your transport carrier.

If required by the regulations, the shipper will include the classifications RQ, MARINE POLLUTANT, BIOHAZARD, HOT, or INHALATION-HAZARD on the package. Cargo containing liquid containers will also have labels indicating arrows pointing in the correct upright direction. The labels depict the hazard class of the material. If more than one label is required, they must be located next to each other and close to the correct shipping name.

## Recognizing Hazardous Materials

Learn how to identify shipments of hazardous materials. Checking the shipping paper will help you determine whether a shipment contains hazardous items. Look for:

- A line item with a correct shipping name, hazard class, and identification number
- An entry that is highlighted, or has an X or RQ in the hazardous materials column

Other indicators of hazardous materials:

- The business category of the shipper. The examples listed below often manufacture hazardous products:
- Paint dealer
- Chemical supply
- Scientific supply house
- Pest control or agricultural supplier
- Explosives, munitions, or fireworks dealer
- Tanks with diamond labels or placards at the shipping location
- The type of package being shipped:
- Cylinders and drums are often used to carry hazardous materials
- A hazard class label, proper shipping name, or identification number on the package
- Any safety precautions

## Hazardous Waste Manifest

If the material you are hauling is considered hazardous wastes, you will be required to sign and carry a Uniform Hazardous Waste Manifest listing the name and EPA registration number of the shippers, carriers, and destination. This manifest must be prepared, dated, and signed by the shipper and should be regarded like a shipping paper while the waste is being transported. Make sure you hand over the waste shipment only to another registered carrier or disposal/treatment facility. The manifest must be hand signed by each carrier transporting the hazardous waste. Retain your copy once the shipment is delivered. Make sure each copy has all the required signatures and dates, including those at the final delivery destination.

## Placarding

Before driving the vehicle, make sure all the necessary placards are in place. An incorrectly placarded vehicle can only be moved during an emergency as a precautionary measure to protect life and property.

Placards must be present on both sides/ends of the vehicle. Each placard must be:

- Clearly seen from its facing direction.
- Situated so that the words or numbers are even and readable from left to right.
- At least three inches away from any other labeling.
- Away from any equipment or components such as ladders, doors, and tarpaulins.
- Clean and free from damage so that the color, format, and message are clearly seen.
- Attached to a background that has a contrasting color.

The front placard may be placed on the front of the tractor or the trailer. “Drive Safely” and other slogans are forbidden.

To decide the which placards are necessary, you will need to know:

- The hazard class of the items.
- The amount of hazardous materials being shipped.
- The total weight of all classes of hazardous materials you are transporting.

## Placard Tables

There are two placard tables to help determine the correct placards to use. Table 1 lists materials that must be placarded whenever any amount is transported. See diagram below for reference.

| Placard Table 1: Any Amount | |
|---|---|
| If your vehicle contains any amount of . . . | Placard as . . . |
| 1.1 Mass Explosives | Explosives 1.1 |
| 1.2 Project Hazards | Explosives 1.2 |
| 1.3 Mass Fire Hazards | Explosives 1.3 |
| 2.3 Poisonous/Toxic Gases | Poison Gas |
| 4.3 Spontaneously combustible when wet | Dangerous When Wet |
| 5.2 (Organic peroxide, Tybe B, liquid or solid, Temperature controlled) | Organic Peroxide |
| 6.1 (Inhalation hazard zone A & B only) | Poison |
| 7 (Radioactive Yellow III label only) | Radioactive |

With the exception of bulk packaging, the hazard classes listed in Table 2 require placards only if the total amount transported is 1,001 pounds or greater, including the package. Include the amount from all the shipping papers for the total number of items listed on Table 2 that you are carrying. See diagram below for reference.

| Placard Table 2: 1,001 Pounds or More | |
|---|---|
| Category of Material (Hazard class or division number and additional description, as appropriate) | Placard Name |
| 1.4 Very Insensitive | Explosives 1.4 |
| 1.5 Extreme Insensitive | Explosives 1.5 |
| 1.6 | Explosives 1.6 |
| 2.1 Flammable Gases | Flammable Gas |
| 2.2 Non-Flammable Gases | Non-Flammable Gas |
| 3 Flammable Liquids | Flammable |
| Combustible Liquid | Combustible* |
| 4.1 Flammable Gases | Flammable Solid |
| 4.2 Spontaneously Combustible | Spontaneously Combustible |
| 5.1 Oxidizers | Oxidizer |
| 5.2 (other than organic peroxide, Type B, liquid or solid, Temperature Controlled | Organic Peroxide |
| 6.1 (other than inhalation hazard zone A or B) | Poison |
| 6.2 Infectious Substances | (None) |
| 8 Corrosives | Corrosive |
| 9 Miscellaneous Hazardous Materials | Class 9** |
| ORM-D | (None) |
| *Flammable may be used in place of a combustible on a cargo tank or portable tank. | |
| **Class 9 Placard is not required for domestic transportation. | |

As an option, you may use DANGEROUS placards instead of separate placards for each Table 2 hazard class when:

- You are carrying 1,001 pounds or more of two or more Table 2 hazard classes, requiring different placards, and

- You have not loaded 2,205 pounds or more of any Table 2 hazard class material at any one location. (You must use the specific placard for this material.)

If the words INHALATION HAZARD are listed on the shipping paper or package, placards with the words POISON GAS or POISON INHALATION must be included in addition to any other placards required as per the product's hazard class. The 1,000-pound exception is not applicable to these items.

Items that have a secondary "dangerous when wet" hazard classification must show the DANGEROUS WHEN WET placard in addition to any others required by the product's hazard class. The 1,000-pound exception is not applicable to these items.

Placards used to distinguish the primary or subsidiary hazard class of a material must have the hazard class or division number clearly visible in the lower corner of the placard. Subsidiary hazard placards without the hazard class number that are permanently attached are permitted as long as they fall within color specifications. Even if they are not required for the cargo type, placards may be used as long as they signify the specific hazard of the material being transported.

A single container with a capacity of 119 gallons or more is called bulk packaging. These items must be placarded, even if the bulk package only contains hazardous material residue. Certain bulk packages are only required to have placarding on the two opposite sides of the vehicle or may display labels. All other bulk packages need to be placarded on all four sides.

## *Loading and Unloading*

Make sure you treat containers of hazardous materials with special care. During the loading process, do not use any tools such as hooks that could damage containers or other packaging.

### General Loading Requirements

Make sure you set the parking brake prior to loading or unloading hazardous material to ensure the vehicle will not move. Hazardous cargo should not be loaded near a heat source, as many products become even more dangerous when exposed to heat.

Be on the lookout for packages that are leaking or damaged. Remember: LEAKS INDICATE TROUBLE! Do not transport any containers that are leaking. Not only could it put you, the vehicle, and others around you in danger, but it is also illegal to drive a vehicle containing hazardous materials that are leaking.

Make sure you securely fasten any hazardous materials cargo prior to a trip to help avoid shifting of packages during transport.

#### No Smoking

Keep away from fire when loading or unloading hazardous materials—do not allow anyone to smoke near your vehicle. Absolutely no smoking around the following items:

- Class 1 (Explosives)
- Class 2.1 (Flammable Gas)
- Class 3 (Flammable Liquids)
- Class 4 (Flammable Solids)
- Class 5 (Oxidizers)

#### Secure Against Movement

Firmly secure all hazardous cargo so that it doesn't fall, shift, or move around during transport. Use caution when loading containers with valves or other fixtures.

After the packages are loaded, do not open any of them during your trip, including transferring hazardous items from one package to another while you are hauling them. The only type of package you are permitted to empty is a cargo tank—do not attempt to empty any other containers while they are on the vehicle.

#### Cargo Heater Rules

There are specific regulations for cargo heaters during the loading process:

- Class 1 (Explosives)
- Class 2.1 (Flammable Gas)
- Class 3 (Flammable Liquids)

Typically the rules prohibit cargo heaters, including automatic cargo heater/air conditioner units. Unless you are familiar with all the corresponding rules, don't load any of the types of material listed above in a cargo space that has a heater.

### Use Closed Cargo Space

Overhang or tailgate loads of the following items are forbidden:

- Class 1 (Explosives)
- Class 4 (Flammable Solids)
- Class 5 (Oxidizers)

You must use a closed cargo space to load these kinds of hazardous items unless all of them are:

- Fire and water-resistant.
- Covered with a tarp that is fire and water-resistant.

## Precautions for Specific Hazards

### Class 1 (Explosives) Materials

Prior to loading or unloading any explosives, turn off your engine and then inspect the cargo area. Make sure to:

- Disable cargo heaters.
- Disconnect the heater power source(s) and drain heater fuel tank(s).
- Check for any sharp points that might damage the items you are transporting. Do a scan for any bolts, screws, nails, broken side panels, and broken floorboards.
- Use a floor lining with Division 1.1, 1.2, or 1.3. The floors need to be tightly sealed and the liner material should be either non-metallic or non-ferrous metal (any metal not made out of iron or iron alloys).
- Use extra care to protect cargo that contains explosives:
- Do not use hooks or other metal tools.
- Never drop, throw, or roll packages.
- Keep it clear of other cargo that might be damaging.

Do not transfer Division 1.1, 1.2, or 1.3 cargo between vehicles while on a public highway except in an emergency. If an emergency transfer is required for safety reasons, make sure you warn other drivers by placing red warning reflectors, flags, or electric lanterns on the road in clear view.

Never transport packages containing explosives that are damaged or show signs of dampness or an oily stain.

Do not transport Division 1.1 or 1.2 in vehicle combinations if:

- One of the vehicles contains a marked or placarded cargo tank.
- The other vehicle in the combination contains:
- Division 1.1 A (Initiating Explosives).

- Packages of Class 7 (Radioactive) materials labeled "Yellow III."
- Division 2.3 (Poisonous Gas) or Division 6.1 (Poisonous) materials.
- Hazardous materials in a portable tank, on a DOT Spec 106A or 110A tank.

## Class 4 (Flammable Solids) and Class 5 (Oxidizers) Materials

Solids that react spontaneously or to water, heat, and air (including fire or explosion) are considered Class 4 materials.

Materials that fall under Class 4 and 5 must be securely sealed off or covered during transport. Cargo that becomes unstable and dangerous when exposed to liquid need to be kept dry during transit and loading and unloading. Items that are susceptible to spontaneous combustion or heat must be transported in properly ventilated vehicles.

## Class 8 (Corrosive) Materials

When loading items by hand, carry breakable containers containing corrosive liquid one at a time, making sure they are right side up. Load them in an area with an even floor surface, being careful not to drop or roll the containers. Stack carboys only if the lower levels can safely handle the weight of the upper tiers.

Nitric acid should not be loaded above any other item. Charged storage batteries should be loaded right side up, so no liquid spills out and away from other cargo that could damage them.

Corrosive liquids should never be loaded next to or above:

- Division 1.4 (Explosives C).
- Division 4.1 (Flammable Solids).
- Division 4.3 (Dangerous When Wet).
- Class 5 (Oxidizers).
- Division 2.3, Zone B (Poisonous Gases).

Corrosive liquids should never be loaded with:

- Division 1.1 or 1.2.
- Division 1.2 or 1.3.
- Division 1.5 (Blasting Agents).
- Division 2.3, Zone A (Poisonous Gases).
- Division 4.2 (Spontaneously Combustible Materials).
- Division 6.1, PGI, Zone A (Poison Liquids).

## Class 2 (Compressed Gases) Including Cryogenic Liquids

If the vehicle does not contain any storage racks for cylinders, the floor area to hold cargo must be flat. Make sure the cylinders are:

- Held upright.
- Stored in racks secured to the vehicle or placed inside boxes to prevent them from rolling over.

Cylinders may be loaded in horizontally (on their side) if the relief valve is in the vapor space.

## Division 2.3 (Poisonous Gas) or Division 6.1 (Poisonous) Materials

Never carry poisonous gas or materials in containers with interconnections. Never load cargo that is labeled POISON or POISON INHALATION HAZARD in the driver's cab, sleeper compartment or near food products meant for humans or animals. You must have specific training in order to load and unload Class 2 materials in cargo tanks and follow the regulations for handling this type of cargo.

## Class 7 (Radioactive) Materials

Some Class 7 (Radioactive) materials have a "transport index" number. They should be classified Radioactive II or Radioactive III by the shipper and have a transport index on the label. These packages will be surrounded by radiation, which will also permeate all packages within close vicinity. To deal with this issue, regulations limit the number of packages that can be loaded together and their proximity to people, animals, and unexposed film. The transport index indicates the required boundaries during transit. The total transport index of all packages within a single vehicle must not be more than fifty. The table below lists the rules for each transport index, indicating the proximity for loading Class 7 (Radioactive) materials to people, animals, or film. For example, a package with a transport index of 1.1 must not be loaded within two feet of people or cargo space walls.

| Radioactive Separation Table A | | | | | | |
|---|---|---|---|---|---|---|
| **Total Index/Transport** | **Minimum distance in feet to nearest undeveloped film** | | | | | **To People or Cargo Compartment Partitions** |
| | 0-2 hours | 2-4 hours | 4-8 hours | 8-12 hours | Over 12 hours | |
| None | 0 | 0 | 0 | 0 | 0 | 0 |
| 0.1 to 1.0 | 1 | 2 | 3 | 4 | 5 | 1 |
| 1.1 to 5.0 | 3 | 4 | 6 | 8 | 11 | 2 |
| 5.1 to 10.0 | 4 | 6 | 9 | 11 | 15 | 3 |
| 10.1 to 20.0 | 5 | 8 | 12 | 16 | 22 | 4 |
| 20.1 to 30.0 | 7 | 10 | 15 | 20 | 29 | 5 |
| 30.1 to 40.0 | 8 | 11 | 17 | 22 | 33 | 6 |
| 40.1 to 50.0 | 9 | 12 | 19 | 24 | 36 | |

### Mixed Loads

Regulations forbid some products to be loaded in the same cargo area—they must be must loaded separately. See table below for examples.

| Do Not Load Table | |
|---|---|
| **Do Not Load** | **In the Same Vehicle With** |
| Division 6.1 or 2.3 (POISON or poison inhalation hazard labeled material) | Animal or human food, unless the poison package is packed in an approved way. Foodstuff means anything a person swallows. Mouthwash, toothpaste, and skin creams are not considered foodstuff. |
| Division 2.3 (Poisonous) gas Zone A or Division 6.1 (Poison) liquids, PGI, Zone A | Division 5.1 (Oxidizers). Class 3 (Flammable Liquids). Class 8 (Corrosive Liquids). Division 5.2 (Organic Peroxides). Division 1.1, 1.2, 1.3 (Class A or B) Explosives. Division 1.5 (Blasting Agents). Division 2.1 (Flammable Gases). Class 4 (Flammable Solids). |
| Charged storage batteries | Division 1.1 (Class A Explosives) |
| Class 1 (Detonating primers) | Any other explosives unless in authorized containers or packages. |
| Division 6.1 (Cyanides or cyanide mixtures) | Acids, corrosive materials, or other acidic materials which could release hydrocyanic acid. For example:<br>Cyanides, Inorganic, n.o.s.<br>Silver cyanide<br>Sodium cyanide |
| Nitric acid (Class B) | Other materials unless the nitric acid is not loaded above any other material. |

Other materials that must be separated are listed on the Segregation Table for Hazardous Materials.

## *Bulk Packaging Marking, Loading and Unloading*

Since cargo tanks are bulk packaging permanently affixed to a vehicle, they remain attached during the loading and unloading process. Portable tanks are bulk packaging that is not permanently fastened to a vehicle. Cargo is loaded or unloaded while these tanks are out of the vehicle and then placed on the vehicle for transport. While there are several different types of cargo tanks in use, the most common are MC306 for liquids and MC331 for gases.

### Markings

The identification number of hazardous materials transported in portable tanks, cargo tanks, and other bulk packaging (such as dump trucks) must be clearly visible. As per regulations, black 100 mm (3.9 inch) numbers on orange panels, placards, or a white, diamond-shaped background must be displayed if placards are not required. Specification cargo tanks must be labeled with a re-test date.

Portable tanks must indicate the name of the lessee or owner and the shipping name of the material being transported on two opposite sides. The shipping name must be prominent (a height of at least two inches) on portable tanks with capacities of more than 1,000 gallons and one-inch tall on portable tanks with capacities of less than 1,000 gallons. The identification number must be listed on each side and each end of a portable tank or other bulk packaging carrying 1,000 gallons or more and on two opposite sides, if the portable tank is hauling less than 1,000 gallons. The identification numbers need to be in clear view when the portable tank is loaded on the CMV. If they are not clearly seen, you will need to show the identification number on both sides and ends of the motor vehicle.

Intermediate bulk containers (IBCs) are bulk packages that do not require the shipping name or owner.

## Tank Loading

The individual responsible for loading and unloading a cargo tank must make sure a qualified person is present and paying attention to the loading/unloading process. This person must:

- Be alert.
- Have clear sight of the cargo tank.
- Be within 25 feet of the tank.
- Be aware of the cargo hazards.
- Know emergency procedures.
- Be sanctioned and able to move the cargo tank if needed

Cargo tanks carrying propane and anhydrous ammonia have special requirements for those who must be present.

In order to prevent leaks, all manholes and valves must be shut before driving a tank containing hazardous materials, regardless of the amount or distance involved. As per 49 CFR 173.29, driving a cargo tank with open valves or covers is against the law unless it is empty.

## Flammable Liquids

Make sure to turn your engine off before loading or unloading any flammable liquids. The engine should be running only if necessary to operate a pump. Ground a cargo tank properly before opening and filling it with the flammable liquid. Make sure the ground is maintained until the filling hole is closed.

## Compressed Gas

Other than during loading and unloading, liquid discharge valves on a compressed gas tank should be closed. Turn off the engine during loading and unloading unless your engine requires a pump for product transfer. If the engine is required, shut it off after product transfer, before you remove the hose. Unfasten all loading/unloading connections prior to coupling, uncoupling, or moving a cargo tank. Make sure trailers and semi-trailers are chocked to prevent movement when unfastened from the power unit.

# *Hazardous Materials—Driving and Parking Rules*

## Parking with Division 1.1, 1.2, or 1.3 Explosives

If you are carrying Division 1.1, 1.2, or 1.3 explosives, never park within five feet of the part of the road used by traffic. Other than necessary vehicle operations (e.g., fueling), do not park within 300 feet of:

- A bridge, tunnel, or building.
- A place where people meet.
- An open fire.

If you need to park because of job responsibilities, make it brief. Don't park on private property unless you make sure the owner knows the risks. Make sure an individual is always supervising the parked vehicle. You may allow another person to look out for your vehicle only if it is:

- On the shipper's property.
- On the carrier's property.
- On the consignee's property

An approved place for parking unattended vehicles containing explosives is called a safe haven. Local authorities typically authorize them.

## Parking a Placarded Vehicle Not Transporting Division 1.1, 1.2, or 1.3 Explosives

You are allowed to park a placarded vehicle (not carrying explosives) within five feet of the trafficked part of the road only if required by your job responsibilities, and only for short amounts of time. You must have someone watch over the vehicle when stopped on a public road or shoulder. Do not unhook a trailer with hazardous materials on a public street and then walk away or park within 300 feet of an open fire.

## Attending Parked Vehicles

The person attending a placarded vehicle must:

- Be inside the vehicle, not sleeping, and not inside the sleeper berth, or within 100 feet of the vehicle and have it clearly within their sight.
- Know the danger level of the materials being transported.
- Be aware of proper emergency procedures.
- Be able to move the vehicle, if necessary.

## No Flares!

If your vehicle breaks down, use reflective triangles or red electric lights to warn other drivers. Make sure never to use burning signals, such as flares or fuses, around a:

- Tank used for Class 3 (Flammable Liquids) or Division 2.1 (Flammable Gas) whether loaded or empty.
- Vehicle loaded with Division 1.1, 1.2, or 1.3 Explosives.

## Route Restrictions

Permits are required to transport hazardous materials or wastes in some states and counties, which may limit your routes in these locations. Since local route and permit regulations often vary, you must determine any deviations and ensure you have the required paperwork prior to starting out.

If you work for a carrier, your dispatcher can convey any route restrictions or permits. If you are an independent trucker and the route is a new one for you, inquire the agencies of the states you will be traveling through before your trip.

Since some areas do not allow hazardous materials to be transported through tunnels, over bridges, or other roadways, it is important to be aware of any restrictions before you start. If the vehicle is placarded, stay clear of heavily populated places, crowded areas, tunnels, narrow streets, and alleys. Even if it is not convenient, choose another route unless that is the only way you can go. Always avoid open fires while driving a placarded vehicle unless you can safely get by without having to stop.

If you are carrying Division 1.1, 1.2, or 1.3 explosives, you must follow a written route plan prepared ahead of time by the carrier. Or, you are allowed to do the route planning if you receive the explosive material at a location separate from your employer's terminal. The plan needs to be formulated ahead of your trip and you need to keep a copy with you while transporting the explosives. When you hand over a shipment of explosive, make sure the person accepting it is authorized or the items are delivered to locked rooms specifically designated for explosives storage.

It is up to the carrier to decide the safest route for transporting placarded radioactive materials. After the route is chosen, the carrier must share details of the radioactive cargo and route plan.

## No Smoking

Make sure you do not smoke within 25 feet of a placarded cargo tank carrying Class 3 (flammable liquids) or Division 2.1 (gases). And do not smoke or carry a lit cigarette, cigar, or pipe within 25 feet of any vehicle, which contains:

- Class 1 (Explosives)
- Class 3 (Flammable Liquids)
- Class 4 (Flammable Solids)
- Class 4.2 (Spontaneously Combustible)

## Refuel with Engine Off

Always turn your engine off before adding fuel to a CMV carrying hazardous materials and make sure someone is standing near the nozzle controlling the flow of fuel.

## 10 B:C Fire Extinguisher

A fire extinguisher with a UL rating of 10 B:C or more must be present on the power unit of placarded vehicles.

## Check Tires

Your vehicle's tires must be properly inflated and not flat or leaking in any way. Check each tire prior to every trip and each time you stop to park using a tire pressure gauge. If a tire is leaking or flat, do not drive unless it is necessary to get to a safe place to get it repaired.

If a tire is overheated, remove it and stow it a safe distance from your vehicle. Don't start up again until the cause of the overheating is determined. The regulations regarding parking and attending placarded vehicles are applicable even when checking, repairing, or replacing tires—make sure to obey them.

## Where to Keep Shipping Papers and Emergency Response Information

Never consent to a hazardous material shipment that does not have a correctly prepared, easily recognizable shipping paper. When you are transporting hazardous materials, it is important for others to be able to quickly locate the shipping paper following a crash. In order to make them easily identifiable from other papers, attach tabs or some other feature or store them on top of the other papers.

Store the shipping papers within reach (without having to remove your seat belt) or in a pouch on the driver's side door while you are driving so they can be located quickly and easily.

When you are not driving, stow shipping papers in the driver's door pouch or on the seat. Make sure emergency response information is stored with the shipping paper.

### Papers for Division 1.1, 1.2 or, 1.3 Explosives

Each driver transporting Division 1.1, 1.2, or 1.3 explosives must obtain the following from their carrier: (1) a copy of Federal Motor Carrier Safety Regulations (FMCSR), Part 397, and (2) written directions about what to do if they are delayed or in an accident. The written instructions should include:

- A contact list of names and phone numbers (including carrier agents or shippers).
- The type of explosives being transported.
- Emergency instructions in case of fires, accidents, or leaks.

Drivers need to sign a receipt for these documents and make sure they have the proper:

- Shipping papers.
- Emergency instructions.
- A written route plan.
- A copy of FMCSR, Part 397

## Equipment for Chlorine

If you are carrying chlorine, the vehicle must have an approved gas mask and an emergency kit on the cargo tank designed to control any leaks in dome cover plate fittings.

### Stop Before Railroad Crossings

You are required to stop at a railroad-crossing if your vehicle:

- Is placarded.
- Is transporting any amount of chlorine.
- Has hazardous material cargo tanks, either loaded or empty.

Make sure you stop fifteen to fifty feet prior to the nearest rail. Drive forward only when you are positive a train is not coming and you can cross the tracks without stopping. Do not shift gears while driving across the tracks.

## *Hazardous Materials: Emergencies*

### Emergency Response Guidebook (ERG)

It is imperative that your shipping papers contain the proper shipping name, identification number, label, and placards of the material(s) you are transporting.

Firefighters, police, and industry personnel use a reference book published by The Department of Transportation that outlines how to use protective measures for hazardous materials. In case of an accident, emergency workers will check the item(s) on the shipping paper against those listed in this guidebook, which is indexed by shipping name and hazardous material identification number.

### Crashes/Incidents

If there's an issue or accident involving your vehicle, your job as a professional driver is to:

- Direct people away from the scene.
- Control the hazardous material if you can do so safely.
- Make first responders aware of the risks of the hazardous cargo.
- Share the shipping papers and emergency response information with emergency personnel.

Follow this checklist:

- Make sure your driving partner is not injured.
- Have the shipping papers with you.
- Make sure people stay away and upwind from the accident.
- Alert others of the cargo's danger.
- Telephone for help.
- Heed the directions of your employer.

### Fires

Although you might have experience dealing with minor truck fires, do not attempt to put out a fire involving hazardous materials unless you have the skill and correct equipment. Specialized training and protective gear is required to fight a hazardous materials fire.

As soon as you notice a fire, telephone for assistance. If it is a minor truck fire, use the fire extinguisher to keep the fire from spreading to the cargo area before firefighters arrive. Before attempting to open the trailer doors, feel the outside to check if it is hot. If so, do not open the doors, as there could be a fire in the cargo area. Opening the door could allow the air to feed the fire—less damage will occur if you keep the doors shut and allow the fire to smolder until firefighters arrive. If the hazardous material is already on fire, you should not attempt to fight it. Keep the shipping papers with you and show them to first responders as soon as they arrive. Make sure to direct others away from the fire and warn them of the risky material.

If you notice a leak in your cargo, use the shipping papers, labels, or package location to help determine the hazardous materials. Use caution when attempting to identify the hazardous material—don't touch any item that is leaking or try to pinpoint the material or source of the leak by its scent. Hazardous materials are very dangerous and could cause injury or cause you to loose your sense of smell even if you can't detect any aroma. Make sure you do not eat, drink, or smoke around a hazardous material leak or spill.

If hazardous materials are leaking out of your vehicle, do not attempt to drive it any further than required, without endangering yourself or other people. Move the vehicle away from the road and any crowded locations, if needed for safety.

If your vehicle is leaking hazardous materials, don't keep driving to try to get help or locate a phone booth or truck stop. Not only is the spillage of hazardous material very dangerous to the environment and other people, but it is also very costly to clean up, a sizable path of contamination. If you notice hazardous materials leaking from your vehicle:

- Park it immediately.
- Secure the area around the vehicle.
- Remain nearby.
- Ask someone else to get help.

When sending someone for help, give that person:

- A description of the incident.
- Your precise location and direction you are travelling.
- Your name, the name of the carrier, and the name of your terminal's location.
- The correct shipping name, hazard class, and identification number of the hazardous materials you are transporting, if you know what they are.

Since this is a good deal of information for someone to relay, it is best to put all the necessary points in writing when you send them to get help. This will help emergency personnel optimally address the situation since they may be a distance away. If they are aware of hazard they are facing, they can bring the correct equipment to deal with it, without having to go back for it.

Make sure you do not operate your vehicle if moving—it could cause contamination, damage or injury. Remain upwind and out of the way of places where people gather, such as rest stops, restaurants, and businesses. Do not attempt to repack a package that is leaking, unless you have the training and equipment to safely repair leaks. Instead, contact your dispatcher or supervisor for directions and any emergency personnel if necessary.

## Responses to Specific Hazards

### Class 1 (Explosives)

If you are transporting explosive materials and your vehicle breaks down or gets into an accident, make sure to warn others nearby and keep people out of the way. Do not let anyone smoke or have any kind of fire near the vehicle. If the material is on fire, warn others of the risk of explosion. If your vehicle has collided with one or more other vehicles, make sure to separate all explosives and place them at least 200 feet from the vehicles and occupied buildings. Make sure you stay a safe distance away from them.

### Class 2 (Compressed Gases)

If you discover compressed gas leaking from your vehicle, make sure to warn others of the danger and only allow emergency personnel authorized to remove the hazard or debris to get close. Any time an incident involves compressed gas, you must let the shipper know.

If you are on a public road, do not transfer flammable compressed gas unless you are filling machinery designed for road construction or maintenance.

### Class 3 (Flammable Liquids)

If you have an accident or vehicle breakdown while carrying a flammable liquid, warn others of the dangerous material, make sure they refrain from smoking, and stay away from the scene. Exit the road if you can safely do so—never drive a cargo tank that is leaking further than absolutely necessary in order to find a safe spot. Except in the case of an emergency, don't transfer flammable liquid between vehicles while on a public road.

### Class 4 (Flammable Solids) and Class 5 (Oxidizing Materials)

If you are transporting a flammable solid or oxidizing material that leaks, make sure to warn others of the chance of fire. Do not open any packages of flammable solids that are smoldering or smoking. If you can do so safely, take them out of the vehicle, as well as any that are intact if it will help lessen the fire hazard.

### Class 6 (Poisonous Materials and Infectious Substances)

It is your responsibility to keep yourself and other people and property around you safe. Keep in mind that many items classified as poisonous are also flammable. If you are transporting any Division 2.3 (Poison Gases) or Division 6.1 (Poison Materials) that you think could be flammable, make sure to take the extra safety precautions that are required for flammable liquids or gases. Warn others of the potential hazards that could result by getting too close to the material, including the chance of fire or inhaling vapors, and make sure nobody smokes, has an open flame, or does any welding nearby.

If a vehicle leaks a Division 2.3 (Poison Gases) or Division 6.1 (Poisons) material, it needs to be checked for any traces of poison before being cleared for use.

Get in touch with your supervisor immediately if you see a Division 6.2 (Infectious Substances) package that shows signs of damage or leaking—you should not accept these.

### Class 7 (Radioactive Materials)

Notify your dispatcher or supervisor immediately if you notice any radioactive material that is leaking or damaged. Stay a distance away—refrain from touching or breathing in the material, and do not operate the vehicle until it can be thoroughly cleaned and scanned by a radiation detection meter.

### Class 8 (Corrosive Materials)

If you notice a leak or spill involving corrosive materials during transport, use extra caution when moving the containers in order to prevent further damage or incident. If any sections of the vehicle have come in contact with a corrosive liquid, they must be completely flushed with water. After you remove all the items, make sure to clean out the inside right away prior to reloading.

Since driving a vehicle with a leaking tank is unsafe, make sure to exit the road as soon as possible and try to prevent any additional leaks if you can do so safely. Stop others from coming near the material and fumes and make sure you do all you can to avoid getting hurt and injury to others.

## Required Notification

The National Response Center is in charge of coordinating emergency response to chemical hazards, including notifying the proper police and firefighter personnel to help. Either you or your employer are required to call their 24-hour toll-free line (listed below) in the event any of the following occurs as a direct result of a hazardous materials incident:

- A death.
- An injured person needs to go to the hospital.
- Property damage estimates are greater than $50,000.
- The general public needs to evacuate an area for more than one hour.
- A major transportation artery or facility is closed for at least an hour.
- There is an incident involving fire, damage, spillage, or suspected radioactive contamination.
- There is an incident involving fire, damage, spillage or suspected contamination of etiologic agents (bacteria or toxins).
- A hazardous material causes an incident that the carrier feels should be reported (e.g., continuing danger to life)

### National Response Center (800) 424-8802

When you or someone else needs to contact the National Response Center, be prepared to disclose:

- Your name.
- The name and address of the carrier.
- The phone number where you or the person calling can be reached.
- The date, time, and location of the incident.
- Any injuries and the severity.
- The class, name, and quantity of hazardous materials involved, if you have access to this information.
- The nature of the incident and hazardous materials involved and whether or not danger to life continues to exist at the scene.

If the hazardous substance is enough to be reportable, the caller must relay the shipper's name and the amount of the hazardous substance that was involved. Your employer will also need this information since carriers are required to file comprehensive written reports within thirty days of an incident.

### CHEMTREC (800) 424-9300

A 24-hour toll-free line is also available via the Chemical Transportation Emergency Center (CHEMTREC) in Washington, D.C., an agency established to supply technical information about the physical properties of hazardous materials to emergency personnel. CHEMTEC and The National Response Center are in close contact with each other. If you get in touch with one, they will communication the issue to the other agency when necessary.

Do not keep packages labeled radioactive yellow-II or yellow-III around people, animals, or film longer than shown in the following diagram:

| Radioactive Separation Table A | | | | | | |
|---|---|---|---|---|---|---|
| **Total Index/Transport** | **Minimum distance in feet to nearest undeveloped film** | | | | | **To People or Cargo Compartment Partitions** |
| | 0-2 hours | 2-4 hours | 4-8 hours | 8-12 hours | Over 12 hours | |
| None | 0 | 0 | 0 | 0 | 0 | 0 |
| 0.1 to 1.0 | 1 | 2 | 3 | 4 | 5 | 1 |
| 1.1 to 5.0 | 3 | 4 | 6 | 8 | 11 | 2 |
| 5.1 to 10.0 | 4 | 6 | 9 | 11 | 15 | 3 |
| 10.1 to 20.0 | 5 | 8 | 12 | 16 | 22 | 4 |
| 20.1 to 30.0 | 7 | 10 | 15 | 20 | 29 | 5 |
| 30.1 to 40.0 | 8 | 11 | 17 | 22 | 33 | 6 |
| 40.1 to 50.0 | 9 | 12 | 19 | 24 | 36 | |

## Classes of Hazardous Materials

Hazardous materials are divided into nine main hazard classifications, as well as two additional categories for consumer commodities and combustible liquids. These are listed in the table below:

| Hazard Class Definitions | | |
|---|---|---|
| **Class** | **Class Name** | **Example** |
| 1 | Explosives | Ammunition, dynamite, fireworks |
| 2 | Gases | Propane, oxygen, helium |
| 3 | Flammable | Gasoline, fuel, acetone |
| 4 | Flammable solids | Matches, fuses |
| 5 | Oxidizers | Ammonium nitrate, hydrogen peroxide |
| 6 | Poisons | Pesticides, arsenic |
| 7 | Radioactive | Uranium, plutonium |
| 8 | Corrosives | Hydrochloric acid, battery acid |
| 9 | Miscellaneous Hazardous Materials | Formaldehyde, asbestos |
| None | ORM-D (other regulated material-domestic) | Hairspray or charcoal |
| None | Combustible liquids | Fuel oils, lighter fluid |

# *Hazardous Materials Glossary*

This glossary serves as a reference for the various definitions of terms used in this section. Please note that a comprehensive glossary is featured in the federal Hazardous Materials Rules (49 CFR 171.8). Make sure you have a current copy of this guide.

Note: This glossary is for reference purposes only; you will not be tested on it.

## Sec. 171.8 Definitions and Abbreviations

### Bulk Packaging

Packaging (except a vessel or barge) including a transport vehicle or freight container that contains hazardous materials not contained by any other means and also has:

- A maximum capacity greater than 450 L (119 gallons) to hold a liquid;
- A maximum net mass greater than 400 kg (882 pounds) or a maximum capacity greater than 450 L (119 gallons) to hold a solid; or
- A water capacity greater than 454 kg (1000 pounds) to hold a gas as defined in Sec. 173.115.

Cargo Tank: Bulk packaging that is:

- A tank meant to transport liquids or gases and includes accessories, reinforcements, fittings, and closures (for "tank", see 49 CFR 178.345-1(c), 178.337-1, or 178.338-1, as applicable);
- Permanently affixed to or part of a motor vehicle, or is loaded or unloaded without being detached from the vehicle due to its size, structure, or the way it is attached and;
- Not manufactured using the specs for cylinders, portable tanks, tank cars, or multi-unit tank car tanks.

Carrier: A person who transports passengers or products by:

- Land or water as a common, contract, or private carrier, or
- Civil aircraft

Consignee: The entity that receives the shipment (can be a business or individual)

Division: A hazard classification subdivision

EPA: U.S. Environmental Protection Agency

FMCSR: The Federal Motor Carrier Safety Regulations

Freight Container: A reusable vessel with a capacity of at least 64 cubic feet that can be shipped with its contents intact and is mainly designed to contain packages (in unit form) during transport.

Fuel Tank: A tank, (except a cargo tank), used to ship flammable or combustible liquid or compressed gas in order to provide fuel for the transport vehicle it is loaded on, or to operate other components of the vehicle

Gross Weight or Gross Mass: The weight of the packaging combined with the weight of the material inside

Hazard Class: The hazard category allocated to a hazardous material as per the Part 173 descriptive standards and the specifications outlined in the Sec. 172.101 Table. Even though an item may fall under more than one hazard category, it is only is assigned to one hazard classification.

Hazardous Materials: A substance or material that the Secretary of Transportation has classified as an extreme risk to health, safety, and property when shipped for business purposes. This includes hazardous substances, wastes, marine pollutants, high temperature materials, materials categorized as hazardous under the hazardous materials table of §172.101, and materials that meet the classification for hazard classes and divisions under §173, subchapter c of this section.

Hazardous Substance: A hazardous material, including any corresponding mixtures and solutions, that:

- Is listed in Appendix A to Sec. 172.101;
- Is an amount within one container that is greater than or equal to the reportable quantity (RQ) listed in Appendix A to Sec. 172.101; and
- When as part of a mixture or solution:
- For radionuclides, conforms to paragraph 7 of Appendix A to Sec. 172.101.
- Is in a weight concentration that is equal to or greater than the amount that corresponds to the material's RQ. See chart below for reference.

| **Hazardous Substance Concentrations** | | |
|---|---|---|
| **RQ Pounds (Kilograms)** | **Concentration by Weight** | |
| | **Percent** | **PPM** |
| 5,000 (2,270) | 10 | 100,000 |
| 1,000 (45) | 2 | 20,000 |
| 100 (45.4) | .2 | 2,000 |
| 10 (4.54) | .02 | 200 |
| 1 (0.454) | .002 | 20 |

This definition is not applicable to petroleum based lubricants or fuels (see 40 CFR 300.6).

Hazardous Waste: In reference to this section, hazardous waste is defined as any material subject to the Hazardous Waste Manifest Requirements of the U.S. Environmental Protection Agency specified in 40 CFR Part 262.

Intermediate Bulk container (IBC): Portable packaging (except a cylinder or portable tank), that is used for mechanical handling. It can be made from either rigid or flexible material. The standards for IBCs manufactured in the United States are listed in subparts N and O §178.

Limited Quantity: The maximum amount of a hazardous material for which there may be a specific exclusion regarding its labeling or packaging.

Marking: The information used on hazardous materials packaging to indicate the danger level of the material. Includes the descriptive name, identification number, instructions, cautions, weight, specification, and/or UN marks.

Mixture: A hazardous material that contains more than one chemical compound or element.

Name of Contents: The material's proper shipping name as outlined in Sec. 172.101.

Non-Bulk Packaging: Packaging with:

- A container for liquids with a maximum capacity of 450 L (119 gallons);
- A container for solids with maximum net mass of less than 400 kg (882 pounds) and a maximum capacity of 450 L (119 gallons) or less; or
- A container for a gas as defined in Sec. 173.115 with a water capacity greater than 454 kg (1,000 pounds) or less.

N.O.S.: Not otherwise specified

Outage or Ullage: The amount (usually expressed in percentage by volume) that a package falls short of being full of liquid

Portable Tank: Bulk packaging (other than a cylinder with a water capacity of 1,000 pounds or less) meant to be loaded onto or temporarily affixed to a vehicle or ship that is equipped with skids, mountings, or accessories in order to mechanically ease the tank handling. This does not include cargo tanks, tank cars, multi-unit tank car tanks, or trailers carrying 3AX, 3AAX, or 3T cylinders.

Proper Shipping Name: The name of the hazardous materials listed with Roman numerals (not italics) in Sec. 172.101

P.s.i. or psi: Pounds per square inch

P.s.i.a. or psia: Pounds per square inch absolute

Reportable Quantity (RQ): The amount listed in Column 2 of the Appendix to Sec. 172.101 for any material specified in Column 1 of the Appendix

RSPA: Now PHMSA—The Pipeline and Hazardous Materials Safety Administration, U.S. Department of Transportation, Washington, DC 20590

Shipper's Certification: A statement on the shipping paper signed by the person who shipped the goods, certifying that he or she correctly prepared the shipment as per legal regulations. For example:

- "This is to certify that the materials listed above are classified, described, packaged, marked and labeled correctly, and are suitable for transport as per the pertinent rules or the Department of Transportation." or
- "I hereby declare that the contents of this shipment are completely and properly described according to the accurate shipping name, are classified, packaged, marked and

labeled/placarded, and are in proper order for transport by * as per appropriate international and national government law."

* Signifies the type of transport (rail, aircraft, motor vehicle, vessel)

# School Buses

Since state and local laws and regulations regulate so many aspects of school transportation and the operation of school bus equipment, much of the information discussed in this section varies from state to state. You will need to be well versed in the specific laws and regulations that pertain to your state and local school district.

## *Danger Zones and Use of Mirrors*

### Danger Zones

The area along the sides of the bus that poses the most danger of impact to children (either via another vehicle or their own bus) is called the danger zone. These zones may reach as far as thirty feet from the front bumper. The first ten feet are considered most dangerous—ten feet from each side and ten feet behind the back bumper. The region to the left of the bus is also deemed dangerous due to the possibility of passing cars. These danger zones are referenced in the diagram below.

**The Danger Zones**

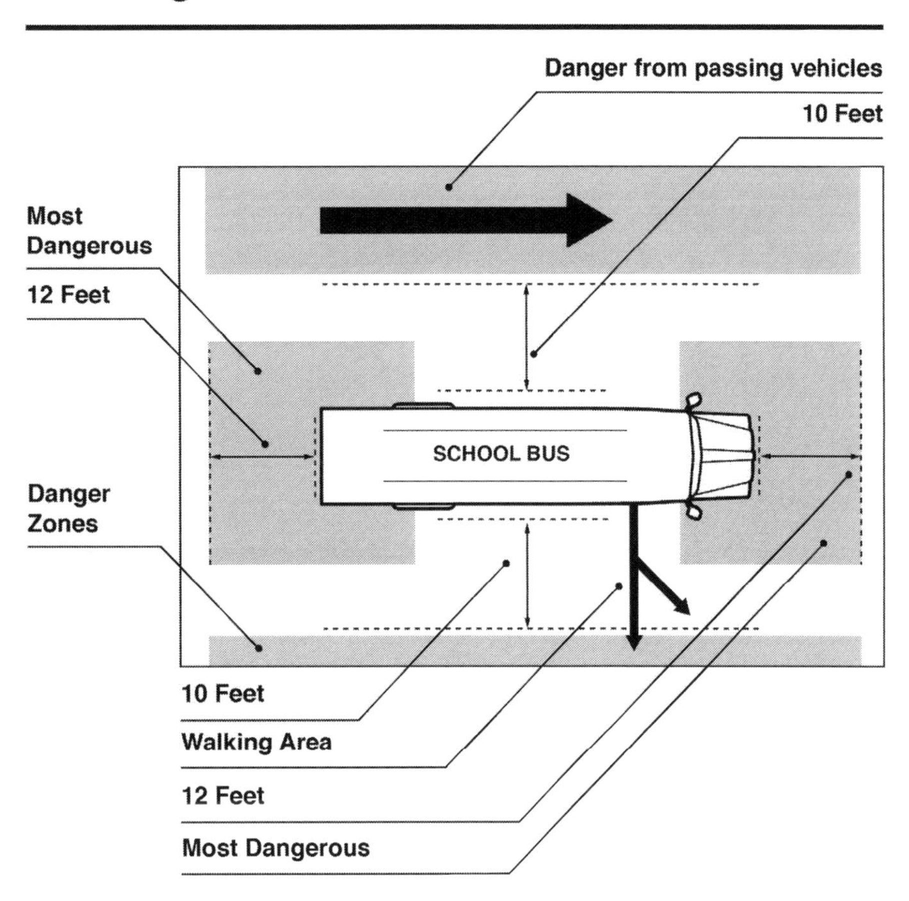

## Correct Mirror Adjustment

In order to safely operate a school bus, you must be able to identify the danger zone around the bus and check for students, traffic, and other hazards. Adjusting and using mirrors correctly is imperative. Always check and adjust each mirror so you have the best possible view.

## Outside Left and Right Side Flat Mirrors

The mirrors located at the left and right front corners of the bus near the side or front of the windshield are used to monitor traffic, check clearances, and watch for students on each side and to the back of the bus. It is important to note that a blind spot is located directly below and in front of each mirror and behind the rear bumper. The blind spot in back of the bus is typically a distance of 50 to 150 feet, but it can extend up to 400 feet depending on the length and width of the bus. Make sure your mirrors are adjusted so you can see:

- 200 feet or four bus lengths in back of the bus.
- Along each side.
- Where the rear tires touch the ground.

The diagram below outlines the method for adjusting the outside left and right side flat mirrors.

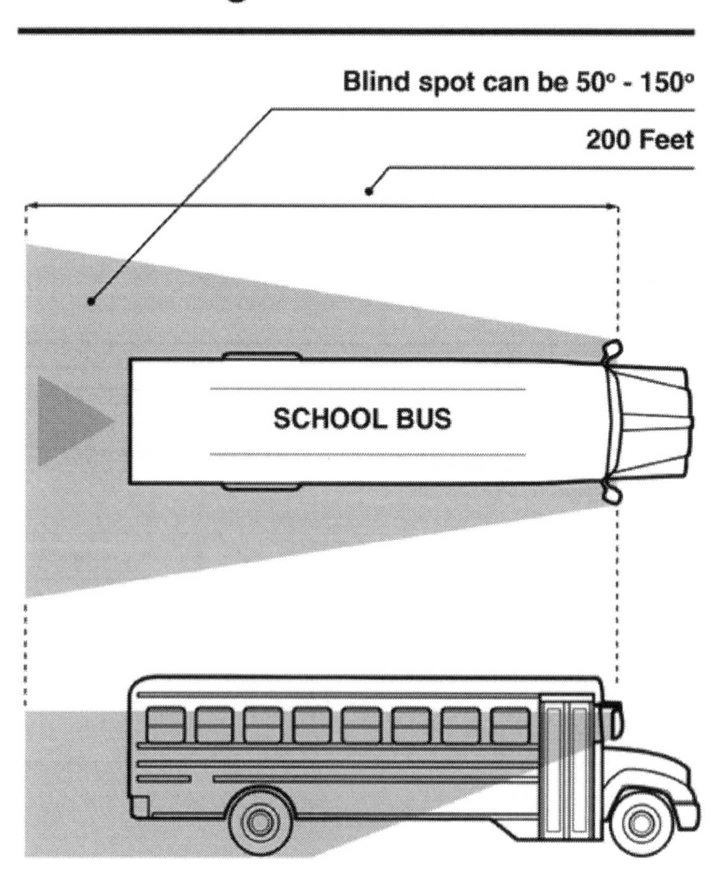

## Outside Left and Right Side Convex Mirrors

The convex mirrors are situated underneath the outside flat mirrors. Designed to show a wide-angle view, they allow the driver to see traffic, clearances, and students on the sides of the bus. However, keep in mind that the image shown by these mirrors is not an accurate reflection of the size and distance from the bus that people and objects appear.

These mirrors should be adjusted to view:

- The whole side of the bus up to the mirror mounts.
- Where the front of the rear tires touch the ground.
- At least one traffic lane on either side of the bus.

The diagram below shows the proper method for adjusting the outside left and right side convex mirrors.

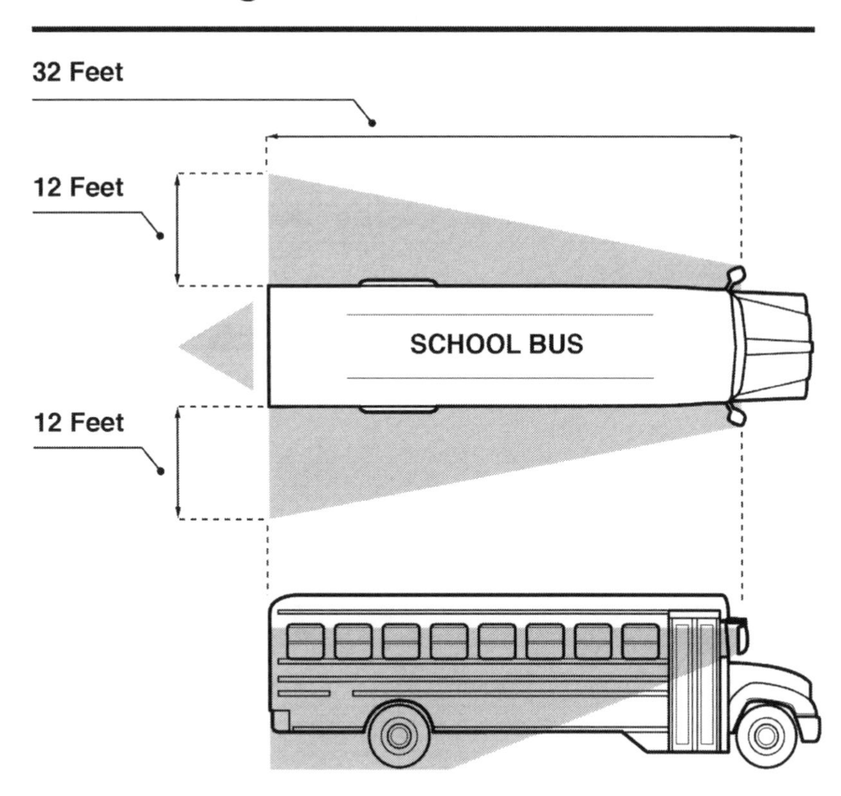


## Outside Left and Right Side Crossover Mirrors

Located at the left and right front corners of the bus, these crossover mirrors are designed to help the driver see the front bumper "danger zone" immediately in front of the bus that is not in direct view, and to see the "danger zone" area on the sides of the bus, including the service door and front wheel area.

Just as with the convex mirrors, keep in mind that the image shown by the crossover mirrors is not an accurate reflection of the size and distance from the bus that people and objects appear.

Make sure these mirrors are adjusted correctly so you can view:

- The area directly in front of the bus ranging from the bottom front bumper to an area where it is possible to see clearly. There should be an overlap between direct and mirror view vision.
- Where the right and left front tires touch the ground.
- The area from the front of the bus to the service door.

Scan these mirrors, along with the convex and flat mirrors, in order to make sure a child or object is not located in any of the danger zones. The diagram below shows the techniques for adjusting the left and right side crossover mirrors.

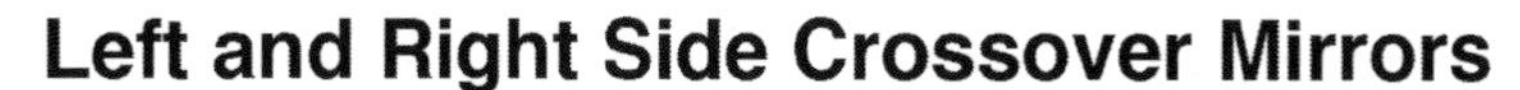


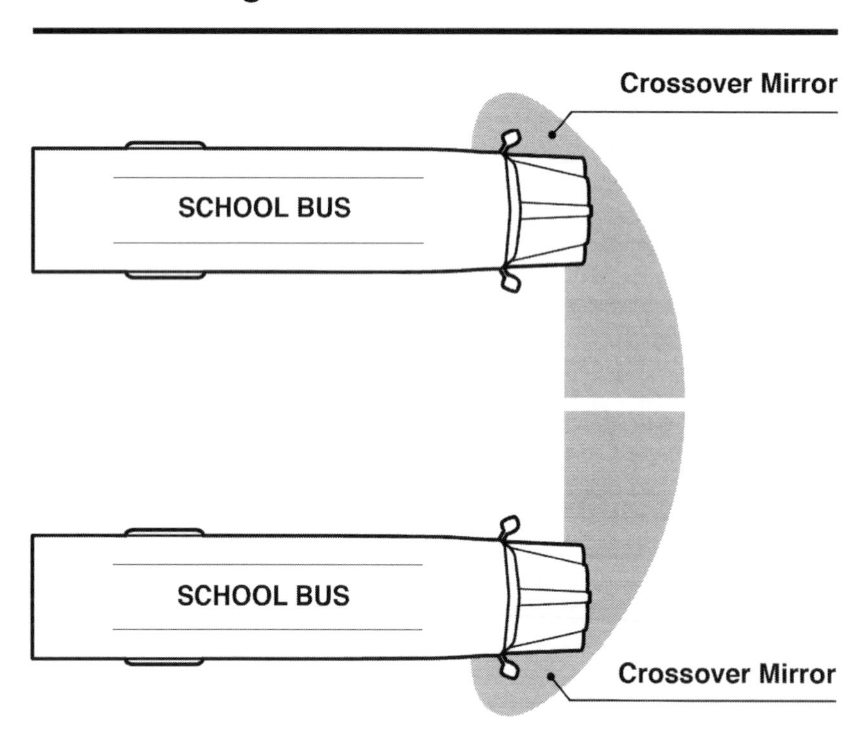


## Overhead Inside Rearview Mirror

Located right above the windshield on the driver's side of the bus, the overhead inside rearview mirror helps the driver check the movement of passengers inside the bus. If the bus has a glass-bottomed rear emergency door, this mirror may offer a limited view in the back of the bus. In addition, keep in mind that blind spots are located right behind the driver's seat in the region starting with the rear bumper and up to 400 feet or more in back of the bus. In order to scan traffic in these zones, use the exterior side mirrors.

You should adjust the mirror so you can view:

- The top of the rear window in the area at the top of the mirror.
- All the students, including those sitting in the seats right behind you.

# *Loading and Unloading*

Since more students are killed or injured while entering or exiting a school bus than while riding as passengers, it is imperative to be thoroughly familiar with the procedure for loading and unloading students. The following paragraphs outline the safety processes to prevent injuries and fatalities during and after loading and unloading students.

This material is not meant to be an absolute set of directions, but rather it is designed offer a broad overview. It is very important to know and follow the state laws and regulations regarding loading/unloading operations in your area.

## Approaching the Stop

Official bus routes and school bus stops are determined by each school district and therefore require approval before stopping at any location. Never deviate from the official route or stops without written approval from the sanctioned school district administrator.

The safety of the students is critical—use extreme caution when approaching a school bus stop. It is imperative that you thoroughly know and observe all state and local laws and regulations, including the correct operation of mirrors, alternating flashing lights, and the moveable stop signal and crossing control arm if the bus is so equipped.

When approaching the stop, you should:

- Enter the area slowly and carefully.
- Scan the area for pedestrians, traffic, or other objects before, during, and after stopping.
- Constantly check all mirrors.
- If the bus has them, turn on the alternating flashing amber warning lights at least 200 feet or five to ten seconds before the school bus stop or as per state regulations.
- Activate the right turn signal about 100 to 300 feet or approximately three to five seconds before pulling over to the stop.
- Scan mirrors regularly in order to check danger zones for students, traffic, and other items.
- Pull the bus over as far to the right as you can away from the traveled portion of the road or street.

When stopping you should:

- Make sure the school bus comes to a complete stop, with the front bumper at a distance of at least ten feet from students waiting at the assigned stop. As a result, the students will need to walk toward the bus to enter, providing a clearer view of their actions.

- At each stop, make sure the transmission in is Park. If the bus is not equipped with a Park function, put the bus in Neutral and engage the parking brake.
- Turn on the alternating red lights when traffic is a safe distance away from the school bus and the stop arm is activated.
- Make a final scan to make sure all traffic has come to a stop before opening the door to signal students can enter.

## Loading Procedures

Stop safely as described in the section above, constantly scanning all mirrors. At each stop, you should see the students waiting in the assigned area facing the bus as you approach. Allow them to board once you give the signal. Make sure you do a headcount of the students waiting at the bus stop so you can check that they all get on board.

If you can, memorize the names of the students at each stop—if you notice one is missing, ask the other students if they know where they are. Check all mirrors and make sure you don't see anyone running to try to catch the bus. If you feel one of the students is missing, stop the bus, take the key, and check outside, around, and under the bus.

Ensure that the students get on board slowly, in single file, and utilize the handrail. If it is dark outside, make sure the dome light is on. Before driving to the next stop, make sure the students have located seats and are sitting in a forward facing position.

When all students are accounted for, get ready to proceed by:

- Shutting the door.
- Engaging the transmission.
- Releasing the parking brake.
- Turning the alternating flashing red lights off.
- Turning on left turn signal.
- Checking all the mirrors one more time.
- Allowing any traffic to clear out of your path.

When it is safe, pull ahead and into the flow of traffic to continue to the next stop. The same basic loading procedure should be followed whenever students are getting on the bus, barring for a few exceptions.

When students are getting on the bus at school, you should:

- Make sure the ignition is off.
- Take the key if you need to exit the bus.
- Oversee the students getting on the bus as per your state or local regulations or recommendations.

## Unloading Procedures on the Route

Stop safely as described in the section above, constantly scanning all mirrors. Make sure the students stay in their seats until you give the signal to exit. Do a headcount of the students getting off to make sure it matches up with the location of the stop before proceeding to the next one. When exiting, instruct students to move at least ten feet away from the side of the bus so you can clearly see all of them.

Do another mirror check, making sure all students are a safe distance away from the bus. If you do not see one of the students who got off at the stop, make sure the bus is stopped and parked and check all around the sides and under the bus.

When all students are accounted for, prepare to leave by:

- Shutting the door.
- Engaging the transmission.
- Releasing the parking brake.
- Turning the alternating flashing red lights off.
- Turning on left turn signal.
- Checking all the mirrors one more time.
- Allowing any traffic to clear out of your path.

When it is safe, pull ahead and into the flow of traffic to continue to the next stop.

Note: Do not back up if you drive past a student's stop. Instead, make sure to follow local procedures.

## Additional Procedures for Students That Must Cross the Roadway

You will need to know the proper procedures students should follow when getting off the school bus and crossing in front of it, bearing in mind they may not always heed the directions correctly.

When crossing the road, a student or group of students should do the following:

- Walk about ten feet away from the side of the school bus to a location where you can spot them.
- Walk at least ten feet in front of the right corner of the bus's bumper, still keeping a distance away from the front of the school bus.
- Stop at the right edge of the road or street. Their feet should be in full view.

When students reach the edge of the road, they should:

- Stop and look both ways, ensuring the path is clear and safe to proceed.
- Check whether or not the red flashing lights on the bus are still flashing.
- Wait to get a signal from you before crossing the road.

After receiving your signal, the students should:

- Keep far enough in front of the school bus when crossing so you can fully see them.
- Pause at the left edge of the bus and once again wait for your signal to continue to cross.
- Scan up and down the road for traffic, making sure it is safe to proceed.
- Cross the road, continuing to check in all directions.

Note: As the school bus driver, you should impose any state or local regulations or recommendations regarding student actions outside the school bus.

## Unloading Procedures at School

When dropping off students at school, keep in mind that state and local laws and regulations often vary from those along the regular school bus route (especially when unloading occurs in the school parking lot or some other place that is not on the travelled road). You will need to fully comprehend and heed these state and local laws and regulations. The procedures listed below are designed to serve as general guidelines to follow.

When unloading students at school, you should:

- Come to a safe stop at the assigned unloading area as described in the above section on "Approaching the Stop."
- Make sure the bus is secure by:
- Turning the ignition switch off.
- Taking the key if you need to exit the driver's seat.
- Direct the students the stay in their seats until it is safe to exit.
- Supervise the students exiting the bus as per state or local requirements or recommendations.
- Make sure students get off the bus in a safe, organized way.
- Check that the students walk away from the unloading region.
- Walk up and down the aisle of the bus to check for hiding/sleeping students and any items left behind.
- Scan all mirrors to make sure there are no students coming back toward the bus.
- If the bus is secure and you cannot account for a student, do a check around and under the bus.

When all students have exited and are accounted for, prepare to drive away by:

- Shutting the door.
- Fastening your safety belt.
- Starting the engine.
- Engaging the transmission.
- Releasing the parking brake.
- Turning the alternating flashing red lights off.
- Turning the left turn signal on.
- Rechecking all the mirrors.
- Waiting until traffic has cleared.

When it is safe to proceed, drive away from the unloading area.

## Special Dangers of Loading and Unloading

### Dropped or Forgotten Objects

Pay attention to students as they near the bus and check for any who suddenly vanish from your view. A student could drop something near the bus during loading or unloading, posing a potential danger if they bend down or go back to pick it up, causing them to disappear from your view.

Students should be instructed not to attempt to pick up a dropped object. Instead, they should move to a safe spot and ask the driver to get the item for them.

### Handrail Hang-Ups

Students have been hurt or killed when an item of clothing, accessories, or even parts of their body get stuck in the handrail or door when getting off the bus. Always carefully account for all students leaving the bus to make sure that they are away from the bus prior to driving away.

## Post-Trip Inspection

You will need to perform a post-trip bus inspection once your route or school activity trip has ended. Walk down the aisle and scan each seat for the following:

- Items left behind by students.
- Sleeping students.
- Open windows or doors.
- Mechanical/operational issues, particularly components specific to school buses, such as mirrors, flashing warning lamps and stop signal arms.
- Damage or vandalism.

Report any problems or special circumstances to your supervisor or school authorities right away.

# *Emergency Exit and Evacuation*

A school bus emergency can occur at any time. This includes an accident, stalling on a railroad-highway crossing or a high-traffic intersection, an electrical fire in the engine area, a medical emergency involving a student, etc. Being aware of how to handle an emergency—before, during and after evacuating the bus—can make all the difference.

## Planning for Emergencies

### Determining Need to Evacuate Bus

Pinpointing the hazard is first and foremost in an emergency situation. If you have enough time, call your dispatcher to relay the issue before deciding to evacuate the school bus. Most of the time, the safety and management of the students is best upheld by retaining them on the bus during an emergency and/or potential danger situation, as long as it does not subject them to any needless hazard(s). Keep in mind that the choice to have the students exit the bus must be done quickly.

When deciding whether or not to evacuate the bus, consider the following circumstances:

- Is there a fire or the potential of fire?
- Do you smell or see leaking fuel?
- Is the bus in the way of other vehicles, increasing the possibility of getting struck?
- Do you see a tornado or rising floodwater?
- Do you see power lines down?
- Would evacuating students put them in harm's way of speeding traffic, extreme weather, or a hazardous environment such as downed power lines?
- If in an accident, would evacuating students intensify fractures and neck and back injuries?
- Is there a hazardous spill in the vicinity? It may be safer for students to stay on the bus and out of the way of this dangerous substance.

### Mandatory Evacuations

The driver must evacuate the bus when:

- The bus is on fire or there is the risk of a fire.
- The bus has stalled or broken down on or near a railroad crossing.
- There is the potential for the bus to shift position, increasing the risk of an accident.
- There is an impending risk of impact.
- There is a hazardous materials spill that requires quick evacuation.

## Evacuation Procedures

### Be Prepared and Plan Ahead

If feasible, ask two responsible, older students to supervise each emergency exit, explaining how to help other students safely exit the bus. Designate another student to take the students to a "safe place" after they have exited the bus. In the event there are no older, responsible students present during an emergency situation, you will need to explain these procedures to all the students, including proper operation of the various emergency exits and the significance of listening to and following directions.

Use these guidelines to help find a safe location:

- It should be at least 100 feet away from the road facing oncoming traffic to help prevent students from being hit by wreckage if another vehicle crashes into the bus.

- If there is a fire on or near the bus, direct students to a place upwind.

- Direct students to a location as far away from railroad tracks as possible and facing the direction of an oncoming train.

- Direct students at least 300 feet upwind of the bus if there is the danger of a hazardous materials spill.

- If you see a tornado directly in the path of the bus and are directed to evacuate, lead students to a nearby ditch or culvert if there is no safe spot in a building. Have them lie face down, with their hands over their head, at enough distance away from the bus so that it can't tip over on top of them. Make sure to keep away from any areas susceptible to flash flooding.

### General Procedures

First decide whether evacuating students is the safest course of action, and if so, the best method to exit the bus:

- Leaving via the front, rear or side doors, or a combination of the three.
- Exiting through the roof or window(s).

Secure the bus by:

- Putting the transmission in Park, or neutral if there is no shift point.
- Engaging the parking brakes.
- Turning the engine off.
- Taking the ignition key.
- Turning on the hazard-warning lights.

If you have the time to do so, alert the dispatch office of your location, circumstances, and the kind of help that is required. Place your telephone or radio (if working) outside the driver's side window so you can use it later. If the radio is not operational, flag down a passing motorist or ask someone nearby to call for assistance. If none of these options are viable, instruct two older, responsible students to go for assistance.

Direct the students to evacuate, assisting where necessary. Make sure you do not attempt to move any student(s) who have a potential neck or spinal injury unless their life is in immediate danger; neck and spinal injuries require special evacuation methods to avoid further harm.

Ask a mature student to direct students to a safe location nearby, and then walk up and down the aisle to make sure all students have exited the bus. Leave the bus to join the students, taking any emergency equipment with you. Once off the bus, do a student headcount and check that they are safe.

Protect the area by placing emergency warning devices around the perimeter where essential and have information ready for emergency personnel.

## *Railroad-Highway Crossings*

### Pavement Markings

Pavement markings have the same meaning as the advance warning sign. They are found on two-lane roads and are marked with an "X," the letters "RR" and a no passing indicator. Two-lane roads will also have a no passing zone sign. At some crossings, a white stop line may be painted on the pavement in front of the railroad tracks. While stopped at the crossing, make sure the school bus stays behind this line. See diagram below for reference.

### Recommended Procedures

The laws and regulations regarding the required procedures for school buses at railroad-highway crossings vary by location. You will need to recognize and follow the laws and regulations in your region. In most cases, school buses need to stop at all crossings, making sure it is absolutely safe before crossing the tracks.

Even though a school bus is one of the safest vehicles on the highway, it is imperative to obey all safety procedures at all train crossings. Due to its much larger size and weight, it takes much longer for a train to stop. Trains do not have an emergency escape plan. The steps listed below will help you avoid school bus/train accidents:

- Approaching the Crossing:
- Slow down, (if the bus has a manual transmission, shift down into a lower gear), and test your brakes.
- When you are about 200 feet from the crossing, turn on the hazard lights to alert others of your objectives.
- Look all around the bus perimeter and check to see if there are any vehicles in back of you.
- If possible, keep to the right.
- Think of an escape route in case your brakes fail or there are issues in back of you.
- At the Crossing:
- To ensure that you have the best view of the tracks, make sure when you stop that the bus is not nearer than fifteen feet and no more than fifty feet from the closest rail.
- Put the transmission in Park. If the bus does not have a Park feature, put the bus in Neutral and engage the service or parking brakes.
- Turn off the radio and any other noisy equipment, and make sure the students are quiet.
- Open the service door and driver's window so you can look and listen for an oncoming train.
- Crossing the Track:
- Prior to going forward, scan the crossing signals one more time.
- If it is a multiple-track crossing, make sure you come to a stop in front of the first set of tracks only.
- Once you are positive that there are no trains coming, drive across the tracks until you have totally cleared them.
- When you are driving across the tracks, stay in a low gear and do not try to change gears while crossing.
- If the gate swings down after you have started driving through the crossing, keep going, even if it means breaking through the gate.

## Special Situations

### Bus Stalls or Trapped on Tracks

If your bus happens to stall or gets stuck on the tracks, evacuate all the students to a spot far away from the tracks at an angle facing the train.

### Police Officer at the Crossing

If a police officer is present at the crossing, follow all instructions. If you think the signal is not working correctly, but there is no police officer at the crossing, call your dispatcher to relay the issue and request directions on the best course of action.

### Obstructed View of Tracks

When approaching highway-rail grade crossings, make sure you can see enough in the distance down the tracks in both directions to be completely sure no trains are coming. Use extra caution at passive crossings (those lacking any type of traffic control device). You still need to look and listen all around even at active railroad crossings with signals indicating the tracks are clear to cross.

### Containment or Storage Areas

Be aware of the size of the bus you are driving and the containment area at highway-rail crossings on your route, in addition to any you come across during a school activity trip. If the bus won't fit, do not proceed. If you encounter a crossing where the signal or stop sign is on the opposite side, size up the amount of room and make sure the containment or storage area of the bus is large enough to completely cross the railroad tracks on the other side if you need to stop. To help verify whether the containment or storage area will clear the tracks, add fifteen feet to the span of the school bus.

# *Student Management*

## Don't Deal with On-bus Problems When Loading and Unloading

To make sure students are safely transported to and from school in a timely manner, you need to fully concentrate on your job responsibilities. Keep in mind that you need to focus all your attention during the loading and unloading process, not what is occurring outside the bus. If one or more students are misbehaving, wait until the students getting off the bus have safely exited and walked away, and then pull the bus over to the side of the road if you need to address the issue.

## Handling Serious Problems

To help deal with serious issues, follow the guidelines below:

- Understand and obey the procedures for your district regarding discipline or refusal of students to ride the bus.
- Find a safe location away from the road, such as a parking lot or a driveway where you can stop and park the bus.
- Make sure the bus is safe; if you need to leave your seat, take the ignition key with you.
- Turn around and face the students, addressing the student(s) acting up in a respectful, considerate, yet firm tone. Remind them of the behavior required when riding the bus. Do not exhibit anger, but do make sure they know you are serious.
- Ask a student to move to a seat near you if you think this is necessary.
- Never remove a student from the bus unless it is at school or his or her assigned bus stop. If you feel the behavior is uncontrollable and it is unsafe to drive, call for a school official or the police to come and get the student. When requesting assistance, always make sure to obey the procedures specific to your region.

# Antilock Braking Systems

## Vehicles Required to Have Antilock Braking Systems

The Department of Transportation requires that the following vehicles have antilock braking systems:

- Air brake vehicles, (trucks, buses, trailers and converter dollies) manufactured on or after March 1, 1998.
- Hydraulically braked trucks and buses with a gross vehicle weight rating of 10,000 pounds or greater built on or after March 1, 1999.

Note: Many school buses built before these dates have been voluntarily outfitted with ABS. If the bus you are driving is so equipped, it will have a yellow ABS malfunction lamp on the instrument panel.

## How ABS Helps You

If your vehicle does not have ABS and you need to brake hard on a slippery surface, your wheels can lock up, causing you to lose control, skid, jackknife, or even spin around. ABS is designed to help prevent your wheels from locking up and enable you to remain in control. Even though ABS might not allow you to stop more quickly, it should enable you to avoid an obstacle while braking, and prevent skidding due to over braking.

## Braking with ABS

If your vehicle is equipped with ABS, use your brakes as you normally would:

- Use only enough brake pressure as is required to safely stop and retain control.
- Use the brakes in the same manner, regardless of whether the bus is equipped with ABS. However, if you need to brake quickly, make sure you do not pump the brakes if the bus has ABS.
- As you slow your speed, watch your bus and decrease brake pressure (if it is safe to do so) to maintain control.

## Braking if ABS is Not Working

Your brakes will still work fine even without ABS—drive and brake just as you normally would. A yellow malfunction light on the dash will turn on if something isn't functioning properly. On newer vehicles, the ABS malfunction light will briefly flash when the vehicle is started up. On some older systems, the light might stay on until you reach a speed of five mph. If the light stays lit even after the bulb check, or turns on after you start driving, you may have lost ABS functionality on one or more wheels. It is important to keep in mind that you still have your standard brakes even if the ABS isn't working properly. You can continue to drive, but make sure to get the system checked soon.

## Safety Reminders

Keep the following in mind when driving an ABS equipped vehicle:

- You won't be able to drive faster, follow behind another vehicle more closely, or drive more recklessly.
- You won't be able to avoid power or turning skids—ABS is designed to prevent brake-induced skids or jackknifes, but not those triggered by spinning the drive wheels or taking a turn too fast.
- Don't assume the distance you need to stop will be shorter—ABS will help you retain control of your vehicle, but it doesn't necessarily decrease stopping distance.
- Your maximum stopping power won't be boosted or reduced—ABS is a supplement for your normal brakes, not a substitute.
- The way you typically brake will not be any different—in normal brake conditions, your vehicle will stop as usual. ABS will only be a factor if one of your wheels would have become locked due to braking too much.
- ABS can't take the place of bad brakes or improper brake maintenance.
- Remember: A safe driver is still the best safety feature on your vehicle.
- Remember: Drive in a manner that you will never need to use your ABS.
- Remember: ABS could help to prevent a serious crash if you need to use it.

# *Special Safety Considerations*

## Strobe Lights

Some school buses have white strobe lights mounted to the top of the roof. If your bus has these, use the overhead strobe light when you do not have a clear view of your surroundings—in the front, rear, or next to the school bus. This pertains whether your view is only a little diminished or so impaired that you cannot see anything. No matter the circumstance, make sure you comprehend and follow your state or local regulations regarding the use of these lights.

## Driving in High Winds

Use extra caution driving a school bus when there are strong winds. Since the height of the bus can mimic the sail on a sailboat, wind gusts can cause the bus to tilt sideways, pushing it off the road or even knocking it over if conditions are intense. If you are caught in strong winds:

- Hold the steering wheel with a strong, steady grip.
- Try to predict strong wind gusts.
- Slow down to buffer the wind's influence, or pull over to the side of the road and wait it out.
- Call your dispatcher to get more information on weather conditions and determine next steps.

## Backing

Backing up a school bus is not recommended, as it is risky and increases your chances of an accident. Only attempt to back up the bus when you have no other method to move it, and never do so when students are near the perimeter.

If there's no other way to proceed, and it is absolutely necessary to back the bus, follow these procedures:

- Assign someone to be a lookout in order to alert you to items in your way, persons walking toward the bus, and other vehicles. This person's job does not involve giving instructions on how to back up the bus.
- Silence your passengers.
- Do frequent scans of all mirrors and rear windows.
- Proceed backing slowly and steadily.
- If there is nobody around to serve as a lookout:
- Engage the parking brake.
- Turn the motor off and take the keys with you.
- Walk around the bus to see if you have a clear path.
- If it is necessary to back up at a spot where you pick up students, make sure all the students are on the bus before you start to back up, and keep on the lookout for any late arrivals.
- Make sure all students are safely in their seats before starting to back up.
- If it is necessary to back up at a spot where you pick up students, make sure all the students have exited after you are done backing up.

## Tail Swing

Keep in mind that a school bus can have up to a three-foot tail swing. Before and while performing any turning maneuvers, monitor the tail swing of the bus by carefully checking your mirrors.

# Pre-Trip Vehicle Inspection Test

Prior to operating your vehicle, you will need to demonstrate that it is safe to drive by participating in a pre-trip inspection. This involves walking around the perimeter of the vehicle, pointing out each item to the examiner, and describing what you are inspecting and for what reason. You will NOT have to crawl under the hood or the vehicle.

## *All Vehicles*

Study the vehicle parts listed below that pertain to the type of vehicle you will be using during the CDL skills tests. You must be able to recognize each component and explain to the examiner what you are seeking or checking.

### Engine Compartment (Engine Off)

Check for puddles of liquid on the ground under the engine and any fluid dripping under the engine and transmission. Check the hoses to see if they are in good condition and whether any are leaking.

Oil Level
Point out the location of the dipstick and check to see that it is within the normal range, with the level above the refill marker.

Coolant Level
Check the reservoir sight glass, or (if the engine is not hot), remove the radiator cap and make sure the coolant level is good.

Power Steering Fluid
Point out the location of the power steering fluid dipstick and check to see that it is within the normal range, with the level above the refill marker.

Engine Compartment Belts
Make sure the following belts are snug enough (up to 3/4 inch of play in the center of the belt), and check for any cracks or frays:

- Power steering belt
- Water pump belt
- Alternator belt
- Air compressor belt

Note: If any of the components listed above are not belt driven, you must:

- Explain which part(s) are not belt driven.
- Check that the part(s) are working correctly, are not damaged or leaking, and are firmly mounted.

Safe Start
Push in the clutch, put the gearshift control in neutral (or park, for automatic transmissions). Start up the engine, then slowly release the clutch.

## Cab Check/Engine Start

### Oil Pressure Gauge

Make sure the oil pressure gauge shows increasing or normal oil pressure or that the warning light goes off. If the vehicle is so equipped, the oil temperature gauge should slowly start to increase to the normal operating range.

### Temperature Gauge

Make sure the temperature gauge indicates a rise in temperature to the normal operating range or the temperature light is off.

### Air Gauge

Make sure the air gauge is in proper working order—the air pressure builds to governor cut-out, roughly 120 to 140 psi.

### Ammeter/Voltmeter

Make sure the gauges indicate that the alternator and/or generator is charging or the warning light is off.

### Mirrors and Windshield

Check that the mirrors are clean and correctly positioned from the inside and the windshield is clear with no illegal stickers, damage, or items obstructing your view.

### Emergency Equipment

Make sure the following items are present:

- Spare electrical fuses
- Three red reflective triangles
- Six fusees or three liquid burning flares
- A fire extinguisher that is fully charged and has the correct rating

Note: If the vehicle does not have electrical fuses, make sure to tell the examiner.

### Wipers/Washers

Make sure windshield wiper arms and blades are safely in place and in good working order. If the vehicle has windshield washers, they must be operational.

### Lights/Reflectors/Reflector Tape Condition (Sides & Rear)

Check that the dash indicators work for the corresponding lights:

- Left turn signal
- Right turn signal
- Four-way emergency flashers
- High beam headlight
- Anti-lock Braking System (ABS) indicator

Make sure all external lights and reflective components are clean and working properly. Light and reflector checks incorporate the following:

- Clearance lights (red in the back of the vehicle, amber in other locations)
- Headlights (both high and low beams)
- Taillights
- Back up lights
- Turn signals
- Four-way flashers
- Brake lights
- Red reflectors (in the back of the vehicle) and amber reflectors (in other locations)
- The condition of the reflector tape

Note: Inspection of the brake, turn signal, and four-way flasher lights must be done separately.

## Horn

Make sure the air horn and/or electric horn work.

## Heater/Defroster

Check that the heater and defroster are in good working condition.

## Parking Brake Check

With the parking brake on (trailer brakes released on combination vehicles), test that the parking brake will hold the vehicle by slowly trying to drive forward.

Release the parking brake and engage the trailer parking brake (combination vehicles only). Test the trailer parking brake by slowly trying to drive forward.

## Hydraulic Brake Check

Test the hydraulic brakes by pumping the brake pedal three times, then pressing on it for five seconds. Make sure the brake pedal does not move during these five seconds. If the vehicle has a hydraulic brake reserve (backup) system, make sure the key is off, and then press down on the brake pedal and listen for noise coming from the reserve system electric motor. Ensure that the warning buzzer or light is turned off.

## Air Brake Check (Air Brake Equipped Vehicles Only)

It is very important to properly inspect all three sections of the air brake check—if you do not, you will automatically fail the vehicle inspection test. The test is intended to make sure that your vehicle's safety component(s) is in proper working order when air pressure drops from normal to a low air condition. If there is a hill where the vehicle is parked, use wheel chocks during the air brake check for safety. Although air brake safety devices differ, use the following method to perform the air brake check:

- Bring the air pressure up to governor cutoff (120 – 140 psi), turn off the engine, chock your wheels (if needed), release the parking brake and tractor protection valve (on combination vehicles only), and completely engage the foot brake. Press down on the foot brake for one full minute and make sure the air pressure drops more than three pounds (single vehicle) or four pounds (combination vehicle).

- With the engine still running, turn the electrical power to the "on" or "battery charge" mark. Release the air pressure by quickly pressing and releasing the foot brake. The low air warning indicators (such as the buzzer, light, flag, etc.) should turn on prior to the air pressure falling under 60 psi or the level designated by the manufacturer.

- Keep releasing air pressure—the tractor protection valve and parking brake valve should shut (pop out) when the level reaches about 40 psi on a tractor-trailer combination vehicle (or level specified by the manufacturer). On combination vehicle types and single vehicle types, just the parking brake valve should close (pop out).

#### Service Brake Check
The air or hydraulic service brakes need to be inspected to ensure that the brakes are in proper working order and that the vehicle is not pulling to one side or the other. Slowly move forward at 5 mph, engage the service brake and come to a stop. Make sure the vehicle is not pulling to either side and that it comes to a complete stop when the brake is engaged.

#### Safety Belt
Make sure the seat belt is securely attached, and that it adjusts, latches properly, and there are no rips or frays.

## *External Inspection (All Vehicles)*

### Steering

#### Steering Box/Hoses
The steering box should be firmly attached, and all nuts, bolts, and cotter keys should be in place. Make sure the power steering fluid is not leaking and the power steering hoses do not show any signs of damage.

#### Steering Linkage
Check for cracks and other wear and tear to the connecting links, arms, and rods that extend from the steering box to the wheel. Make sure the joints and sockets are not damaged or coming loose and all nuts, bolts, and cotter keys are in place.

### Suspension

#### Springs/Air/Torque
Check that all leaf and coil springs are in place and none are loose, cracked, or damaged in any way.

If the vehicle has torsion bars, torque arms, or is equipped with some other kind of suspension, make sure they are in good working order and firmly fastened. Check the air ride suspension for any signs of leaking and wear and tear.

#### Mounts
Make sure spring hangers do not show signs of cracks or damage, bushings are in place and undamaged, and bolts, U-bolts and other axle mounting parts are not broken, loose, or missing. (Inspect the mounts at each point where they are fastened to the vehicle frame and axle[s]).

### Shock Absorbers
Check that shock absorbers are in proper working order and no leaks are present.

Note: Make sure you inspect the suspension parts on every axle (both the tractor and trailer, if the vehicle is so equipped).

## Brakes

### Slack Adjustors and Pushrods
Make sure none of the components are broken, loose, or missing. If the vehicle has a manual slack adjustor, the brake pushrod should not budge more than an inch (with the brakes released) when manipulated by hand.

### Brake Chambers
Make sure the brake chambers have no leaks, cracks, or dents and are firmly fastened.

### Brake Hoses/Lines
Check to see that hoses do not show any signs of cracks, wear and tear, leaking hoses, lines, or couplings.

### Drum Brake
Make sure there are no visible cracks, dents, holes, or loose or missing bolts, and the drum brake is not tainted with dirt or oil/grease. Check that the brake linings are not worn dangerously thin.

### Brake Linings
Some types of brake drums have openings where the brake linings are visible from outside the drum. If your vehicle is so equipped, make sure that you can see a portion of the brake lining.

Note: Make sure you inspect the brake parts on every axle (both the tractor and trailer, if the vehicle is so equipped.

## Wheels

### Rims
Make sure rims are not dented or damaged and there are no signs of have welding repairs.

### Tires
Check every tire for the following:

- Tread depth: Needs to be at least 4/32 on steering axle tires and 2/32 on all other tires.
- Tire condition: Make sure the tread wear is consistent on each tire, there are no signs of cuts or other damage to the tread or sidewalls, and the valve caps and stems are not missing, broken, or damaged.
- Tire inflation: Use a tire gauge to make sure the tires are inflated to the correct level.

Note: You will not receive positive marks on the CDL exam if you kick the tires to check to see if the tires are inflated properly.

### Hub Oil Seals/Axle Seals
Make sure there are no leaks coming from the axle or hub oil/grease seals and that the oil level is in the proper range if the wheel has a sight glass.

### Lug Nuts
Make sure none of the lug nuts or boltholes are cracked or distorted, all the lug nuts are in place, and there are no rust trails or shiny threads (an indicator of looseness).

### Spacers or Budd Spacing
If the vehicle has spacers, make sure they are squarely positioned and do not show any signs of damage or rust, with the dual wheels and tires evenly separated.

Note: Be ready to do the same type of check on every axle (both the tractor and trailer, if the vehicle is so equipped).

## Side of Vehicle

### Door(s)/Mirror(s)
Make sure the door(s) and hinges do not show any signs of damage and they open and close correctly from the outside. Make sure the mirror(s) and mirror brackets are clear and without cracks or scratches and are firmly attached with no loose fittings.

### Fuel Tank
Make sure the fuel tank(s) are firmly in place, the cap(s) fit snugly, and you do not see any signs of leaking from the tank(s) or lines.

### Drive Shaft
Check that the drive shaft is not damaged and the couplings are firmly in place without any obstructions.

### Exhaust System
Make sure the exhaust system is undamaged, firmly connected and attached and free of any signs of leaking such as rust or carbon soot.

### Frame
Check for signs of damage such as cracks, broken welds, holes, etc. to the longitudinal frame members, cross members, box, and floor.

## Rear of Vehicle

### Splash Guards
If the vehicle has splashguards or mud flaps, make sure they are undamaged and firmly attached.

### Doors/Ties/Lifts
Make sure all doors and hinges do not display any signs of damage and they are in good working order, including outside latches if the vehicle has them.

Check that all ties, straps, chains, and binders are firmly in place.

If the vehicle has a cargo lift, make sure it is fully retracted and securely fastened and there are no signs of leaks, damage, or missing parts. You must be able to describe the inspection process to the examiner to determine that it is in good working order.

## Tractor/Coupling

### Air/Electric Lines

Make sure air hoses and electrical lines do not show any signs of having been cut, scraped, spliced, or worn (you should not see the steel braid underneath), and listen carefully for any leaking air. Make sure the air and electrical lines are not twisted, pinched, or brushing against tractor components.

### Catwalk/Steps

Make sure the steps to the cab entrance and catwalk (if the vehicle has one) are in good condition, free of obstructions, and firmly attached to tractor frame.

### Mounting Bolts

Make sure all mounting brackets, clamps, bolts, and nuts are in place and securely attached, including the fifth wheel and slide mounting. If the coupling system is a different type (i.e., ball hitch, pintle hook, etc.), make sure all coupling parts and mounting brackets are in place and undamaged.

### Hitch Release Lever

The hitch release lever should be firmly in place.

### Locking Jaws

Check the fifth wheel gap and make sure locking jaws are fully surrounding the kingpin. Other types of coupling systems (i.e., ball hitch, pintle hook, etc.) should be checked to make sure the locking mechanism is working and locked correctly and no components are missing or damaged. If so equipped, the safety cables/chains must be firm and without any kinks and/or excessive slack.

### 5th Wheel Skid Plate

Make sure the 5th wheel skid plate is lubricated correctly, firmly attached to the platform, and all bolts and pins are securely in place.

### Platform (Fifth Wheel)

Make sure the platform structure supporting the fifth wheel skid plate does not show any signs of damage such as cracks or fractures.

### Release Arm (Fifth Wheel)

If the vehicle has a release arm, make sure it is engaged and the safety latch is secure.

### Kingpin/Apron/Gap

Make sure the kingpin and the exposed section of the apron do not show any signs of damage such as bending, cracks, or fractures. Make sure the trailer is flush on the fifth wheel skid plate (you should not see any spaces).

### Locking Pins (Fifth Wheel)

If the vehicle has a fifth wheel, make sure none of the pins in the slide mechanism of the sliding fifth wheel are loose or missing. If it is air powered, check for signs of leaking. Check that the locking pins are properly connected and the fifth wheel is properly situated so the tractor frame can clear the landing gear when turning.

#### Sliding Pintle

Make sure the sliding pintle, nuts, bolts and cotter pin are firmly in place.

#### Tongue or Draw-Bar

Make sure that the tongue/draw-bar does not show any signs of damage such as bending, twisting, fractured welds or stress cracks, and extreme wear and tear.

#### Tongue Storage Area

Make sure the storage area is firm and attached to the tongue, and the cargo in the storage area, such as chains, binders, etc., is securely in place.

## *School Bus Only*

### Emergency Equipment

When inspecting a school bus, check for the following:

- Spare electrical fuses (if the bus is so equipped)
- Three red reflective triangles
- Charged and rated fire extinguisher
- Emergency Kit
- Body Fluid Cleanup Kit

### Lighting Indicators

Besides checking the lighting indicators listed in the previous section, when inspecting a school bus, make sure to check the following lighting indicators (internal panel lights):

- Alternately flashing amber lights, (if so equipped).
- Alternately flashing red lights.
- Strobe light (if so equipped).

### Lights/Reflectors

Besides checking the lights and reflective devices listed in the previous section, when inspecting a school bus, make sure to check the following (external) lights and reflectors:

- Strobe light (if the bus has one).
- Stop arm light (if the bus has one).
- Alternately flashing amber lights (if the bus has one).
- Alternately flashing red lights.

### Student Mirrors

Besides checking the outside mirrors, those driving a school bus also need to inspect the inside and outside mirrors that are used to keep an eye on students. Check for:

- Proper adjustment.
- Any damage to mirrors and mirror brackets and make sure they are firmly attached and no fittings have come loose.
- Cleanliness—make sure mirrors are clear so you can see properly.

### Stop Arm

If the bus has a stop arm, make sure it is firmly attached to the frame and there is no damage or loose fittings.

### Passenger Entry/Lift

Make sure the entrance to the bus is free from damage and that it is in proper working order, including closing securely from the inside. Check that the handrails are firmly attached, the steps are free from any obstructions with no loose or extremely worn treads, and the step light is working, if the bus has one.

If there is a handicap lift, make sure it is fully retracted and firmly locked. Check for any leaks, damage, or missing parts and demonstrate how to inspect the lift to make sure it is working correctly.

### Emergency Exit

Check all emergency exits to make sure they do no show any signs of damage, and are in good working order, including closing completely from the inside. Make sure emergency exit warning devices are working properly.

### Seating

Make sure seat frames are undamaged and securely fastened to the floor, and seat cushions are firmly fastened to the seat frames.

## *Trailer*

### Trailer Front

#### Air/Electrical Connections

Make sure trailer air connectors are firmly closed and undamaged. Check that the glad hands are securely fastened and show no signs of damage or air leaks. Ensure that the trailer electrical plug is secured and tightly locked in place.

#### Header Board

If the vehicle has a header board, make sure it is firmly in place, undamaged, and sturdy enough to properly stow cargo. If there is a canvas or tarp carrier, check that it is firmly attached. If the vehicle has an enclosed trailer, inspect the front section for any damage such as cracks, warps, or holes.

### Side of Trailer

#### Landing Gear
Make sure the landing gear is in a completely raised position, the crank handle is firmly in place, the support frame is undamaged and there are no missing parts. If it is power operated, make sure there are no air or hydraulic leaks.

#### Doors/Ties/Lifts
If the vehicle has door ties or lifts, make sure the doors show no signs of damage and they open, close, and latch correctly from the outside. Check that the ties, straps, chains, and binders are firmly in place. If the vehicle has a cargo lift, make sure it is fully retracted and firmly latched, with no signs of leaks, damage or missing components. Be prepared to demonstrate how it should be checked for proper operation.

#### Frame
Check for damage to the frame, cross members, box, and floor such as cracks, broken welds, fractures or holes.

#### Tandem Release Arm/Locking Pins
If the vehicle has a tandem release arm/locking pins, make sure the locking pins are firmly fastened and the release arm is locked.

### Remainder of Trailer

Please refer to the previous section "External Inspection (All Vehicles)" for detailed inspection methods regarding the following components:

- Wheels
- Suspension system
- Brakes
- Doors/ties/lift
- Splash guards

## *Coach/Transit Bus*

### Passenger Items

#### Passenger Entry/Lift
Make sure the entrance to the bus is free from damage and that it is in proper working order, including closing securely from the inside. Check that the handrails are firmly attached, the steps are free from any obstructions with no loose or extremely worn treads, and the step light is working, if the bus has one.

If there is a handicap lift, make sure it is fully retracted and firmly locked. Check for any leaks, damage, or missing parts and demonstrate how to inspect the lift to make sure it is working correctly.

### Emergency Exits
Check all emergency exits to make sure they do not show any signs of damage, and are in good working order, including closing completely from the inside. Make sure emergency exit warning devices are working properly.

### Passenger Seating
Make sure seat frames are undamaged and securely fastened to the floor, and seat cushions are firmly fastened to the seat frames.

## Entry/Exit

### Doors/Mirrors
Make sure the entrance and exit doors do not show any signs of damage and work properly from the outside. Check that the hinges are firmly in place and the seals are not cracked or broken.

Inspect the passenger exit mirrors and all external mirrors and mirror brackets for signs of damage and to make sure they are undamaged and firmly fastened with no loose fittings.

## External Inspection of Coach/Transit Bus

### Level/Air Leaks
Confirm that the vehicle is level (both the front and back), and check for any signs of air leaks coming from the suspension system if it is air-equipped.

### Fuel Tank(s)
Make sure the fuel tank(s) are firmly in place and no leaks are coming from the tank(s) or lines.

### Baggage Compartments
Make sure the baggage and other outside compartment doors are undamaged and in good working order, including locking firmly.

### Battery/Box
Make sure battery(s) are properly situated, cell caps are in place and connections are firm, without any signs of extreme corrosion. Make sure the battery box and cover/door is securely attached and there are no signs of damage.

## Remainder of Coach/Transit Bus

Please refer to the previous section "External Inspection (All Vehicles)" for detailed inspection methods for the rest of the vehicle's components. Keep in mind that you must pass the pre-trip vehicle inspection prior to taking the basic vehicle control skills test.

# *Taking the CDL Pre-Trip Inspection Test*

## Class A Pre-Trip Inspection Test

If applying for a Class A CDL, you will need to complete one of the four types of pre-trip inspections in the vehicle you have brought to the exam. The tests are similar and you will not know in advance which one you will be taking.

All four tests include starting the engine and an inspection of the cab and the coupling system. For the rest of the test, you might need to inspect the entire vehicle or only certain section(s) pointed out by the CDL Examiner.

## Class B and C Pre-Trip Inspection Test

If applying for a Class B CDL, you will need to complete one of the three types of pre-trip inspection in the vehicle you have brought with you for testing. The tests are similar and you will not know in advance which one you will be taking.

All three tests include starting the engine and an inspection of the cab. For the rest of the test, you might need to inspect the entire vehicle or only certain section(s) pointed out by the CDL Examiner. You will also be required to check any features specific to the type of vehicle (e.g, school or transit bus).

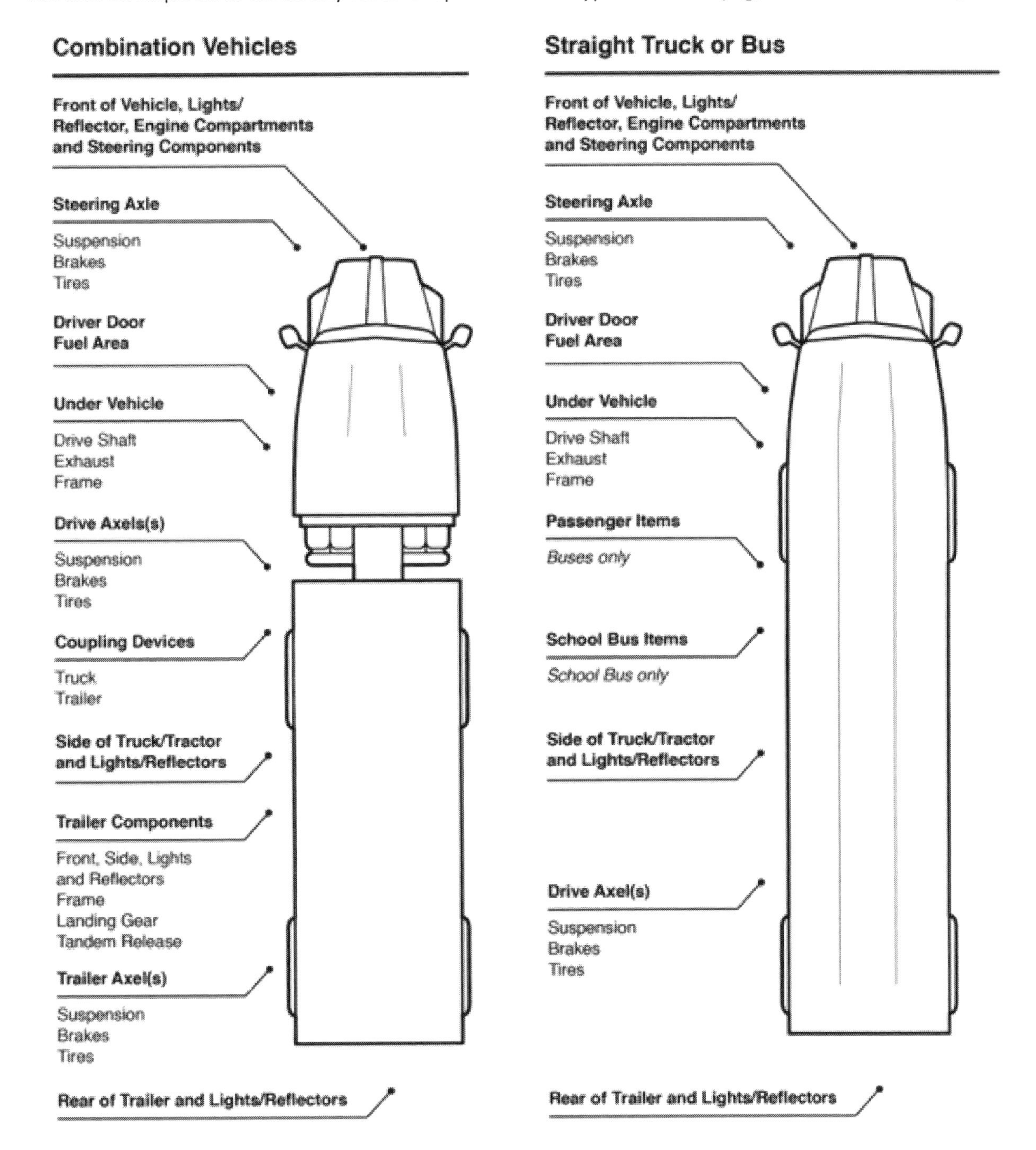

# Basic Vehicle Control Skills Test

The basic control skills exam you need to take during the road test could include one or more of the following maneuvers, in a location that is off-road or somewhere along the street:

- Straight line backing
- Offset back/right
- Offset back/left
- Parallel park (driver side)
- Parallel park (conventional)
- Alley dock

These exercises are outlined below.

## *Scoring*

- Crossing Boundaries (encroachments)
- Pull-ups
- Vehicle Exits
- Final Position

### Encroachments

You will be marked down for each time you touch or cross a boundary line or cone with any part of your vehicle.

### Pull-Ups

If you pull forward to clear an encroachment or to reposition the vehicle, it is scored as a "pull-up." Stopping without changing direction does not count as a pull-up. At first you will not receive a negative score for pull-ups; however, if you do this several times, you will get marked down.

### Outside Vehicle Observations (Looks)

The examiner may allow you to come to a complete stop and get out of the vehicle in order to check on its position (look). If this is the case, put the vehicle in neutral and set the parking brake(s). When you leave, continuously maintain three points of contact with the vehicle (if it is a bus, always keep a firm grip on the handrail). If you neglect to safely stop and leave the vehicle, you may automatically fail the basic control skills test.

You are allowed to check the position of your vehicle twice, except in the case of the Straight Line Backing exercise, which permits one chance only. You will receive one "look" score for each time you open the door and/or give up physical control of the vehicle by moving from a seated position or walk to the back of a bus to get a better view.

### Final Position

Keep in mind that you must complete each part of the test precisely as directed by the examiner. If you do not move the vehicle into its final position as instructed by the examiner, you will be marked down and could potentially fail the basic skills test.

# *Exercises*

## Straight Line Backing

The examiner may direct you to back up your vehicle in a straight line between two rows of cones without touching or crossing over the boundaries. (See the diagram below for reference.)

## Offset Back/Right

The examiner may direct you to back into a space located on the right rear side of your vehicle after pulling straight ahead to the outer boundary. Starting from that location, you must be able to back the vehicle into the opposite lane until the front of your vehicle has cleared the first set of cones without hitting any cones or border lines. (See the diagram below for reference.)

## Offset Back/Left

The examiner may direct you to back into a space located on the left rear side of your vehicle after pulling straight ahead to the outer boundary. Starting from that location, you must be able to back the vehicle into the opposite lane until the front of your vehicle has cleared the first set of cones without hitting any cones or border lines. (See the diagram below for reference.)

## Parallel Park (Driver Side)

The examiner may direct you to back into a space located on your left. You must be able to:

- Drive past the designated parking space, pulling your vehicle parallel to the parking area.
- Back into the space without cutting into the front, side or rear boundaries marked by cones.
- Park your whole vehicle entirely into the space. (See the diagram below for reference.)

## Parallel Park (Conventional)

The examiner may direct you to back into a space located on your right. You must be able to:

- Drive past the designated parking space, pulling your vehicle parallel to the parking area.
- Back into the space without cutting into the front, side, or rear boundaries marked by cones.
- Park your whole vehicle entirely into the space. (See the diagram below for reference.)

## Alley Dock

The examiner may direct you to sight-side back your vehicle into an alley. You must be able to:

- Drive past the alley, pulling your vehicle parallel to the outside boundary.
- Back into the alley, moving the rear of your vehicle within three feet of the back of the alley without touching the boundary lines or cones.
- When parked, your vehicle must be straight within the alley/lane. (See the diagram below for reference.)

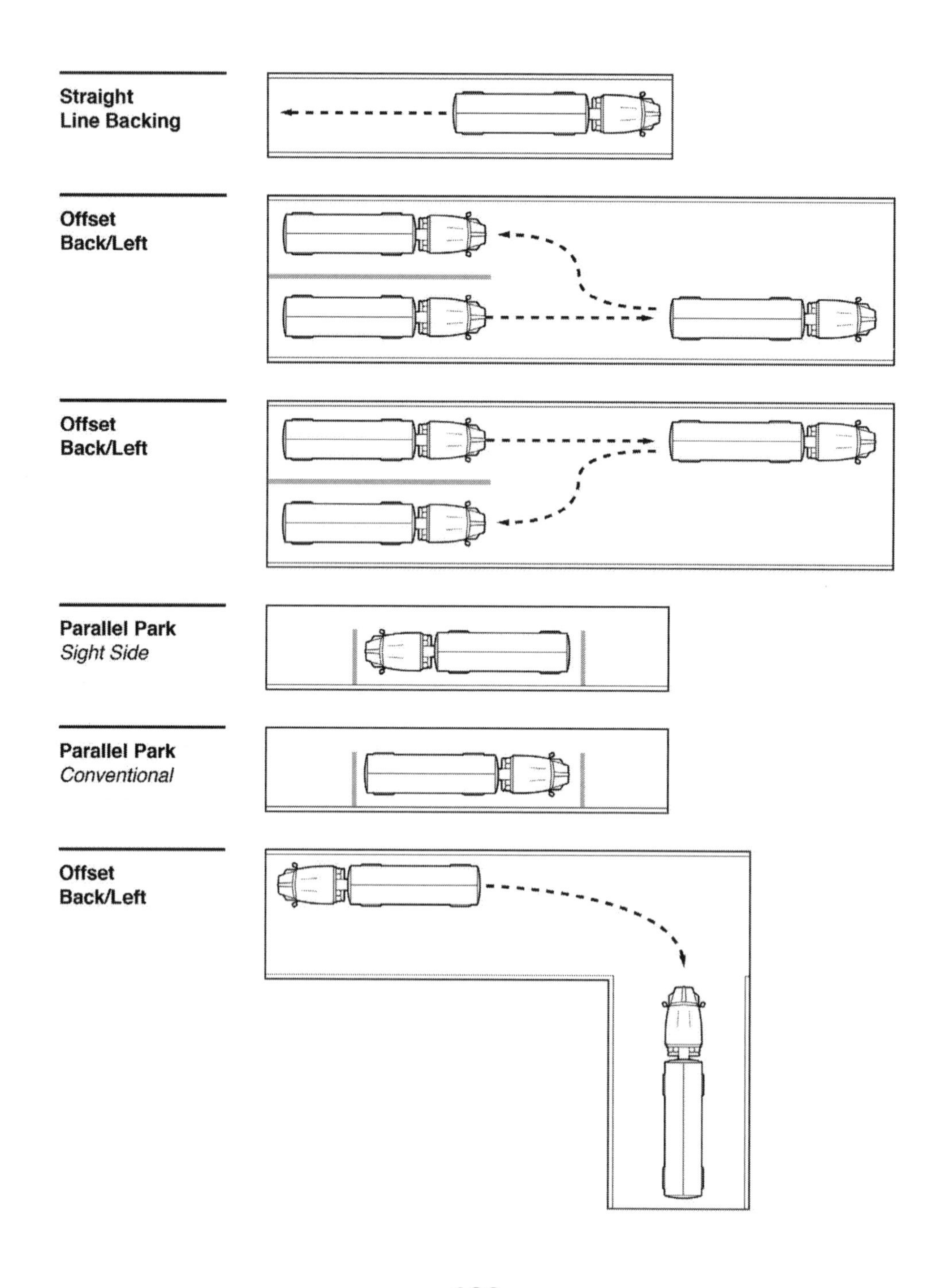

# On-Road Driving

This section covers how you will be tested. Your exam route will cover a wide range of traffic situations. Throughout the duration of the test, you must drive safely and responsibly; and

- Keep your safety belt fastened.
- Yield to all traffic signs, signals, and regulations.
- Finish the exam without an accident or moving violation.

During the driving portion of the exam, follow the tester's instructions. He or she will be grading you on specific driving exercises as well as your general driving performance.

The examiner will give you the instructions in advance so you will have plenty of time to execute the various maneuvers. You will not be asked to do anything considered unsafe. If the test route lacks a specific traffic condition, the examiner may ask you to do a simulation, which will require explaining how you would handle that particular situation.

## *How You Will Be Tested*

### Turns

When asked to turn, make sure to:

- Scan traffic in all directions.
- Use turn signals and safely maneuver into the required lane to make the turn.

As you approach the turn, be sure to:

- Use turn signals to warn others around you that you are turning.
- Smoothly begin to slow the vehicle, changing gears as necessary to maintain power, but do not coast in an unsafe manner—unsafe coasting occurs when your vehicle is not in gear (the clutch is pushed in or the gearshift is in the neutral position) for longer than the distance of your vehicle.

If you need to stop before making the turn, make sure to:

- Stop smoothly without skidding.
- Stop completely behind the stop line, crosswalk, or stop sign. If you are stopping behind another vehicle, make sure to allow enough distance so you can see the other vehicle's back tires.
- Keep the front wheels pointing straight ahead.
- Prevent your vehicle from rolling.

When ready to turn:

- Scan traffic in all directions.
- Keep both hands firmly on the steering wheel during the turn.
- Check your mirror frequently to make sure you do not scrape anything on the inside of the turn.
- Make sure you do not drive into oncoming traffic, and you finish the turn in the proper lane.

After turn:

- Check that the turn signal is off.
- Increase speed, turn on your turn signal, and slowly merge into the right-hand lane when you can safely do so (if not there already).
- Check mirrors and traffic.

## Intersections

As you approach an intersection:

- Thoroughly scan traffic in all directions.
- Gradually start slowing down.
- Put gentle pressure on the brakes and change gears if needed.
- Completely stop (without coasting) at any stop signs, signals, sidewalks, or stop lines, making sure to keep a safe distance behind any vehicle in front of you.
- Make sure you do not roll forward or backward.

When driving through an intersection:

- Thoroughly scan traffic in all directions.
- Gradually start slowing down and give the right of way to any pedestrians and/or traffic in the intersection.
- Do not make any lane changes.
- Keep both hands firmly on the steering wheel.

Once through the intersection:

- Continue scanning mirrors and traffic.
- Slowly and smoothly speed up and make gear changes as needed.

## Urban Business

For this section of the exam, you will be required to check traffic frequently and keep a safe following distance between your vehicle and those in front of you. You should stay in the middle of the right-hand lane and drive with the traffic flow (but not above the posted speed limit).

## Lane Changes

For this section of the exam, you will be required to change lanes to the left, and then back to the right. Make sure you first do any essential traffic checks, then use the correct signals and change lanes smoothly when you can safely do so.

## Expressway/Rural/Limited Access Highway

Before entering the expressway:

- Scan traffic.
- Use correct signals.
- Smoothly merge into the correct traffic lane.

Once on the expressway:

- Stay in the correct lane and maintain speed and enough space around your vehicle.
- Continue to systematically scan traffic in all directions.

When exiting the expressway:

- Check traffic as needed.
- Use correct signals.
- Slow down smoothly while in the exit lane.
- Once on the exit ramp, continue to slow down while staying within the lane margins, and keep enough distance between your vehicle and others around you.

## Stop/Start

For this part of the test, you will need to pull your vehicle over to the side of the road and stop as if you were going to exit the vehicle to check something.

Make sure to completely scan traffic in all directions and then carefully guide the vehicle to the right-hand lane or shoulder.

As you prepare for the stop:

- Check traffic.
- Turn your right turn signal on.
- Slow down and brake smoothly and steadily, changing gears as needed.
- Bring your vehicle to a complete stop without coasting.

Once stopped:

- Make sure your vehicle is parallel to the curb or shoulder and out of the way of the traffic flow—it should not be obstructing driveways, fire hydrants, intersections, signs, etc.
- Make sure your turn signal is off.
- Turn on your four-way emergency flashers.
- Engage the parking brake.
- Put the gearshift into neutral or park.
- Take your feet off of the brake and clutch pedals.

When instructed to resume:

- Scan traffic and check all mirrors completely in all directions.
- Switch your four-way flashers off.
- Turn on your left turn signal.
- When it is safe to enter traffic, release the parking brake and slowly pull straight ahead.
- Do not turn the steering wheel before starting to drive.
- Scan traffic in every direction, especially on your left side.
- Guide the vehicle slowly into the correct lane when you can safely do so.
- Once you have entered the traffic flow, turn your left turn signal off.

## Curve

When approaching a curve:

- Thoroughly scan traffic in all directions.
- Slow down prior to taking the curve so you will not need to brake or shift down while in the curve.
- Keep the vehicle within the lane boundaries.
- Keep scanning traffic in all directions.

## Railroad Crossing

Prior to reaching a railroad crossing, you should:

- Slow down, brake steadily and shift gears as needed.
- Look and listen for trains.
- Scan traffic in every direction.
- Do not stop, change gears, switch lanes, or attempt to pass another vehicle while in the crossing.

If you are taking the test in a bus, a school bus, or a vehicle displaying placards, you must be ready to obey the following procedures at every railroad crossing (unless the crossing is exempt):

- Turn on the four-way flashers as you approach the crossing.
- Come to a stop within 50 feet but not less than 15 feet from the nearest track.
- Look and listen in both directions up and down the track for any trains and signals that signify a train is approaching. If you are driving a bus, you may also need to open the window and door before crossing the tracks.
- Keep both hands firmly on the steering wheel as you cross. Do not stop, switch gears, or make any lane changes while any component of your vehicle is passing over the tracks.
- Turn off your four-way flashers once you are across.
- Keep scanning mirrors and traffic.

Note: CDL procedures for scoring railroad crossings may vary from state to state. Make sure to check with your state DMV for specifics.

Keep in mind that some routes will not have railroad crossings. For your test, you may be required to describe and show your examiner the proper railroad crossing procedures at a simulated location.

## Bridge/Overpass/Sign

After driving under an overpass or over a bridge, the examiner may ask you to recite the figure for posted clearance, height, or weight. If there are no bridges or overpasses on your test route, he or she may ask you for information about some other traffic sign. Be ready to recognize and describe any traffic sign that could appear along the route.

## Student Discharge (School Bus)

If you are applying for a School Bus endorsement, you will need to show the proper method for loading and unloading students. Please refer to the "School Bus" section of this guide for specifics.

## General Driving Behaviors

You will receive a score regarding your overall performance in the following general driving behavior categories:

### Clutch Usage (for Manual Transmission)

- Always push in the clutch when you need to shift.
- Double-clutch while shifting—make sure you do not rev or lug the engine.
- Make sure you do ride the clutch to control your speed, coast with the clutch pushed in, or "pop" the clutch.

### Gear Usage (for Manual Transmission)

- Do not grind or clash the gears.
- Choose the gear that does not rev or lug the engine.
- Do not shift gears while in turns or intersections.

### Brake Usage

- Do not ride or pump the brakes.
- Do not slam on the brakes or use a jerky motion—brake smoothly and steadily.

### Lane Usage

- Do not run over or onto curbs, sidewalks, or lane markings.
- Make sure to stop behind stop lines, crosswalks, or stop signs.
- When driving on a multi-lane road, make sure you finish a turn in the correct lane (a left turn should be completed in the lane directly to the right of the center line).
- Right turns should be completed in the right-hand lane.
- Always stay in or switch over the right-hand lane unless it is blocked.

### Steering

- Do not steer the vehicle too much or too little.
- Make sure both hands are always firmly gripping the steering wheel (except while shifting). As soon as you are done shifting, bring both hands back to the wheel.

### Regular Traffic Checks

- Check traffic and mirrors frequently, especially when entering, in the middle of, and exiting an intersection.
- Continuously scan traffic in high volume and pedestrian-heavy areas.

### Use of Turn Signals

- Use our turn signals correctly.
- Switch on turn signals when required and applicable.
- Switch off turn signals when you finish turning or make a lane change.

# CDL Practice Test

## Section: Driving Safely

1. Commercial drivers need to inspect their vehicles according to:
   a. State and local regulation
   b. Federal and state regulations
   c. Federal, state, and local regulations
   d. The regulations set forth by their employer

2. How many steps are included in the CDL pre-trip vehicle inspection test?
   a. Ten
   b. Five
   c. Eight
   d. Seven

3. When starting the engine, the Anti-Lock Braking System (ABS) indicator light on the dashboard should do the following:
   a. Stay illuminated
   b. Blink periodically
   c. Light up briefly and then turn off
   d. Never light up

4. When backing up, the safest method is to back and turn toward the:
   a. Right side
   b. Driver's side
   c. Middle
   d. Front

5. You should turn off the retarder when:
   a. The road is wet, icy, or snow covered
   b. Road conditions are dry
   c. Driving up a hill
   d. Driving down a hill

6. Curved or convex mirrors show items as appearing
   a. Larger and closer than they really are
   b. Larger and farther away than they really are
   c. Smaller and closer than they really are
   d. Smaller and farther away than they really are

7. If you must stop on or by a one-way or divided highway, place warning devices:
   a. 10 feet, 100 feet, and 200 feet toward the approaching traffic
   b. 20 feet, 50 feet, and 200 feet toward the approaching traffic
   c. Within 10 feet of the front or rear corners to mark the location of the vehicle and 100 feet behind and ahead of the vehicle
   d. Within 20 feet of the front or rear corners to mark the location of the vehicle and 200 feet behind and ahead of the vehicle

8. When driving in heavy traffic, the safest speed is:
   a. 10 mph slower than other vehicles
   b. 5 mph slower than other vehicles
   c. The speed of the other vehicles
   d. 10 mph faster than other vehicles

9. If you are driving a 50-foot vehicle traveling over 40 mph, how many seconds of following distance should you allow?
   a. Two seconds
   b. Five seconds
   c. Six seconds
   d. Ten seconds

10. Some states have enacted "move-over laws." These regulations require drivers to slow and change lanes when approaching a roadside incident.
   a. True
   b. False

11. Your CDL will be disqualified after ________ convictions of any state law for using a hand-held mobile telephone while operating a CMV.
   a. One or more
   b. Two or more
   c. Three or more
   d. Five or more

12. If confronted by an aggressive driver, you should:
   a. Speed up
   b. Shake your head and try to change lanes if possible
   c. Follow behind them
   d. Avoid any eye contact

13. The risk of having a crash due to drowsy driving is most likely to occur:
   a. In the early evening and late at night
   b. At night and in the mid-afternoon
   c. During the morning and mid-afternoon
   d. Mid-morning and early evening

14. The best advice for driving in fog is to:
   a. Drive past any vehicles going too slow
   b. Pull over to the side of the road immediately
   c. Not drive at all
   d. Use your high beams to see better

15. When driving in winter conditions, your vehicle should have at least ______ tread depth in every major groove on front tires and at least _______ tread depth on the other tires.
   a. 2/32 inch and 4/32 inch
   b. 2/16 inch and 4/16 inch
   c. 4/16 inch and 2/32 inch
   d. 4/32 inch and 2/32 inch

16. Before driving in hot weather, you need to make sure your vehicle has a sufficient amount of both water and antifreeze.
   a. True
   b. False

17. When approaching a railroad crossing marked by a round, black-on-yellow warning sign, all commercial vehicles carrying passengers or hazardous materials are required to:
   a. Proceed with caution
   b. Pull over to the side and let other vehicles go ahead
   c. Stop completely
   d. Activate their emergency flashers while crossing

18. When driving down a hill, when should you shift the transmission to a low gear?
   a. When you reach the bottom
   b. Before starting down the hill
   c. As you are driving down
   d. You don't need to shift down at all

19. If an oncoming driver drifts into your lane, it is best to:
   a. Move to your right
   b. Move to your left
   c. Brake hard
   d. Honk your horn

20. Antilock Braking Systems (ABS) increase your normal braking capability.
   a. True
   b. False

21. Skids are most commonly caused by acceleration:
   a. On hills
   b. When cargo is overloaded
   c. When taking a turn too fast
   d. On ice or snow

22. If you are in an accident, the first thing to do at the scene is:
   a. Notify authorities
   b. Care for any injured people
   c. Prevent another accident from happening in the same spot by protecting the accident area
   d. Stay in the vehicle until help arrives

23. If you a driving a van or box trailer and discover a fire in the cargo area, you should:
   a. Keep the doors shut
   b. Try to put out the fire
   c. Pull into a service station or truck stop to check on the fire
   d. Carefully read all the instructions on the vehicle's fire extinguisher

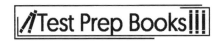

24. All of the following drinks contain the same amount of alcohol:
    a. A 16-ounce glass of 5% beer, a 6-ounce glass of 12% wine, and a 1-ounce shot of 80 proof liquor
    b. A 12-ounce glass of 5% beer, a 5-ounce glass of 12% wine, and a 1 ½-ounce shot of 80 proof liquor
    c. A 10-ounce glass of 5% beer, a 7-ounce glass of 12% wine, and a 2-ounce shot of 80 proof liquor
    d. A 10-ounce glass of 5% beer; a 6-ounce glass of 12% wine, and a 1-ounce shot of 80 proof liquor

25. Hazardous Material Identification Numbers are a ______ digit code used by first responders to identify hazardous materials.
    a. Two
    b. Three
    c. Four
    d. Five

## Section: Transporting Cargo Safely

26. The Gross Vehicle Weight Rating (GVWR) is:
    a. The value specified by the manufacturer as the loaded weight of a combination vehicle
    b. The value specified by the manufacturer as the loaded weight of a single vehicle
    c. The value specified by the manufacturer as the weight of a combination vehicle before any cargo is loaded
    d. The value specified by the manufacturer as the weight of a single vehicle before any cargo is loaded

27. Maximum axle weights are set by a bridge formula. A bridge formula permits less maximum axle weight for axles that are:
    a. Closer together
    b. Farther apart
    c. Located in the rear
    d. Located in the front

28. It is very important to make sure cargo is distributed:
    a. In the front of the cargo area
    b. In the back of the cargo area
    c. As high as possible
    d. As low as possible

29. Cargo should have at least one tie down for each _______ feet of cargo.
    a. Five
    b. Ten
    c. Fifteen
    d. Twenty

30. There are two basic reasons for covering cargo on an open bed:
    a. To hide the contents and to make sure nothing is stolen
    b. To make sure nothing falls off and to help streamline the vehicle
    c. To protect people from spilled cargo and to protect the cargo from weather
    d. To make sure nothing gets wet or stolen in transit

31. Before driving a bus, you must review the inspection report submitted by:
    a. Your employer
    b. Your state's Department of Motor Vehicles
    c. The bus company
    d. The previous driver

**Section: Transporting Passengers**

32. The following hazardous materials are allowed on buses: Small-arms ammunition labeled ORM-D, emergency hospital supplies, and drugs.
    a. True
    b. False

33. If driving a bus, you must stop between ______ and _____ feet before railroad crossings.
    a. 10 and 50
    b. 10 and 25
    c. 15 and 50
    d. 25 and 50

34. When approaching a drawbridge in a bus, you need to stop:
    a. At any type of drawbridge
    b. At those that do not have a signal light or traffic control attendant
    c. When there is a traffic light, even if it is green
    d. If the bridge has an attendant or traffic officer who controls traffic

35. If you work for an interstate bus carrier, you must complete a written inspection report at the end of each shift for:
    a. Each bus you drove
    b. The first bus you drove
    c. The last bus you drove
    d. The bus(es) instructed by the carrier

36. On vehicles with air brakes, what device controls when the air compressor will pump air into the air storage tanks?
    a. The air tank drain valves
    b. The safety valve
    c. The alcohol evaporator
    d. The governor

## Section: Air Brakes

37. In an air brake system, foundation brakes are used at each wheel. The most common type are:
    a. Wedge brakes
    b. S-cam drum brakes
    c. Disc brakes
    d. Anti-lock brakes

38. Spring brakes on tractor and straight trucks will fully engage when air pressure drops to a range of:
    a. 10 to 50 psi
    b. 15 to 45 psi
    c. 20 to 45 psi
    d. 20 to 50 psi

39. Anti-lock braking systems (ABS) will help shorten your stopping distance and keep the vehicle under control during hard braking.
    a. True
    b. False

40. To test the air leakage rate of your air brakes, apply the foot brake and hold it for one minute. If the air pressure on the air gauge drops more than ____ psi for a single vehicle and more than _____ for a combination vehicle, you are losing too much air.
    a. Three, four
    b. Four, five
    c. Two, three
    d. Two, four

## Section: Combination Vehicles

41. To help prevent rollover when driving a combination vehicle, stick to the following two guidelines:
    a. Make sure the cargo is positioned in the front of the vehicle, and brake hard when traveling around turns.
    b. Make sure the cargo is positioned in the back of the vehicle, and drive slowly around turns.
    c. Make sure the cargo is piled high, and brake hard when traveling around turns.
    d. Make sure the cargo is as low to the ground as possible, and drive slowly around turns.

42. The earliest and best way to determine if your trailer has started to skid is:
    a. By feeling the skid
    b. By noticing other vehicles getting out of your way
    c. By seeing it in your mirrors
    d. By seeing the ABS light activate

43. When backing up with a trailer:
    a. Turn the top of the steering wheel in the direction you want to go.
    b. Turn the top of the steering wheel in the opposite direction you want to go.
    c. Try to position your vehicle so you can back in a curved path.
    d. Correct drift by turning the top of the steering wheel in the opposite direction of the drift.

44. The trailer hand valve (also called the trolley valve or Johnson bar) should only be used:
    a. To test the trailer brakes
    b. When driving
    c. When parking
    d. When in a skid

45. Each trailer and converter dolly has _______ air tank(s).
    a. One
    b. Two
    c. One or more
    d. Two or more

46. When you drive a tractor-trailer combination equipped with ABS, you should
    a. Brake more frequently
    b. Brake less frequently
    c. Brake more forcefully
    d. Brake as you normally would

47. When coupling a combination vehicle, the first step is to:
    a. Inspect the fifth wheel
    b. Inspect the area around the vehicle and chock wheels
    c. Position the tractor in front of the trailer
    d. Secure the tractor

48. The first step when uncoupling a combination vehicle is to:
    a. Unlock the fifth wheel
    b. Position the rig
    c. Chock trailer wheels
    d. Lower the landing gear

49. When uncoupling a combination vehicle, ease pressure on the fifth wheel locking jaws by
    a. Chocking the wheels
    b. Braking gently
    c. Slowly backing up
    d. Slowly pulling forward

50. When inspecting a combination vehicle, you should be able to see some space between the upper and lower fifth wheel.
    a. True
    b. False

## Section: Doubles and Triples

51. Which trailer in a double/triple combination is most likely to turn over?
    a. The likelihood is the same for all trailers
    b. The first trailer
    c. The middle trailer
    d. The last trailer

52. For safety reasons, where should the trailer with the heaviest cargo be positioned?
    a. Right behind the tractor
    b. In the last position
    c. In the middle
    d. It makes no difference

53. A converter gear on a dolly is a coupling device of ____________ axle(s) and a fifth wheel.
   a. One
   b. Two
   c. One or two
   d. Two or three

54. When inspecting the coupling system areas of double and triple combination vehicles, make sure the locking jaws of the lower fifth wheel are positioned:
   a. Around the head of the kingpin
   b. Around the shank
   c. Around the release arm
   d. Around the locking pins

55. To test the emergency brakes on double and triple combination vehicles, you first need to:
   a. Charge the trailer air brake system and make sure the trailer moves freely
   b. Pull out the trailer air supply control or place it in the "emergency" position
   c. Pull gently on the trailer using the tractor to make sure the trailer emergency brakes are on
   d. Check for normal air pressure

## Section: Tank Vehicles

56. A tank endorsement is required for certain vehicles that transport:
   a. Military equipment
   b. Hazardous liquids or gases
   c. Weapons
   d. Liquids or gases

57. On all tank vehicles, what is the most important item to check?
   a. The brakes
   b. Signs of leaking
   c. The doors
   d. The locking mechanism(s)

58. Which of the following is not considered Special Purpose Equipment for tank vehicles?
   a. Emergency shut-off systems
   b. Grounding and bonding cables
   c. Fire extinguisher
   d. Vapor recovery kit

59. Always try to load a cargo tank so that it is completely full.
   a. True
   b. False

60. Some tanks are divided into several smaller sections by:
   a. Baffles
   b. Bulkheads
   c. Cables
   d. Doors

## Section: Hazardous Materials

61. The handling of hazardous materials is regulated by
    a. All levels of government
    b. Local municipalities
    c. Each state's DMV
    d. The federal government

62. Who is required to provide training and testing for drivers who transport hazardous materials?
    a. The federal government
    b. Each state's DMV
    c. The company who employs the driver or a designated representative
    d. It varies from state to state

63. Who is required to report accidents and incidents involving hazardous materials to the proper government agency?
    a. The carrier
    b. The driver
    c. The shipper
    d. It varies from state to state

64. There are _______ different classes of hazardous materials.
    a. Five
    b. Ten
    c. Eight
    d. Nine

65. A placarded vehicle must have at least how many identical placards?
    a. Two
    b. Three
    c. Four
    d. Five

66. Six different symbols may appear in Column 1 of the Hazardous Materials table. The symbol (A) means:
    a. The hazardous material described in Column 2 is subject to the Hazardous Materials Regulations (HMR) only when slated for water transport unless it is a hazardous substance, hazardous waste, or marine pollutant.
    b. The hazardous material described in Column 2 is subject to the HMR only when slated for air transport, unless it is a hazardous substance or hazardous waste.
    c. The proper shipping name is suitable for labeling materials for domestic transport, but not necessarily international transport.
    d. The hazardous material described in Column 2 is a generic shipping name. This all-purpose name must be supplemented by a technical name on the shipping paper.

67. Which of these hazardous material characteristics will NOT help decide the proper placards to use?
    a. The material's hazard class
    b. The amount being shipped
    c. The amount of all hazardous materials of all classes on your vehicle
    d. The material's identification number

68. If a shipping paper describes both hazardous and non-hazardous products, the hazardous materials must be:
    a. Entered first
    b. Entered last
    c. Written in all capital letters
    d. Written using boldface type

69. What items must be listed on a Uniform Hazardous Waste Manifest?
    a. The name and FDA registration number of the shippers, carriers, and destination
    b. The name and EPA registration number of the driver, shippers, carriers, and destination
    c. The name and EPA registration number of the shippers, carriers, and destination
    d. The name and EPA registration number of the driver, carriers, and destination

70. Bulk packaging is a single container with a capacity of _____ gallons or more.
    a. 115
    b. 119
    c. 125
    d. 129

71. Which three classes of hazardous materials must be loaded into a closed cargo space unless all packages are fire and water resistant or protected by a fire and water resistant covering?
    a. Class 1 (Explosives), Class 4 (Flammable Solids), and Class 5 (Oxidizers)
    b. Class 1 (Explosives), Class 2 (Compressed Gases), and Class 4 (Flammable Solids)
    c. Class 2 (Compressed Gases), Class 7 (Radioactive Materials), and Class 8 (Corrosive Materials)
    d. Class 4 (Flammable Solids), Class 5 (Oxidizers), and Class 7 (Radioactive Materials)

72. When you are transporting hazardous materials, keep shipping papers:
    a. Locked in the glove compartment or in a pouch on the driver side door
    b. Locked in the glove compartment or in a pouch on the passenger side door
    c. Within reach (while still wearing your seat belt), or in a pouch on the passenger side door
    d. Within reach (while still wearing your seat belt), or in a pouch on the driver side door

## Section: School Buses

73. When driving a bus, make sure the outside left and right side flat mirrors are properly adjusted so you can see:
    a. 50 feet or 1 bus length behind the bus
    b. 100 feet or 2 bus lengths behind the bus
    c. 200 feet or 4 bus lengths behind the bus
    d. 300 feet or 6 bus lengths behind the bus

74. The convex mirrors on a bus are located:
    a. Above the outside flat mirrors
    b. Below the outside flat mirrors
    c. Next to the outside flat mirrors
    d. On the front corners of the bus

75. When approaching a school bus stop to pick up students, come to a complete stop with the front bumper at least _______ feet away from students at the assigned stop.
    a. Five
    b. Ten
    c. Fifteen
    d. Twenty

76. If you miss a student bus stop, you should do the following:
    a. Obey local procedures.
    b. Back up to get the student(s).
    c. Call your supervisor.
    d. Stop and wait for instructions.

77. Which of the following situations is NOT considered a mandatory bus evacuation?
    a. The bus is stalled on or next to a railroad highway crossing.
    b. There is an impending danger of collision.
    c. The bus is on fire or there is a threat of a fire.
    d. The bus gets in an accident.

78. What is the difference between active and passive railroad crossings?
    a. Pavement markings are only present at active crossings.
    b. Passive crossings have flashing red lights to mark the crossing.
    c. Passive crossings do not have any type of traffic control device.
    d. Active crossings do not have any type of traffic control device.

79. What should you do if you think a railroad-crossing signal is malfunctioning and no police officer is present?
    a. Call the police
    b. Call your dispatcher to report the situation and get directions on how to proceed
    c. Turn around and seek another route
    d. Get out and see if there is a sign nearby with an emergency number to call

80. If your bus is equipped with ABS, it will help you:
    a. Avoid wheel lock up and maintain control
    b. Shorten stopping distance
    c. Compensate for bad brakes or poor brake maintenance
    d. Prevent power or turning skids

81. If you are driving a bus and experience strong winds, which of the following should you NOT do:
    a. Keep a strong grip on the steering wheel and try to anticipate gusts.
    b. Slow down to lessen the effect of the wind, or pull off the roadway and wait.
    c. Contact your dispatcher to get more information on how to proceed.
    d. Proceed immediately to the school as quickly as you can.

82. If you need to back up a bus, you should try to post a lookout to help. This person's job is to:
   a. Give you directions on how to back the bus
   b. Warn you about obstacles, approaching persons, and other vehicles
   c. Ask other vehicles to move away
   d. Get the students off the bus before you begin backing up

## Section: Pre-Trip Inspection

83. When doing a pre-trip inspection, which of the following will you NOT have to do?
   a. Walk around the vehicle
   b. Identify each item and explain to the examiner what you are checking and why
   c. Crawl under the hood or the vehicle
   d. Start the engine

84. To perform a hydraulic brake check, pump the brake pedal ______ times, then hold it down for _____ seconds.
   a. Five, three
   b. Three, five
   c. Five, ten
   d. Ten, five

85. When checking the brake manual slack adjustors, the brake pushrod should not move more than ____ (with the brakes released) when pulled by hand.
   a. One inch
   b. Two inches
   c. One half inch
   d. One quarter inch

86. The following items must be inspected on every tire:
   a. Tread depth, tire inflation, and tire size
   b. Tire inflation and tire condition
   c. Tire size, tire inflation, and tire condition
   d. Tread depth, tire condition, and inflation

87. Which of the following is NOT included as bus emergency equipment?
   a. A properly charged and rated fire extinguisher
   b. Flares
   c. Three red reflective triangles
   d. Body fluid cleanup kit

88. When checking the air/electrical connections on a trailer, what two items should be locked in place?
   a. Trailer air connectors and glad hands
   b. Trailer electrical plug and header board
   c. Glad hands and header board
   d. Glad hands and trailer electrical plug

89. Which of the following items is NOT included as part of an External Inspection of a Coach/ Transit Bus:
   a. Fuel tank(s)
   b. Battery/Box
   c. Radio antenna
   d. Fuel tanks

90. When applying for a Class A CDL, you will be required to perform one of the _______ versions of a pre-trip inspection in the vehicle you have brought with you for testing.
   a. Four
   b. Three
   c. Two
   d. Five

## Section: Basic Control Skills test

91. Which of the following is not one of the basic control skills that are tested on the Basic Vehicle Control Skills Test?
   a. Straight line backing
   b. Parallel parking
   c. Alley dock
   d. Dashboard control check

92. On the Basic Vehicle Control Skills Test, you may look to check the position of your vehicle a maximum of ______ time(s), except for the Straight Line Backing exercise, which allows _____ look(s).
   a. One, two
   b. Two, one
   c. Two, three
   d. Three, two

93. On the Basic Vehicle Control Skills Test, stopping without changing direction counts as a pull-up.
   a. True
   b. False

94. If you fail to maneuver your vehicle into its final position as described by the examiner on the Basic Vehicle Control Skills Test:
   a. You will be penalized and could fail the basic skills test.
   b. You will get another chance to do it correctly.
   c. It is up to the discretion of the examiner how to proceed.
   d. You will have to wait 30 days before taking the test again.

95. If asked to sight-side back your vehicle into an alley, you will need to drive the back of your vehicle within ______ feet of the rear of the alley without touching the boundary lines or cones.
   a. Two
   b. Five
   c. Three
   d. Four

## Section: On-Road Driving

96. If your test route on the on-road driving portion of the test does not have certain traffic situations, you may be asked:
   a. To skip this part
   b. To drive to another location to test the particular situation
   c. To come back another time so you can test this portion
   d. To simulate the circumstance by telling the examiner what you are or would be doing if you were in that traffic situation.

97. Which of the following is incorrect when driving through an intersection?
   a. Check traffic thoroughly in all directions
   b. Decelerate and yield to any pedestrians and traffic in the intersection
   c. Change lanes as needed while proceeding through the intersection
   d. Keep your hands on the wheel

98. For a Stop/Start maneuver, you will be asked to:
   a. Pull your vehicle over to the side of the road and stop as if you were going to get out and check something on your vehicle, then merge back into traffic.
   b. Come to a complete stop and start at a stop sign.
   c. Stop and start at a traffic light.
   d. Stop and start as if you were in "stop and go" traffic.

99. If driving a bus, what is one thing you may be required to do when navigating railroad tracks?
   a. Turn on your headlights
   b. Open the window and/or door prior to crossing tracks
   c. Change gears while crossing
   d. Turn the radio off prior to crossing

100. When tested on clutch usage while driving a manual transmission vehicle, which of the following should you never do?
   a. Use the clutch to shift
   b. Double clutch when shifting
   c. Select a gear that does not rev or lug the engine
   d. Coast with the clutch depressed

## Answers and Explanations

**1. B:** Federal and state laws require that drivers inspect their vehicles.

**2. D:** Seven. These are the steps included in the CDL pre-trip vehicle inspection test: 1) Vehicle Overview, 2) Check Engine Compartment, 3) Start Engine and Inspect Inside the Cab, 4) Turn Off Engine and Check Lights, 5) Do Walkaround Inspection, 6) Check Signal Lights, 7) Start the Engine and Check.

**3. C:** Upon engine startup, the ABS indicator lights on the dash should come on and then turn off. If the light stays on, as in Choice *A*, the ABS is not working properly.

**4. B:** Back and turn toward the driver's side whenever possible to get the best view. Backing toward the right side, Choice *A*, is very dangerous because it is more difficult to see.

**5. A:** You should turn the retarder off whenever the road is wet, icy, or snow covered—when the drive wheels have poor traction, the retarder may cause them to skid.

**6. D:** In a convex mirror, everything appears smaller and farther away than it would if you were looking at it directly.

**7. A:** If you must stop on or by a one-way or divided highway, place warning devices 10 feet, 100 feet, and 200 feet toward the approaching traffic. Choice *C* is the scenario for stopping on a two-lane road carrying traffic in both directions or on an undivided highway.

**8. C:** When driving in heavy traffic, the safest speed is the speed of other vehicles. Vehicles going the same direction at the same speed are not likely to run into one another. Drive at the speed of traffic without going an illegal or unsafe speed.

**9. C:** Six seconds. The best formula is to keep a distance of least one second for each ten feet of vehicle length at speeds lower than 40 mph, adding one second for safety when traveling at higher speeds. If the vehicle were traveling less than 40 mph, then 5 seconds, Choice *B*, would be the correct answer.

**10. A:** True. The incidence of enforcement officers, emergency medical services, fire department personnel and people working on the road being hit while performing roadside duties have significantly increased. Some states have enacted move-over laws to lessen the problem. Signs are posted on roadways in states that have such laws.

**11. B:** Two or more. Your CDL will be disqualified after two or more convictions of any state law on hand-held mobile telephone use while operating a CMV. Disqualification is sixty days for the second offense within three years and 120 days for three or more offenses within three years.

**12. D:** Avoid eye contact. Do not: challenge the driver by speeding up or attempting to "hold-your-own" in your lane (Choice *A*), make any gestures that might anger another driver (Choice *B*), even seemingly harmless expressions of irritation like shaking your head, or follow behind (Choice *C*)—make sure to keep a reasonable distance.

**13. B:** Crashes tend to occur at times when sleepiness is most pronounced, typically during the night and in the mid-afternoon.

**14. C:** The best advice for driving in fog is to not drive at all. It is preferable to pull off the road into a rest area or truck stop until visibility improves. Do not: pass any other vehicles (Choice *A*), stop along the side of the road (Choice *B*), unless absolutely necessary, or use high beams (Choice *D*)—use low-beam headlights and fog lights for the best visibility even during the day.

**15. D:** You must have at least 4/32 inch tread depth in every major groove on front tires and at least 2/32 inch on other tires; more than this is even better. Use a gauge to determine whether your vehicle has enough tread to drive safely in winter conditions.

**16. A:** True. During hot weather, make sure the engine cooling system has the correct amount of water and antifreeze as per the engine manufacturer's directions. (Antifreeze helps the engine under hot as well as cold conditions.)

**17. C:** All passenger and hazmat carrying vehicles are required to stop at a public railroad-highway crossing marked by a round, black-on-yellow warning sign.

**18. B:** Shift the transmission to a low gear before starting down the hill. Do not try to downshift once the vehicle has built up speed—it will be impossible to shift into a lower gear.

**19. A:** Swerving to the right is best. If the driver suddenly realizes the mistake, the natural response will be to return to his or her own lane.

**20. B:** False. ABS is an *addition to* your vehicle's normal brakes, helping to prevent the wheels from locking up during hard brake applications. ABS only activates when the wheels are about to lock up, and does not decrease or increase your vehicle's normal braking capability.

**21. D:** The most common type of skid is when the rear wheels lose traction through excessive braking or acceleration. Skids caused by acceleration usually happen on ice or snow.

**22. C:** The first thing to do at the scene of an accident is to prevent another accident from happening in the same location by protecting the accident area. Notifying authorities (Choice *A*) is the second step to follow and caring for any injured people (Choice *B*) is step three.

**23. A:** For a cargo fire in a van or box trailer, keep the doors shut, especially if the cargo contains hazardous materials. Opening the van doors will fuel the fire with oxygen, potentially increasing the fire's strength. Do not try to put out this type of fire yourself (Choice *B*), pull into a service station or area where there other people, buildings, or vehicles (Choice *C*) (try to find an open space), or wait until a fire occurs to know how the fire extinguisher works (Choice *D*). Study and know the instructions printed on the extinguisher before you need it.

**24. B:** All of the following drinks contain the same amount of alcohol: A 12-ounce glass of 5% beer, a 5-ounce glass of 12% wine, and a 1 ½-ounce shot of 80 proof liquor. It is the alcohol in drinks that affects driving performance. The source of the alcohol doesn't make any difference.

**25. C:** Hazardous Material Identification Numbers are a four-digit code used by first responders to identify hazardous materials.

**26. B:** The Gross Vehicle Weight Rating (GVWR) is the amount specified by the manufacturer as the loaded weight of a *single* vehicle. Gross Combination Weight Rating (GCWR) (Choice *A*) is the amount specified by the manufacturer as the loaded weight of a *combination* vehicle.

**27. A:** A bridge formula permits less maximum axle weight for axles that are *closer together*. This is to prevent overloading bridges and roadways.

**28. D:** It is very important to distribute the cargo as low as possible and to load the heaviest items under the lightest ones. Loading too much weight on the steering axle (Choice *A*) can cause hard steering and damage the steering axle and tires. Loading the cargo too far to the rear (Choice *B*) can make the steering axle weight too light to steer safely. A high center of gravity (Choice *C*), caused by loading cargo too high or placing heavy cargo on top, makes the vehicle more likely to tip over.

**29. B:** Cargo should have at least one tie down for each ten feet of cargo.

**30. C:** The two main reasons for covering cargo are: To protect people from spilled cargo and to protect the cargo from the weather.

**31. D:** Before driving a bus, you must be sure it is safe by reviewing the inspection report made by the previous driver.

**32. A:** True. Buses may carry small-arms ammunition labeled ORM-D, emergency hospital supplies, and drugs.

**33. C:** Stop your bus between 15 and 50 feet before railroad crossings.

**34. B:** Stop at drawbridges that do not have a signal light or traffic control attendant. You do not need to stop, but must slow down and make sure it's safe, when: There is a traffic light showing green (Choice *C*), or the bridge has an attendant or traffic officer who controls traffic whenever the bridge opens (Choice *D*).

**35. A:** If you work for an interstate carrier, you must complete a written inspection report for each bus driven.

**36. D:** The governor controls when the air compressor will pump air into the air storage tanks. The air tank drain valves (Choice *A*) are located on each air tank to allow extra water and oil to drain away, the safety valve (Choice *B*) protects the tank and the rest of the system from too much pressure, and the alcohol evaporator (Choice *C*) puts alcohol into the air system.

**37. B:** The S-cam drum brake is the most common type of foundation brake. Wedge (Choice *A*) and disc brakes (Choice *C*) are also considered foundation brakes, but they are less common. Anti-lock brakes (Choice *D*) are a different type of brake.

**38. C:** Spring brakes on tractor and straight trucks will fully come on when air pressure drops to a range of *20 to 45 psi* (typically 20 to 30 psi).

**39. B:** False. ABS does not necessarily shorten a vehicle's stopping distance, but it does help the vehicle maintain control during hard braking.

**40. A:** If the air pressure falls more than *three* psi in one minute for single vehicles and more than *four* psi for combination vehicles, the air loss rate is too high.

**41. D:** To help prevent your vehicle from rolling over, make sure the cargo is as close to the ground as possible, and drive slowly around turns.

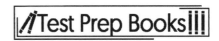

**42. C:** The earliest and best way to recognize that the trailer is starting to skid is by seeing it in your mirrors. Any time you need to brake hard, check your mirrors to make sure the trailer is in the location it should be.

**43. B:** When backing a trailer, turn the steering wheel in the *opposite direction you want to go*. Once the trailer starts to turn, rotate the wheel the other way to follow the trailer. Turning the steering wheel in the direction you want to go (Choice *A*) is the proper procedure for backing a car, straight truck, or bus. Do not seek a curved path (Choice *C*)—try to position the vehicle so you can back in a straight line. Finally, you should correct drift by turning the top of the steering wheel in the *same* direction of the drift, not the opposite (Choice *D*).

**44. A:** The trailer hand valve (also called the trolley valve or Johnson bar) should only be used to test the trailer brakes. Do not use it while driving (Choice *B*) because it might cause the trailer to skid, or parking (Choice *C*) because all the air might leak out unlocking the brakes (in trailers lacking spring brakes).

**45. C:** Each trailer and converter dolly has one or more air tanks.

**46. D:** When you drive a tractor-trailer combination equipped with ABS, you should brake as you normally would.

**47. A:** The first step to coupling a combination vehicle is to inspect the fifth wheel.

**48. B:** The first step to uncoupling a combination vehicle is to position the rig.

**49. C:** When uncoupling a combination vehicle, ease pressure on the fifth wheel locking jaws by slowly backing up.

**50. B:** False. When inspecting a combination vehicle, there should be NO visible space between the upper and lower fifth wheel.

**51. D:** The last trailer in a double/triple combination is most likely to tip over, due to the "crack-the-whip" effect.

**52. A:** To be safe, the most heavily loaded trailer should be positioned in the first position right behind the tractor; the lighter trailer should be in the rear.

**53. C:** A dolly's converter gear is a coupling device of one or two axles and a fifth wheel used to couple a semitrailer to the rear of a tractor-trailer combination, creating a double bottom rig.

**54. B:** The locking jaws of the lower fifth wheel should be positioned *around the shank*, not the head of kingpin.

**55. A:** The first step in testing the trailer emergency brakes in a double or triple combination vehicle is to *charge the trailer air brake system and check that the trailer rolls freely*. The next step is to stop and pull out the trailer air supply control (Choice *B*) (also referred to as the tractor protection valve control or trailer emergency valve) or place it in the "emergency" position, and the third step is to use the tractor to gently tug on the trailer to ensure that the trailer emergency brakes are on (Choice *C*).

**56. D:** A tank endorsement is required for certain vehicles that transport liquids or gases. The liquid or gas does not have to be a hazardous material (Choice *B*).

**57. B:** When inspecting a tank vehicle, the most important item to check for is leaks.

**58. C:** A regular fire extinguisher is not considered special purpose equipment for tanks—only one that is built-in.

**59. B:** False. *Never* load a cargo tank so that it is completely full. You must leave room, since liquids will expand as they heat up, a term referred to as "outage."

**60. B:** Some liquid tanks are divided into several smaller tanks by *bulkheads*.

**61. A:** Because of the danger posed by hazardous materials, *all levels of government* regulate the handling of this type of cargo.

**62. C:** Your employer or a designated representative is required to provide hazardous materials training and testing.

**63. A:** The carrier is responsible for reporting accidents and incidents involving hazardous materials to the proper government agency.

**64. D:** There are nine different hazard classes.

**65. C:** A placarded vehicle must have at least four identical placards.

**66. B:** The symbol (A) means that the hazardous material described in Column 2 is subject to the HMR only when meant for transport by air unless it is a hazardous substance or hazardous waste.

**67. D:** The identification number is assigned for each proper shipping name. The other three choices WILL help decide which placards to use: The material's hazard class (Choice *A*), the amount being shipped (Choice *B*), and the amount of all hazardous materials of all classes on your vehicle (Choice *C*).

**68. A:** If a shipping paper describes both hazardous and non-hazardous products, the hazardous materials must be *entered first*. They also must be highlighted using a contrasting color or identified by an "X" or "RQ" placed in front of the shipping description.

**69. C:** When transporting hazardous wastes, drivers must sign and carry a Uniform Hazardous Waste Manifest that lists the name and EPA registration number of the shippers, carriers, and destination.

**70. B:** Bulk packaging is a single container with a capacity of 119 gallons or more.

**71. A:** Class 1 (Explosives), Class 4 (Flammable Solids), and Class 5 (Oxidizers) must be loaded into a closed cargo space unless all packages are fire and water resistant or protected by a fire and water resistant covering.

**72. D:** When you are behind the wheel, keep shipping papers within reach (while still wearing your seat belt), or in a pouch on the driver's door. Shipping papers must be in full view by someone entering the cab.

**73. C:** When driving a bus, make sure the outside left and ride side front mirrors are properly adjusted so you can see 200 feet or 4 bus lengths behind the bus.

**74. B:** The convex mirrors on a bus are located below the outside flat mirrors. They are used to monitor the left and right sides at a wide angle.

**75. B:** When approaching a school bus stop to pick up students, come to a complete stop with the front bumper at least *ten* feet away from students at the assigned stop.

**76. A:** If you have missed a student's unloading stop, follow local procedures. Do not back up (Choice *B*).

**77. D:** The bus gets in an accident. Generally, having students stay on the bus is best to maintain student safety and control during an emergency and/or impending crisis situation, as long as it does not expose them to unnecessary risk or injury. The remaining answers (Choices *A*, *B*, and *C*) are all considered mandatory evacuations.

**78. C:** Passive crossings do not have any type of traffic control device. Pavement markings can be found at both active and passive crossings, making Choice *A* incorrect. Active crossings have flashing red lights to mark the crossing, making Choice *B* incorrect. Active crossings DO have some kind of traffic control device to regulate traffic, making Choice *D* incorrect.

**79. B:** Call your dispatcher to report the situation and get directions on how to proceed.

**80. A:** ABS helps to avoid wheel lock up and maintain control. ABS will NOT necessarily shorten stopping distance (Choice *B*), compensate for bad brakes or poor brake maintenance (Choice *C*), or prevent power or turning skids (Choice *D*).

**81. D:** Proceed immediately to the school as quickly as you can. The other answers (Choices *A, B,* and *C*) are all correct procedures to follow.

**82. B:** The purpose of the lookout is to warn you about obstacles, approaching persons, and other vehicles. The lookout should not give directions on how to back the bus (Choice *A*).

**83. C:** Crawl under the hood or under the vehicle. You WILL have to do the remaining procedures as described in the answers (Choices *A, B* and *D*).

**84. B:** To do a hydraulic brake check, pump the brake pedal *three* times, then hold it down for *five* seconds.

**85. A:** For manual slack adjustors, the brake pushrod should not move more than *one inch* (with the brakes released) when pulled by hand.

**86. D:** The following items must be inspected on every tire: Tread depth, tire condition, and tire inflation.

**87. B:** Flares. The other answers (Choices *A*, *C*, and *D*) should all be included as part of a bus emergency kit.

**88. D:** Glad hands and trailer electrical plug.

**89. C:** Radio antenna. The remaining items ARE included as part of an external inspection of a coach or transit bus.

**90. A:** When applying for a Class A CDL, you will need to perform one of the *four* versions of a pre-trip inspection in the vehicle you have brought with you for testing. For a Class B CDL, there are three versions (Choice *B*).

**91. D:** Dashboard control check is not one of the basic control skills that are tested on the Basic Vehicle Control Skills Test.

**92. B:** Two, one. Every time you open the door, move from a seated position when in control of the vehicle, or walk to the back of a bus to get a better view, which is scored as a "look."

**93. B:** False. Stopping without changing direction *does not* count as a pull-up.

**94. A:** You will be penalized and could fail the basic skills test.

**95. C:** You will need to drive the back of your vehicle within three feet of the rear of the alley without touching the boundary lines or cones.

**96. D:** To simulate the circumstance by telling the examiner what you are or would be doing if you were in that traffic situation.

**97. C:** You should NEVER change lanes while proceeding through an intersection.

**98. A:** Pull your vehicle over to the side of the road and stop as if you were going to get out and check something on your vehicle, then merge back into traffic.

**99. B:** Open the window and door prior to crossing tracks.

**100. D:** Coast with the clutch depressed. The other answers (Choices *A, B,* and *C*) are all perfectly fine.

Dear CDL Test Taker,

We would like to start by thanking you for purchasing this study guide for your CDL exam. We hope that we exceeded your expectations.

Our goal in creating this study guide was to cover all of the topics that you will see on the test. We also strove to make our practice questions as similar as possible to what you will encounter on test day. With that being said, if you found something that you feel was not up to your standards, please send us an email and let us know.

We have study guides in a wide variety of fields. If you're interested in one, try searching for it on Amazon or send us an email.

Thanks Again and Happy Testing!
Product Development Team
info@studyguideteam.com

# FREE Test Taking Tips DVD Offer

To help us better serve you, we have developed a Test Taking Tips DVD that we would like to give you for FREE. **This DVD covers world-class test taking tips that you can use to be even more successful when you are taking your test.**

All that we ask is that you email us your feedback about your study guide. Please let us know what you thought about it – whether that is good, bad or indifferent.

To get your **FREE Test Taking Tips DVD**, email freedvd@studyguideteam.com with "FREE DVD" in the subject line and the following information in the body of the email:

a. The title of your study guide.

b. Your product rating on a scale of 1-5, with 5 being the highest rating.

c. Your feedback about the study guide. What did you think of it?

d. Your full name and shipping address to send your free DVD.

If you have any questions or concerns, please don't hesitate to contact us at freedvd@studyguideteam.com.

Thanks again!

Made in the USA
Columbia, SC
22 October 2020